MANUFACTURING
THE EMPLOYEE

MANUFACTURING THE EMPLOYEE

Management Knowledge from the 19th to 21st Centuries

Roy Jacques

SAGE Publications

London • Thousand Oaks • New Delhi

First published 1996

SAGE Publications Ltd
6 Bonhill Street
London EC2A 4PU

SAGE Publications Inc
2455 Teller Road
Thousand Oaks, California 91320

SAGE Publications India Pvt Ltd
32, M-Block Market
Greater Kailash - I
New Delhi 110 048

British Library Cataloguing in Publication data

A catalogue record for this book is
available from the British Library

ISBN 0 8039 7915-0
ISBN 0 8039 7916-9 (pbk)

Library of Congress catalog card number 95-072174

Typeset by Type Study, Scarborough. UK

Contents

Preface

No industrial relation can long survive the reasons for its being.

(Margaret Schaffner, 1907)

This book is a history of *l'employé* – the employee. By telling his/her story, I will attempt to show that contemporary management knowledge forms a culturally and historically specific way of thinking about work and society. I will show the incompatibility between the context from which management thinking arose and the problems of 'managing for the twenty-first century' as posed in today's business and academic press. I will question the dominant habits of thought which, having become 'common sense', prevent constructive analysis of today's organizational problems.

'. . . And the Wisdom to Know the Difference'

'The pretense that corporations are necessary for the better government of the trade, is without any foundation.'

This anti-corporate rhetoric is not from Karl Marx, but Adam Smith, whose *Wealth of Nations* is a cornerstone of modern economic thinking. According to Smith, 'The real and effectual discipline which is exercised over a workman, is not that of his corporation, but that of his customers' (1776/1937: 129). How is one to interpret this observation? Was Smith an early advocate of self-managing work teams? Was he more radical than Marx? Was he pro- or anti-capitalist? Without a context to aid interpretation, this observation can mean anything and thus means nothing. Yet, to have an opinion on Smith is important today because his metaphor of the invisible hand is one of the central icons used to defend the positive social value of corporate capitalism.

Alfred Sloan, who with Pierre DuPont was one of the chief architects of General Motors, claimed in his memoir not to be anti-union. Rather, he explained, 'our initial reaction to unionism was negative,' because of

the persistent union attempt to invade basic management prerogatives. Our rights to determine production schedules, to set work standards, and to discipline workers were all suddenly called into question. Add to this the recurrent tendency of the union to inject itself into pricing policy. (Sloan, 1964: 406)

What is a 'basic management prerogative'? Is worker possession of these responsibilities and privileges the only 'real and effective discipline' preventing corporate 'fraud' and 'negligence' as Adam Smith contended? If so, how can management's rights to them be a 'basic' prerogative? Without a context for thinking about these inconsistencies, we will organize and manage based on the tyranny of 'common sense,' which is nothing more than our unexamined and entrenched biases.

The complexity of societies and their institutions gives them a great deal of inertia; they change slowly. At any point in time, *almost* everything is unchangeable. This supports deterministic views that change results from societal 'evolution' or autonomous forces in 'the environment.' I consider this an abdication of social responsibility. My (stereotypically American) assumption is that the main purpose of inquiry is to identify the little which can be changed, to assess the limits of the possible and to anticipate the consequences of various actions. Societies are not voluntaristic in the sense that they can be rationally planned, but a central component of social action has to do with taking responsibility for one's choices and acting purposefully in relation to one's values.

But, when change can be effected only in localized pockets of the complex web of social relationships, how can one best leverage one's efforts to work for change where change is actually possible? This is the main contribution an historical perspective can make. If one has a sense of where a social relationship began and how it changed, one can better understand where it is currently heading. If one knows past points of rigidity and of responsiveness, one can analogize profitably to present situations. As this book will hopefully illustrate, historical perspective can lead one to seriously reconsider both what constitutes a problem and what possible paths exist to address problems.

Bear in mind that even if one's goal in theorizing about organizations is to have an effect on them, not every aspect of theorizing is best directed toward immediate action. Sometimes, one should stand back and reflect on the process of effecting change. If this book gives the reader insights s/he can apply in organizations, so much the better, but three goals are more important. The first, for those of us who engage directly in organizations, is to reflect on the absence of norms, processes and institutions to foster dialogue about issues that go beyond immediate problems. Second, for those of us engaged in theorizing, how can the current obsession with hypothesis confirmation be broadened to include reflection on the role of the management disciplines within the broader currents of the social sciences and on the role of academic knowledge within today's, and tomorrow's, societies? Third, for both theorists and practitioners, how can a dialogue be developed between contemporary problems/problem-solvers and expert knowledge production? Knowledge about organizations can be thought of as a set of tools. In a changing world, it is periodically useful to step back from asking how tools can be used, asking instead what tools need repair or replacement and what new tools – and new tool-users – are appearing or are needed.

Some Issues of Method, Perspective and Scope

This book is not an attempt to reclaim the meanings of the past. It is an effort to better understand the post-industrial future into which the most-industrialized countries are now heading – with the rest of the world in tow. It is becoming less and less controversial to allege that these are times of transformational change. Some proclaim the advent of the post-industrial, others the postmodern. Where these changes are heading is still anybody's guess, but they pose a serious problem for knowledge about organizing: *in times of transformation, not only do new **problems** arise; old **ways** of looking at problems become problems themselves.* Ways of thinking that evolved in response to the problems of a previous era sediment over time into 'common sense.' Because such sedimented belief forms the structure of assumptions into which one places problems for analysis, new problems must be represented using old frameworks, old language and concepts. Only the portions of new problems reflecting the past era are representable; that which is genuinely novel is both unrepresented and unsuspected. As Thomas Kuhn has argued, a system of thinking is never refuted by mere data.

This book will show that current attempts to theorize this emerging future embody a common sense that is a product of industrialism. I do not proffer an agenda for managing tomorrow's organizations. To do so would be necessarily superficial and premature. First, we must create a more comprehensive forum for discussing the problems of tomorrow by articulating ways that *today's* problems are constrained by *yesterday's*. Whether one focuses on industrial management, industrial unionism or industrialized practices of education, there is reason to ask *whether* – not simply how – these institutions will be related to organizational practice in the presently emerging world.

Because it is the purpose of this book to present and question broad currents of change over a wide-ranging area of analysis, it should not be judged by the same standards as a specialized study. I am not as expert in historiography as the historians, in sociology as the sociologists and so forth. My argument draws freely on secondary sources as well as original texts. In this project, I believe I hold true to the vision of organizational research as an applied social science. I have merely used some reference disciplines less commonly drawn upon as resources for understanding the management of organizations. Those familiar with these other disciplines will see that much of what I have 'discovered' might better be described as *re*covered. Much of the forgotten history of management knowledge lies 'hidden' right before our eyes – the original texts of Taylor or McGregor, the statements of those who engineered the first large bureaucratic organizations in the US within the last century, critiques existing in sociology, and so much more. One of the amazing aspects of researching this book has been the accessibility of this history. My claim is not to have produced a great deal of new material, but to have organized this material in a way that may contribute to thinking differently about problems that currently perplex those seeking to adapt today's organizations to changing times.

Hopefully, this book will be an equal opportunity offender. Nobody is likely to agree with all of my points. Critical theorists may find my incrementalist views too accommodating to the *status quo*. Many managerialist theorists will object to the mere fact that I brand as an *ism* what they view as disinterested, socially neutral science. A few of my propositions go well beyond 'the data' (although no more so than ideas such as the Big Bang and evolution). Some are intended to be outrageous (though never frivolous or insincere) to discourage passive consumption by you, the reader. It is not my desire to precisely grasp some small element of today's organizational world, but to roughly map the broad currents flowing through this world. If I am occasionally washed overboard, so much the better. To have made no errors is to have taken no risks. This book is in no way intended to be the final word on anything. I offer it as fodder for a discussion I hope to see beginning regarding values, social life and the role of organizing. In the workplace, this dialogue has already begun – haltingly. It remains an open question whether and in what role the dialogue will include academic 'organizational science.' What this book is not is an ivory-tower polemic; it is intended as a tool for managing and organizing. Perhaps some personal background can help to show how this may be so.

Background

When I first applied to doctoral programs a decade ago I saw (and see) myself as a pragmatic person, a practicing manager in the field of financial software development. My decision to return to school was motivated by two very concrete questions: (1)   why don't organizations work better than they do?; (2)   why was my MBA degree of so little use in answering the first question?

When I finally entered my doctoral program, I quickly learned two things about management education. First, having returned to school with what I considered relatively specific interests and problems for study, I was quite amazed to find that in what I would now call the 'disciplinary' school of business there are no business problems. There are only accounting problems, finance problems, human resource problems, and so forth. Even within the department where I finally got my degree, problems were divided into human resource management (HRM), organizational behavior (OB), organizational theory (OT) and policy. Thinking like 'the practitioner,' I found my interests transected the school's disciplinary boundaries. Nobody in business has 'an OB problem.' There is an OB *aspect* to every problem, but there is also an accounting aspect, a policy aspect and so forth. So my first lesson as an academic was that I must choose between working on the problems of business *people* or those of the business *disciplines* (and we perpetually wonder why 'the practitioner' fails to read our research or come to our conferences!).

The second thing I learned was that, even compared to the relative conservatism of business, the boundaries of business school discourse are surprisingly narrow. As it is with most of the mid-career doctoral students I meet in my current teaching position, issues of organizational power were central to the questions I brought from the business world. I quickly learned that power was a peripheral topic and one the savvy management scholar avoided lest s/he be branded insufficiently soft on Marxism. There was also the question of language. The business world is a pidgin language,[1] a polyglot of overlapping dialects. The business school speaks the artificially clarified and semantically impoverished language of hypothesis testing alone. Because of my training in biology, computer information systems and business, and my work background supporting financial forecasting software for hospital budgeting analysts, I find the language of statistics useful – where appropriate[2] – but the paradigmatic insistence that *anything* of value in organizational studies can be expressed as a statistically significant difference struck me (then and now) as unnecessarily limiting, counterproductive and, frankly, somewhat silly. One can produce useful knowledge without being a scientist and one does not become a scientist simply by adopting the forms of scientific inquiry.

As my socialization as a management scholar continued, I learned that expressing any doubts about the adequacy of probability theory to produce a paradigmatic science of business and any resistance to reshaping problems to fit the disciplinary structure of the academy was 'radical;' lockstep conformity to restrictive norms of inquiry was enforced informally, yet effectively, by The Four But's. 'You can do that but . . .' one is told by those presumed to know: '. . . it won't constitute a dissertation,' '. . . it won't be publishable,' '. . . you won't get a job if you write that,' or '. . . you won't get tenured.' Thus, potentially fresh insights are put on ice for a decade or more, by which time the subject is encrusted like a barnacle in research s/he has been told is 'safe.' Thus, the boundaries of the discipline continue to narrow, solidify and become ever more out of step with the broader society. I am no bolder than my peers, but I had the good fortune to enter a doctoral program that never enforced conformance to these norms. Even those who thought my studies a bit odd were generally tolerant and often constructive. As a result, I could remain 'pragmatic;' that is, I could follow the interests I had developed as a manager and pursue whatever studies helped me answer the questions I had brought with me from the business world.

As these interests led into comparative literature, philosophy and nursing, even I began to wonder if my studies were turning into an academic

---

1 Linguistically, a pidgin is any language with no native speakers; one used for communication between cultures of origin.

2 In this context, I would define 'appropriate' as providing answers to problems that are found useful by those posing the problems and by their client constituencies.

shell game. These doubts accumulated as the years passed. The turning point came in 1991 when I was doing field research on a nursing unit in a large teaching hospital. What I saw and how I saw it were profoundly shaped by the detours I had taken into post-analytic thought and feminist theorizing. To paraphrase an overly quoted aphorism, I found there was nothing quite so practical as a good feminist-poststructuralist theory.

Given the emotionally laden fault lines in academia, it would be easy to pigeonhole this book, based on terms or topics, as the work of a theorist congenitally suffering from nihilistic, Nietzschean relativism (to synthesize the three most common epithets). I ask your forbearance. This book developed from an attempt to better understand concrete workplace problems; it is presented as a means for better addressing them. If the story occasionally disappears into the ozone layer of epistemology, it is for a reason – this ozone layer is also becoming thin and we deplete it, too, at our own peril. If my story is sometimes critical, it is because I believe critique is necessary to dislodge long-established habits of doing and thinking that increasingly block, rather than facilitate, useful action. You will not find this book offering five points you can apply at the office next Tuesday. Still, it emerges from the problems of a practitioner and is intended to offer insights useful for changing practice.

You, the Reader

This book has been written to reflect the needs of several distinct readerships. I believe it has potential value for both the academic and the student or practicing manager, as well as for the US reader and the reader in other countries.

For academics

My primary goal in writing this book has been to provide a short history of American management discourse that can be used as a supplemental text in HRM, general management, OB, OT and other classes. In that role, I hope the book contextualizes the history of management and the employee in a way that stimulates discussion of today's emerging trends and their implications for organizing. At the same time, I have attempted to produce a work that can be taken on its own merits by scholars. Much of the detail necessary to support such an essay has been placed in footnotes, outside the main text, but accessible to the serious reader.

For managers and students

For the reader who is not a theoretician, most of the footnote material will contain unnecessary detail. I have made a sustained attempt to trim the main text to contain only a story that helps the practitioner, future practitioner or change agent to think about contemporary problems of organizing. Granted, this story often moves a long way from the nuts and bolts of organizational how-to lists. For the reader who will exercise a bit of patience, however, I believe this distance brings the reward of additional perspective not available to those who keep their noses pressed to the proverbial grindstone. Sometimes, especially in times of discontinuous change, stepping back to re-assess is more practical than obsessively pushing ahead at the same old problems in habitual ways.

For US readers

In writing this book, my own perspective has been changed. My initial goal was to show how industrial-era US values interfere with understanding emerging problems of a post-industrial society. As my research progressed, I learned that the problem went deeper. Although the American Dream within which management thought and institutions developed was significantly reshaped by industrialism, its core elements are pre-industrial. They depend upon a conceptual language of frontier, community, small-town life and individual self-sufficiency which are not part of the lived experience of most contemporary US workers. For the US reader, this book is intended to create new possibilities for dialogue, problem-solving and action by helping to show how this Federalist mythology restricts our theory and our practice.

For readers outside the US

If you are reading this book in Bombay or Liverpool, Jakarta or Rio, of what interest is a past era of US history? Is this not merely another example of American ethnocentrism? Hopefully not. The MBA, the business school, managerial publishing and consulting are all US export products. Little or no attempt is made by 'the manufacturer' to determine whether this product is compatible with your culture, history or values. Demystifying this product and articulating its limitations can be facilitated by better understanding the processes through which the industrial Northeast of the US colonized the rest of the country, which then proceeded to economically and culturally colonize the world.

This has been especially true since the Second World War, after which the only intact major industrial economy in the world was that of the US. In the decades following, this historical coincidence has often been mistaken for genuine superiority (most often, of course, in the US itself). From the Marshall Plan to the more recent gold rush to 'help' the benighted former Soviet economies, Americans have quite unreflectively proselytized our culturally specific management beliefs to others as objective and universal truths for organizing work relationships. You in other countries cannot separate the wheat from the chaff in US management knowledge without understanding it as a cultural product. By contextualizing the history of management as culturally bound up with the Euro-American tradition, we can re-frame questions of other races from 'why don't they get it?' to 'how did the question get narrowed to this particular subset of experience?' For instance, Americans regularly publish articles about 'the troubled Black family' or 'saving the Black family,' when a stronger appreciation of African cultures could lead to reformulating the question as 'what could be learned about families from the survival of Black America through three centuries of exclusion from white culture?'

Hopefully, this book will contribute to the possibility of other analyses dealing with the specific history of capital formation and industrialization in other cultures. The British, German or French reader especially will note many points of similarity between this history and his/her own, but the overall patterns, the structuring of business relations, interactions between business and culture, are different in quite important ways. This complex pattern of similarity/difference will be still greater for the Brazilian, the Japanese, the Indian reader and others. In each of these cultures, the interacting patterns of cultural and economic colonization and resistance have been different, yet these stories are currently absent from the history of the development of management knowledge. Chandler (1990) has begun the project of telling the multiple stories of organizing that emerge from different countries, but much more needs to be done.

Indigenizing Management Knowledges

I hope this book will strengthen arguments for the development of indigenous management knowledges by indigenizing 'organizational science'[3] itself as a discourse shaped by its culture of origin. In studying the management books, courses and seminars imported from the US, does one not find the ghost of Freeman Hunt (see Chapter 1) – the endlessly self-actualizing Protestant perfectionist, the pioneer, the self-determining and omnicompetent social participant, the 'man [sic] of action' who scorns reflection as impractical, the self which denies its fundamental embeddedness in complex organizations – haunting the text as 'the employee,' the implicitly generic worker? To shape contemporary work practices, even in the US, to this view of the working subject is of questionable value. To export this subject worldwide is indefensible. Until texts come with a product warning ('caution: contents are historically and culturally specific'), let the buyer beware. Particularly in the post-colonial world – the politically self-determining nations who entered industrialized world capitalism as colonies of the most industrialized nations – there is searching for regionally appropriate voices that neither fantasize about an unretrievable pre-colonial

---

3 This is not to overlook the contributions of other countries, especially the UK, to this knowledge. As the US has become the preeminent economic world power, however, its ability to export a US-influenced model of the working subject worldwide has become the foremost cultural problem of organizational knowledge.

essence nor slavishly accept Western technologies and knowledge as representative of 'development' or 'progress'. This book will not and should not attempt to contribute to the production of regional knowledges. It can, however, offer valuable assistance by helping to show that the knowledge currently exported as universally applicable objective science is profoundly shaped by its culture of origin. Hopefully, armed with this knowledge, scholars and practitioners worldwide will be better prepared to argue for the possibility of regional knowledges – a possibility foreclosed by the dominance of a form of knowledge claiming to transcend history and culture.

Finally, I must say that it is not my intention to replace one universal account of management development with another. Rather, by identifying the cultural and historical specificity of the account that currently presents itself as universal, I am attempting to contribute to the possibility of producing many, localized stories, each of which is understood, produced by and productive of the community to which it applies. Neither internationalism nor respect for diversity are possible as long as one cultural system is able to present itself as the objective, neutral and universal framework within which all other cultures' artifacts can be hung.

'America' the Country/the Myth System

In order to appreciate this book, the reader must understand 'America' at two levels. At one level, 'America' is a geopolitical entity, a national affiliation claimed by most of the people who live south of Canada and north of Mexico. When speaking of this entity, I have attempted to consistently speak of the 'US' or, where appropriate, 'North America', 'Anglo North America' and so on. After all, the other residents of the North, Central and South Americas are also 'American.' But 'America' is also a powerful metaphor, an ethos, a vision of the good society. This imagery is not the common property of all residents of the hemisphere. The 'American Dream' is not equally a cultural artifact of the *Québecois*, the Ixtapan and the New Yorker. It is an ethos identified worldwide with the mainstream culture of the US. Baudrillard, writing primarily to a French audience, wonderfully captures the spirit of this dream in his book *America*:

> [America] is the land of the 'just as it is' . . . yet it is all the stuff of dreams too . . . What you have to do is enter the fiction of America. . . . It is, indeed, on this fictive basis that it dominates the world. . . . [T]he tragedy of a utopian dream made reality. . . . This is America's problem and, through America, it has become the whole world's problem. . . . If you are prepared to accept the consequences of your dreams – not just the political and sentimental ones, but the theoretical and cultural ones as well – then you must still regard America today with the same naive enthusiasm as the generations that discovered the New World. . . . If not, you have no understanding of the situation, and you will not be able to understand your own history – or the end of your history – either, because Europe can no longer be understood by starting out from Europe itself. (Baudrillard, 1989: 28–30, 98)

An often-missed connection Baudrillard makes explicit is that the 'American' Dream is not indigenous to the Americas. It is Modern and Western European. In this sense, I will argue, the colonization of the world by American management theories and institutions represents a 'return of the repressed' of the first order. For those outside the US, of course, it is unlikely that these values are a part of one's cultural heritage. But, even for those within the US, this cultural context is critical to assess. As the US moves into a post-industrial and perhaps postmodern world, the core values structuring public discourse are not those of the *industrial*, but of the *pre*-industrial, the rhetoric of frontier and community that have been increasingly marginal to lived experience for decades.

In this respect, the present book could be looked at as a case study in one country's experience with capitalism, organizing and managing work. US history may represent the closest thing one can find to capitalism growing up in a vacuum, untainted by the influence of other social institutions. When industrialism recast the social topography of the US between 1870 and about 1920, neither history nor common culture, church, central government nor aristocracy was capable of effectively constituting an axis of opposition. As a result of this history, if one wishes today to examine the curious mix of benefits and weaknesses of a society where meaning must be found in one's work and in mass market consumption, the case of the US can be illustrative – and perhaps partially a warning.

Sexist Language

How we speak and how we think are not independent. Thus, the old documents used in this book pose a problem regarding sexist usage of pronouns. Usually, I call attention to sexist usage in citations because I strongly believe the use of 'he/him/his' to represent people in general perpetuates the practice of treating men as humanity and women as a special-interest subgroup. In the historical period emphasized in this book, however, standard English usage was consistently sexist in this respect. To call attention to each instance would be distracting. Accordingly, I have adopted the following general guidelines: in my own narrative, every attempt is made to avoid sexist usage. For contemporary citations (roughly since 1970), I have denoted sexist usage through the use of '[*sic*],' on the assumption that these authors wrote when sexist usage was being actively questioned. For historical citations, I pass on the sexist usage verbatim.

Is This a 'Postmodern' Book?

It is sometimes said of me by colleagues that I am a postmodernist. What that might mean continues to elude me. I do believe that a relatively specific mode of consciousness and system of social relations which is exemplified by the dominant strands of European and Anglo North American cultures between roughly 1600–1700 and the present can be identified. So, for that matter, did Max Weber. I also believe that *certain* (not all) aspects of this culture may presently be in flux. Thus, I find modernity both a sensible and an important object for analysis. If modernity is to be regarded as having an historically specific existence, it is logically necessary that there be a pre-modern and a post-modern.[4] This logical categorizing, however, in no way indicates the content of these bracketing periods other than that they be 'not modern.' Certain things can be known or inferred about premodern Europe, but to recapture the meanings of this time as it was experienced by those within it is impossible. One can only speculate. Similarly, to imagine the postmodern from our current position within the modern should be taken as tentatively as one would take Cotton Mather's Puritan views about life in the twentieth century. After all, about five centuries elapsed between the fall of Rome and the establishment of a thoroughly non-Roman feudal order in Northern Europe. Similarly, several centuries separate the early empiricist such as Roger Bacon (1214–92) Descartes (1596–1650) and the eruption of a secular, modern social order in the eighteenth or nineteenth centuries. How much perspective, then, is it possible to expect from these early decades of analyzing the post-industrial or postmodern?

Whether the present time represents the dawn of a post-industrial or postmodern era at all is still a matter for debate. Still more contestable are opinions regarding the meanings such a transition would entail. What the postmodern/post-industrial debates *should* signal for business people, management professors and consultants is that these are times for thinking carefully about change, for examining the taken-for-granted, and for asking how relevant our habits of practice are to the future we participate in constructing.

This has implications for understanding the ideology embodied in this book. Like the work of Foucault, this ideology advocates questioning the *status quo*, but it does not do so within an established 'radical' context of seeking to replace one system with another. Questioning of disciplinary society cannot be reduced to 'opposition'. That would be simplistic, a nostalgic atavism. If, today, certain aspects of hierarchy and control are becoming less prominent, the social relations that intersected to produce the normalized or 'disciplinary' individual – standardization, massification, interconnection, and so on – continue to exist. In fact, these networks are becoming *more* elaborated in post-industrial society. A view of the future cannot simply announce 'emancipation' from disciplinary relationships. It

---

4 While I have found no standardized usage of hyphenation regarding the term 'post-modern,' I have found the hyphen used more frequently by authors whose views diverge from mine than by those with whom I am in agreement. Thus, I do not hyphenate. In contrast, there appears to be something close to consensus on the hyphenation of 'post-industrial,' so I follow that usage.

must be more subtle, articulating different possibilities and implications that exist *within* these relationships.

Whatever your geographical, cultural and intellectual place of origin, welcome to my history of 'managing for the twenty-first century.' May your journey be an uncomfortable one!

San Francisco
July, 1995

Acknowledgements

What is an author? As Foucault notes in his famous essay of this title, 'discourses are objects of appropriation.' The author is not a creator, but a borrower; not a source, but a filter of meaning. Indeed, I share Foucault's view that in a consumer society, authorship functions more to control than to disseminate[1] knowledge. Granting special status to appropriately authorized texts is an effective means of limiting and neutralizing the 'dangerous proliferation of significations.' Aided by this acknowledgement section (and by norms of citation), practices of authorship create a network of legitimation, permit establishment of a pedigree for knowledge and fix it in a relatively stable system of evaluation and control. As we who produce texts collude with this system, we make it unnecessary for the police to see that our papers are in order. In the auto-panoptic world of disciplinary knowledge production, we bait increasingly clever traps to catch ourselves. Merely by accepting the position of author, I implicate myself in the modern/industrial mode of rationality whose common sense this book was written to question. After all, everyone I have met and everything I have read is present in this text as a silent (perhaps a horrified) co-author. Nonetheless, my modernist sense of gratitude to several perhaps-mythical subjectivities must be gratified.

Three people deserve special mention as conditions of this book's possibility. First, Lisa Yamilkoski, my wife through the years this book took shape, has served every possible collaborative role *except* typing. She has been a source of intellectual, emotional and financial support; a scrutinizing editor; a proxy for that elusive creature, 'the practitioner,' and a very tolerant companion to a husband who can find Cotton Mather in contemporary management writing more dependably than he can find milk at the corner store. Along with Lisa, Linda Smircich and Marta Calás, dissertation mentors and friends, have been so integrally involved in the production of these ideas that it is quite impossible to imagine this book without the influence of either. If they are seldom explicitly present in the text it is because this topic only indirectly overlaps with their published work. They have done much more than producing a few ideas, however. They have been instrumental in producing the author. Every word of this book bears the mark of my relationship with these two good friends and outstanding scholars.

---

1 The sexualized connotation of this term should not pass without notice. It says more than it means to about knowledge as the pedigreed progeny of our patriarchs.

In other capacities, many have made identifiable contributions to this work. Albert Mills has been instrumental in convincing me to better reflect the role of gender in the text. Joyce Fletcher has been a partner in the development of our ideas regarding relational practices. My other dissertation committee members, Genevieve Chandler, Ann Ferguson and Tony Butterfield, have, in very different ways, each contributed valuably to my thinking. I am grateful to the doctoral students in my classes at the California School of Professional Psychology for repeatedly asking me how these ideas might influence practice in concrete organizational settings and to my program dean, Jo Sanzgiri, for doing everything possible to give a junior faculty member the space within which to write a book. For creating the incubator in which my thinking was nurtured, I thank Sarah Jacobson, Pushkala and Anshuman Prasad, Michael Cavanaugh and the rest of 'those U. Mass. people.' To the rest of my friends and colleagues, I apologize for not being able to recognize each of you individually. Finally, I thank Sue Jones of Sage for her encouragement and support, Hans Lock and Jane Evans for editorial assistance.

And, of course, since this book perpetuates the fiction of the author, I must recognize that while all of the above deserve to share whatever credit this book may receive, its sins of commission and omission are claimed as my exclusive property.

1

Managing for the Next Century – or the Last?

> The revolution we started almost two years ago with the publication of *Reengineering the Corporation* [Hammer and Champy, 1993] continues . . .
>
> (Hammer, 1995: xi)

The New Revolutionaries

The subtitle of Hammer and Champy (1993) is 'a manifesto for business revolution.' Manifesto? Revolution? Ever since that underdog victory of 1776–84, we Americans seem to have been consistently revolting (so to speak), but today a curious 'radical' is emerging. No less a management-consulting supernova than Tom Peters announced in the preface to his 1987 book that it was 'about a revolution.' In 1989, Rosabeth Moss Kanter threw in with the cause, announcing 'a far-reaching revolution in business management.' By 1992, Peters judged his previous work too reactionary, coopting the rhetoric of liberation theology for his new book, *Liberation Management*. By 1993, Peter Drucker confidently announced the arrival of 'post-capitalist society.'[1]

Peters, Kanter, Drucker; hardly a group of wild-eyed radicals. Yet they are talking revolution. And they are only three of the more visible voices in a growing chorus of prominent managers, consultants and theorists who claim today's organizations are changing in transformational, not merely incremental ways. These assorted voices are beginning to coalesce into a fairly standard litany about the conditions and challenges of so-called 'post-industrial' management. One aspect of these changes, we are told, has to do with changing markets and technologies (Table 1.1). Global markets, hypercompetition, smart technologies and so forth are transforming the environment external to the organization. Internally, we are told that this changing environment is producing a new employee, the proactive, self-managing, team-oriented 'knowledge worker,' who embodies the firm's most valuable capital asset (Table 1.2). Look closely at Tables 1.1 and 1.2. It's beginning to sound familiar, isn't it? It should; the newest observation in these lists is more than sixty years old! If management thought has been

---

1 Drucker (1993), Kanter (1989a: 9), Peters (1987: xi, 1992: xxxi).

Table 1.1   *Themes in managing for the new century: changing markets and technologies*

Forty years of the most rapid growth in production, the doubling of the population, and the conquest of the international markets were accomplished with a decrease in the number of firms in the leading industries.[1] The stupendous wave of industrial consolidations which began in the late eighties . . . culminated at the climax of feverish speculation [and] was abruptly terminated in conditions verging on a panic.[2]

Americans, in the first flush of their international victories, may have assumed foolish airs of 'US first and the rest nowhere,'[3] but if we wish to compete with products made in countries where lower wages prevail we shall need to make a superior article. Not only will there be a need in the future for fewer workers to produce a given amount of product but those workers will need to be highly skilled . . . there will be more specialists. . . . In less than ten years more than 2,000,000 people have been thrown out of employment in the United States. They are finding re-employment in relatively new kinds of work, mostly of the service type.[4]

Table 1.2   *Themes in managing for the new century: The new worker – 'making capital' from knowledge work*

The *mechanical* phase . . . [of industrial organization was followed by] the *organic* phase . . . [which] maintained that society ought to be regarded as a complex organism, or at least as analogous to an organism. . . . At the present time the discussion has entered on a third phase. . . . Neither [the mechanical nor organic views] is adequate, or carries us far enough.[5] In the industrial era just passed and now drawing to a close, it was to have been expected that employers, with their chief attention absorbed by questions relating to machines and methods, should neglect the greatest of all their assets . . . their employees. Our records show that the average employee in the average institution represents a capitalized value of between $32,000 and $38,000 to his or her employer. [The organization must] protect that investment from depreciation and loss in every way possible [and] develop and increase its value.[6]

The increased competition that has come in recent years . . . will have to be met, if it is to be met successfully, through education.[7] [The] manager of the future will have to be first of all an educator . . . The contest ahead of us is an educational rivalry.[8] The thoughtful observer of contemporary scientific affairs must have noticed the gradual dissolution of the artificial barriers between different realms of knowledge. There is considerable traffic over the borders of all disciplines.[9] *The greatest thought of this century is the transference of value from property to the human being.*[10]

Machines must more and more be made to do the work for which labor is becoming scarce. . . . But instead of workers being mated to a single machine . . . one individual will supervise the work of a chain of machines . . . requiring, instead of a brainless and emotionless automaton, a well-trained mind and a knowing touch.[11] The employer who does not avail him or herself of the natural, healthy love of work in employees as a motive for excellence loses much.[12] Women [especially], we find, are absolutely loyal. They do not work for us awhile and then quit, which is sometimes urged as one of the objections against woman workers.[13] It is an important part of [the manager's] duties to find out what [the workers'] ideas and opinions are . . . and thus to *make capital out of their originality and their suggestions*.[14]

'evolving,' as our textbooks almost universally claim, why does 'managing for the twenty-first century' look so much like managing for the twentieth?

Table 1.3   *Managing for* which *century? Sources of Tables 1.1 and 1.2 quotations*

[1] Simons, A.M. (1912) *Social Forces in American History*, New York: Macmillan: 309.
[2] Dewing, A.S. (1920) 'The early trust movement outlined,' in R.E. Curtis (ed.), *The Trusts and Economic Control*, New York: McGraw-Hill: 14.
[3] Lawson, W.R. (1903) *American Industrial Problems*, Edinburgh: William Blackwood & Sons: 5.
[4] Struck, F.T. (1930) *Foundations of Industrial Education*, New York: John Wiley & Sons: 16, 69, 72.
[5] Drever, J. (1929) 'The human factor in industrial relations,' in C.S. Myers (ed.), *Industrial Psychology*, London: Thornton Butterworth Ltd: 26.
[6] Blackford, K.M.H. and Newcomb, A. (1914) *The Job, The Man, The Boss*, Garden City, NY: Doubleday, Page & Co.: 22, 38, 60. [Values given in the original of $2,500 to $3,000 have been adjusted for inflation to amounts *c.* 1990.]
[7] Struck, F.T. (1930) *Foundations of Industrial Education*, New York: John Wiley & Sons: 67.
[8] Fagan, J.O. (1909) *Labor and the Railroads*, New York: Houghton Mifflin: 26–7.
[9] Moore, B.V. and Hartmann, G.W. (eds) (1931) *Readings in Industrial Psychology*, New York: D. Appleton-Century Company: 1.
[10] Crowther, S. (1917) 'There's a solution for labor troubles, an interview with John D. Rockefeller, Jr,' in A.W. Shaw Co. (ed.), *Handling Men*, Chicago, IL: A.W. Shaw Co.: 90; emphasis added.
[11] Link, H.C. (1924) *Employment Psychology*, New York: Macmillan: 385–6.
[12] Blackford, K.M.H. and Newcomb, A. (1914: 50, 51, 57).
[13] Ommer, W.I. (1917) 'Why we are replacing men with women,' in A.W. Shaw Co. (ed.), *Handling Men*, Chicago, IL: A.W. Shaw Co.: 54.
[14] Edison, T.A. (1917) Aphorism cited in A.W. Shaw Co. (ed.), *Handling Men*, Chicago, IL: A.W. Shaw Co.: 81; emphasis added.

The Industrial Logic of 'Post-industrial' Management Discourse

What is the key challenge to organizations in the upcoming decades? It is no longer radical to suggest that present-day organizations may be in the midst of transformational change. While the specific topics said to indicate this change vary widely – from multiculturalism and self-management to flexible manufacturing and business process re-engineering – there is an archetypal question structuring the way each issue is approached. That question, today's management mantra, could be phrased as: *how can organizations develop new and innovative ways of managing the employee to achieve world-class efficiency, productivity and competitiveness?* This is the key challenge to 'managing for the twenty-first century,' right?

Wrong.

This sentence has the 'ring of truth' because it is a familiar platitude supported by 'common sense.' On examination, it reflects many key assumptions of industrial, not post-industrial, societies. Precisely because they are assumptions, these beliefs are not available for examination. Before one even begins a discussion of managing in the post-industrial future, one is locked into a phenomenological factory, a factory of the mind. Consider the above platitude phrase by phrase:

Organizations must come up with new and innovative ways . . . Who or what is 'the organization?' Suppliers, customers, and society are not conventionally thought to be part of 'the organization.' Employees are most often conceptualized as contractors who exchange their labor with 'the organization' for compensation. Management as a group is often identified with 'the good of the organization,' but this mandate is contingent upon the claim that managers act as stewards for the stockholders; examples can easily be found, both of managers acting in their self-interest (golden parachutes, poison pills, greenmail) or of stockholders treating managers as disposable employees. For that matter, is the board of directors itself synonymous with the interest of the stockholders in the large organization? How much proportional representation does the proverbial hundred-share grandmother in Hoboken really have? There appears to be *no* concrete entity necessarily represented by 'the organization.' Indeed, as long ago as 1932, Adolf Berle and Gardiner Means, a lawyer and an economist affiliated with Harvard University, saw clearly that:

> Grown to tremendous proportions, there may be said to have evolved a 'corporate system' [within which] . . . [p]hysical control over the instruments of production has been surrendered in ever growing degree to centralized groups who manage property in bulk, *supposedly, but by no means necessarily, for the benefit of the security holders*. . . . Since the corporation is a distinct legal identity, separate and apart from the stockholders . . . the owners of passive property, by surrendering control and responsibility over the active property, have surrendered the right that the corporation should be operated in their sole interest. . . . They have placed the community in a position to demand that the modern corporation serve not alone the owners or the control but all of society. (Berle and Means, 1932: 1, 7, 221, 222, 355, 356; my emphasis)

Consider an example common in US business rhetoric. IBM manufacturing facilities in South Korea may be portrayed as creating jobs for the Korean people and 'developing' their economy. Simultaneously, Sony's purchase of Columbia pictures could be (and was) represented as a Japanese 'attack,' on Hollywood, depleting US wealth and threatening the US economy. These views are consistent with common sense, but they are incompatible with each other. Who or what constitutes 'the organization' changes fundamentally between one example and the other.

. . . **of managing the employee** . . . Speaking of people in organizations as 'managers' and 'employees' will seldom raise an eyebrow. This distinction is deeply ingrained in common sense. Yet, managers are also employees. When is one speaking about manager-employees and when is one speaking about managed-employees? Associating the *tasks* of management with the *persons* called managers makes invisible the numerous ways non-management employees also 'manage' work activities.[2] What is made invisible through this common sense is precisely what one wishes to understand when dealing with the increasing number of situations where worker self-management is desirable. Unless entrenched habits of thought

2 Cf., Fletcher (1994a); Jacques (1992a, 1993); Jacques and Fletcher (1994).

are questioned, one is unlikely to notice the process described by Hollway (1991) through which the domain of management discourse has narrowed over several decades from the general problem of organizing the work of society to the much narrower – and decreasingly relevant – issue of controlling the worker at task-level actions.

. . . **to achieve world-class** . . . In the 1980s 'international management' became a hot topic in the US. While management is highly international today, one might also ask 'why now?' The US *entered* industrial society as an international power in the late 1800s.[3] The US multinational was a dominating force in world markets in the decades immediately after the Second World War.[4] Could the drive to be 'world-class' simply represent the American response to the erosion of a temporary privilege enjoyed while the other major industrialized countries were being devastated by two World Wars? Industrial common sense focuses us on the question 'how can one become world-class?' but never challenges us to ask why the idea of being world-class has become an icon of success at this time.

. . . **efficiency, productivity** . . . It may seem self-evident that business must make efficiency and productivity its first priority, but history suggests that this also may be simply an industrial habit of thought. Economic analysis was once centered on the subject of *wealth*. This changed in the eighteenth century to analysis of *production*. A further shift from production to *productivity* did not occur in the US until the latter 1800s. Today, efficiency and productivity are often enshrined as timeless icons. One can literally not imagine a responsible challenge to their importance. But what of the need for organizational flexibility? Creativity? Social citizenship? Building and balancing a long-term web of relationships and commitments?[5] Might these or other values be necessary for achieving efficiency and productivity? Might the direct pursuit of efficiency and productivity be paradoxically *un*productive in at least some important instances? Industrial common sense makes it all but impossible to think in these terms, even as emerging organizational realities demand it.

. . . **and competitiveness** . . . In the US, to question the goodness of competition is blasphemous, but organizations in market economies are hardly combatants. Systematic and exclusive focus on competitive action obscures a network of cooperative relationships essential to the success of any enterprise. These relational practices are familiar to anyone who engages in business, but they are marginal in both popular and academic

---

3 This is, for instance, the subject of Lawson's *American Industrial Problems* (1903).

4 For instance, Jean Jacques Servan-Schreiber's *The American Challenge* (1967), foresaw the US dominating Europe.

5 One concrete example is the report prepared by Clegg et al. (1994) on the development of 'embryonic industries,' in which corporate self-interest is intertwined with industry and cross-industry alliances as well as multinational social policies. To understand the nurturance of embryonic industries in terms of productivity would be *counter*productive when it is the health of the overall web of developing relationships that one must foster. This report affirms that it is 'decreasingly production costs' that are responsible for 'driving competitive success' (1994: 95).

management writing, which more often reinforces the 'common sense' notion that only competition need be analyzed. One would be surprised today to read of the degree to which the architects of the US industrial order – builders of quasi-monopolistic, government regulated, socially scrutinized empires, the likes of Andrew Carnegie, J.P. Morgan, and John D. Rockefeller – openly identified the advent of the industrial era with a shift from 'invisible-hand' style competition to industry-wide cooperation between employers (some might say collusion, but collusion is not competitive either). Paradoxically, many would support the observation that lack of awareness of the value of relationships is one of the main disadvantages of US business culture relative to that of Japan. But, how does one discuss cooperation as a competitive advantage and competition as a barrier to competitiveness? Industrial common sense gives the very thought an oxymoronic quality.

Walking Away from the Wall

*A co-worker once told me of a recurring dream she has. In this dream, she is facing a high wall. On the other side of the wall she hears a sound and knows, with the certainty of a dreamer, that it comes from a large, hostile animal. In fear, she begins to run along the wall, but the sound follows her as the animal runs along the wall on the other side. She runs faster and faster, her terror increasing until she is stunned awake. Only after she wakes up does she remember that she could have walked **away** from the wall!*

The central idea of this book is that if management knowledge is to have relevance to the emerging post-industrial world(s) both managers and management scholars must learn to 'walk away from the wall.' But before we can do that, we have to see how current ways of knowing constitute running along the wall, our increasing terror prodding us to more of the same rather than to creative responses. How is it that our dialogue about a society increasingly called post-industrial, post-bureaucratic, postmodern – even post-capitalist – unintentionally reinforces patterns of thought and habits of practice that have been coalescing since the emergence of industrialized societies? How is it that we no longer even see the wall itself?

In the following chapters I will first describe the wall and the process of its construction. I will trace the growth of the animals the wall was built to keep out and the reasons industrialized society began to run along the wall it built. Hopefully, the reader who follows me through this part of the book will come to see that, in Kafkaesque fashion, we are fleeing a beast which began to die generations ago, while ignoring the beasts gathering on *our* side of the wall.

What do I mean by 'our'? This will vary with you, the reader. The management knowledge I trace is that of the US, but like Coca Cola and Levi jeans, it is exported worldwide. In the US, we must come to see the degree to which our knowledge of contemporary work is shaped by past eras and past problems. We Americans will be able to understand the specificity of other cultures only to the degree we are able to become reflective about the cultural assumptions structuring our own. For those of you outside the US, studying the cultural roots of American knowledge may help to contextualize the role it will play as it is consumed abroad.

The Need for Critically Reflective Practice

Management has not been a philosophical discipline. The US business hero, real or fictional, has been the 'man [*sic*] of action.' Getting to 'the bottom line' is highly valued. Even management scholarship has aspired to be eminently pragmatic. In the founding issue of *Administrative Science Quarterly*, Thompson expresses a vision of administrative science as the applied arm of the social sciences 'as engineering stands with respect to the physical sciences, or as medicine to the biological' (1956: 103). During times of incremental change, this pragmatic approach allows one to focus one's efforts on solving concrete problems. Treating the work, the worker and the world as objects of common sense allows one to deal with what Thomas Kuhn (1962/1970) called puzzle-solving science. It facilitates the accumulation of knowledge within a well-defined domain. During times of transformational change, however, not only do new problems arise; old *ways* of understanding problems become problems *themselves*. To be successful, puzzle-solving must assume a certain structure of assumptions; thus it does not permit examination *of* assumptions. If present times are indeed times of discontinuous change, prudence suggests inquiring how puzzle-solving science may constitute a barrier to dealing with today's central issues.

Paradoxically, during times such as these, 'pragmatic' approaches to problem-solving are *obstacles* to solving concrete problems while questioning basic values and assumptions – philosophy – is pragmatic. Such times of transformation require critically reflective practice, a blending of the poles of the traditional theorist/practitioner dichotomy. Both practice uninformed by theoretical reflection and theory disconnected from the workplace are sterile and reinforce the *status quo*. All too often we see this manifested in theory which accepts as 'normal' an assembly-line or hardhat workplace that has been declining in importance since the 1930s. Correspondingly, practicing managers often accept, as given, management principles developed in the 1960s or before as well as workplace structures that emerged in response to the needs of industrialization a century ago.

In order to break this cycle of reliance on obsolete expertise, managers, consultants and management scholars must become, in a sense, applied philosophers. These critically reflective practitioners (both theoretical practitioners and practical theorists) must raise issues that were once of central importance to business writing, but have been dormant within mainstream managerial literature for decades: What is 'the organization?' Who is 'the employee?' What is the purpose of the organization in society? What are the rights, responsibilities and values of organization members?

What power relationships currently structure the workplace? How are these relationships changing? What can/should be done about them?

The challenge to what Douglas McGregor (1960) called 'the human side of enterprise' is shown by the topics emergent in the last decade and a half – organizational culture, quality of work life, 'Japanese' management, gender and diversity, international management, business ethics, entrepreneurship, Total Quality Management. These are not simply new topics which can be conveniently added to accumulated theory in behavioral science. Each represents a new 'root metaphor'[6] for viewing work, the worker and the world. Knowledge can no longer be treated as transparent; one must know *from* a specific perspective, incompatible with other perspectives.[7]

One might think that times of transformation would be exciting for theorists of organizing. Surprisingly, this is not the case. In the last decade major figures in organization theory have increasingly described the results of this effort as 'trivial,' 'disappointing,' 'meaningless,' 'out of fashion,' or even 'disintegrating,'[8] but it is still fashionable, after a century, to state that organizational research is on the verge of producing a paradigmatic science. Accordingly, the mainstream of organizational research continues to call for more scientific rigor, more data, more draconian norms requiring conformance to already formulated theory.[9] This puts organization science into a tight position. The last period of major theory development seems to have begun faltering in the early 1970s.[10] Indeed, it is only a slight exaggeration to say that what today's business student is taught about behavior in organizations represents what was known about the white, male, American (and sometimes British) assembly-line worker and college sophomore in 1960. Organizational science is caught in a 'truth-trap.' Scientific rigor dictates that knowledge be developed cumulatively, based on prior knowledge about a presumably stable system. Business needs for knowledge are based on an already turbulent world where the pace of change is increasing. Where rigor and relevance diverge, the norms of the field tend to favor

6 Smircich (1983) has distinguished between views of organizational culture which treat culture as a 'variable,' something to be tacked onto the current way of viewing organizations, and culture as a 'root metaphor,' an altogether different way of viewing *everything* that goes on in organizations.

7 Burrell and Morgan (1979) still make this argument better than any other source with which I am familiar. While some continue to argue that divergent paradigmatic positions can be unified, my experience as a knower does not support this view. Learning about race, gender and philosophy (i.e., the ongoing process of learning that I am white, male and Western/modern) has led me to adopt assumptions that cannot be integrated with the views I once held. I can view my experience through a number of lenses, but each leads to conclusions that are incompatible with the others and only one at a time 'really' reflects my belief. Others may argue that *they* do not have this experience, but I cannot accept the argument from others that I do not.

8 Sequentially: Weick (1989); Daft and Lewin (1990), Webster and Starbuck (1988), Ashmos and Huber (1987) and Perrow (1981).

9 E.g., Bettis and Donaldson (1990), Mitchell and James (1989), Pfeffer (1993), Van de Ven (1989), Webster and Starbuck (1988).

10 Ashmos and Huber (1987), Perrow (1973).

rigor.[11] The presumption that current organizational knowledge represents a fledgling science leads researchers to cling more tightly to this past knowledge the more its relevance is questioned. As a result, old knowledge is recycled and applied in procrustean fashion to new problems.

Example: The 1980s (and continuing) infatuation with so-called 'Japanese' management has made Total Quality Management and its successor, Business Process Re-engineering, a deservedly 'hot' idea. But, W. Edwards Deming, the guru of TQM, is a statistical quality control engineer, born at the turn of the century; he started his career when the 'hot' management concept was Scientific Management. The Deming system was fully articulated before the Second World War. While TQM concepts can be valuable to today's organizations, what does it say about the state of knowledge development in organizational theorizing that the latest theory for organizing people at work comes from half-century old ideas developed by a century-old engineer?

Example: Peter Senge became the celebrity author regarding post-industrial 'learning organizations' with his book, *The Fifth Discipline* (1990). Senge offers a number of tips that could be quite valuable to the reader, but his theoretical position rests on systems theory developed and popularized four decades ago. Theoretically, much of *The Fifth Discipline* could be viewed as application of Karl Weick's *The Social Psychology of Organizing*, first published in 1969.

To summarize, we are living through a curious moment when a 'revolution' is being announced whose *avant garde* sit at the heart of the current power elite and whose *internationale* is composed from minor variations on a nineteenth-century theme. One might be tempted to dismiss the whole show as a lot of empty noise except for the growing conviction that transformational changes of some kind are indeed sweeping the organizational world. How is one to make sense of these mixed messages? Chapter 2 will outline some of the main ideas and conclusions presented in this book and will make a case for the practical value of historical perspective as a tool for understanding these current problems. It will briefly sketch the 'discursive' perspective of this book, contrasting it to managerialist and critical histories a reader is more likely to have encountered. We can then proceed, in Chapter 3, with the main thread of the story – the historical construction of *l'employé*.

11 Cf., Staw (1985).

2

Evolutionary and Discursive Histories of Knowledge

The 'Evolution' of Management Knowledge: The First Century and a Half

> It would be no difficult task to compile . . . [a] Hand-Book of Mercantile practice. It would be still more profitable to arrange this mass of material into something like a system, and to construct out of them a true theory of business. (Freeman Hunt, 1857: vi; *Worth and Wealth: Maxims for Merchants and Men of Business*)

> Unless we admit that rules of thumb, the limited experience of the executives in each individual business, and the general sentiment of the street, are the sole possible guides for executive decisions of major importance, it is pertinent to inquire . . . how a proper theory of business is to be obtained. . . . Otherwise, business will continue unsystematic, haphazard, and for many men a pathetic gamble. (Wallace B. Donham, 1922: 1; inaugural issue of the *Harvard Business Review*)

> [T]he possibility of a science of administration is only now coming to be taken seriously. . . . There is now every reason to believe that an administrative science can be built, although the building will not be easy. (James D. Thompson, 1956: 103; inaugural issue of *Administrative Science Quarterly*)

> [T]he field of organization studies is characterized by a fairly low level of paradigm development. . . . [I]f anything, the field is more fragmented and diverse than it has been. (Jeffrey Pfeffer, 1993: 607–8; widely debated article in *Academy of Management Review*)

Don't Know Much About History

Abraham Zaleznik is angry. *The Managerial Mystique* (1989) is a sustained polemic against the atrophy of leadership in business. Judith Bardwick (1991) is upset also, claiming that the 'psychology of entitlement' – believing that one is owed an income by society – is a 'habit that is killing American business.' The chapter in which she first makes these points is entitled 'The American Dream Shattered.' Zaleznik's appears to hold today's managers personally responsible for failing to exhibit the leadership qualities of their predecessors. Similarly, Bardwick's target is the moral turpitude of workers who lack the old-fashioned work ethic. Both authors observe important problems, but, moral outrage is not the same as a plan of action; what is to be done about these issues?

Both the managerial mystique and the entitled worker are quite reasonable results of work practices and structures deliberately put in place and reinforced for nearly a century. Entrepreneurial leadership has not disappeared by chance; one can follow its systematic exclusion from large industrial organizations – and for very good reasons. Today's 'entitled' worker was produced slowly and painfully over two generations because workers centered on output and seeking a voice in the work process were obstacles to production of the industrial corporate order as it has developed. The 'entitled' attitude is a byproduct of wage systems, work relationships and job design deliberately introduced to create a task-centered worker. If that worker is today a problem, should one look for a solution in the worker's morality or in the systems reinforcing worker disinterest?

In other words, if one wishes to change today's behaviors, one must change systems of authority, reward and work design. To criticize organization members for exhibiting behaviors produced by organizational systems amounts to blaming the victim. This applies equally to those who would seek greater workplace democracy and those who simply seek more efficient methods of controlling productivity. But, how does one better understand these forces? How can one influence them? One source of insight is to follow the construction of the system over time, to study how the relationships Bardwick and Zaleznik find so repugnant were produced as the answers to problems now forgotten. In reflecting on the conflicts surrounding the introduction of these relationships and on the other possibilities foreclosed by their establishment, one can find new insights for understanding today's issues. If one still wishes to express moral indignation, that is one's prerogative, as long as one does not imagine this to be a step toward changing work practices.

Challenging Common Sense

The employee has a history of little more than a century. My interest in writing this 'history of the employee' has developed from the observation that the 'human nature' of the person in work organizations has been surprisingly malleable for something presumed to change at the slow pace of biological evolution. I have documented the changing work relationships and assumptions about the rights, duties, interests and innate 'nature' of the worker associated with the emergence of this term in the US for the purpose of clarifying the great depth to which individual 'nature' is socially conditioned. I have no interest in attempting to 'correct' the historical record. Rather, I believe this analysis is necessary as a prologue to developing knowledge about the post-industrial worker. Without an appreciation of the role played by industrial work relationships in producing today's worker, we will imagine these qualities to be 'natural' – that is, a basic property of human beings. In so doing, we will import into our theorizing about the future of work, assumptions, values and beliefs which are a legacy of the (American) industrial past.

Emerging with the employee is the manager, a worker who is also an employee. A third actor, also an employee, is the employed professional. None of these subjects has a pre-industrial antecedent. It is possible that in a century none of them will remain important. Other actors – the slave, the vassal, the clerk – have come and gone. Perhaps the present-day search for the 'knowledge worker' represents another shift in work's cast of characters. Researching the history of the employee has led me to a number of conclusions that may initially strike a reader as counterintuitive. Good; common sense is the enemy.[1] The story I will tell goes something like this:

Professional knowledge, certified by the university and legitimated by association with scientific objectivity, was the key social power relation through which the US was restructured after the demise of nineteenth-century Federalist social institutions. This network of relationships both played a key role in creating the very possibility of modern management and was instrumental in constructing the 'discourse of objectivity.' This objectivist discourse was appealing to a society torn apart by vested interests, but, over a century, it has also sedimented into an extremely powerful form of authority. Today, because its origin is forgotten, this discourse has assumed the status of being self-evidently good and necessary. Scientific Management, the initial carrier of the discourse of objectivity, does not constitute the beginning of management history, but the end of its prehistory. Within this discourse, 'hard' and 'soft' approaches to management have not been antithetical, but reciprocal and complementary. During this period, the relationship between knowledge and industry produced an 'industrial revolution' in education. Business itself went through a 'mercantile[2] revolution' and a 'financial revolution,' as important as its industrial revolution.

This revolution also represented a 'masculinization' of work practices and of organizational knowledge.[3] That is, relative to today's sex-role norms,

1 I am grateful to Anshuman Prasad for the phrase 'common sense is the enemy.'
2 References to 'mercantile' society are unrelated to European Mercantilism, the economic doctrine. Mercantilism was dead before the US mercantile order emerged.
3 This conception of masculinization draws heavily from Bordo (1986). According to Bordo, '"masculine" describes not a biological category but a cognitive style, an epistemological stance' (1986: 450). She draws a parallel between individual masculine socialization (characterized by development of an individuated self) and the growth of Enlightenment Europe whose increasingly empirical and rationalist worldview removed God from the world of immediate experience, leaving a world characterized by 'autonomy, separation and distance' (1986: 450). The world, which had been a living and breathing (if often cruel) mother, 'becomes inert *res extensa*: dead, mechanically interacting matter' (1986: 452). With a society, as with an individual, Bordo reasons that, '[o]ne mode of dealing with that separation is through the denial of any longing for that lost union through an assertion of self against the mother and all that she represents and a rejection of all dependency on her. In this way, the pain of separateness is assuaged, paradoxically, by an even more definitive separation – but one that is chosen this time

forms of social practice once integral to the world of business were devalued, consigned to the domestic sphere and stigmatized as 'women's work.' The domestic sphere itself atrophied as the role of the middle-class homemaker metamorphosed from producing to 'shopping.' Today, this devaluation constitutes a major barrier to effectively managing 'knowledge work' because such management requires metaphorically feminine qualities long since driven to the invisible margins of the business world.

From his/her point of appearance (*c.* 1920), the employee was *already* a knowledge worker. Through all of this, the boundaries of management were conditioned by traditional American values and ideology – especially the frontier and Protestant perfectionism – which it was also instrumental in transforming. From the turn of the last century to the turn of the next, the central issue of organizational studies has moved from understanding problems of the person in the organization to understanding problems of the organization in society.

History? What Can You Do With It?

The French philosopher Jean Baudrillard (1989: 28, 76) was close to the mark when he said of America that it 'has no past' and 'lives in a perpetual present;' this is, he said, 'the land of the "just as it is."' Neither do we Americans particularly value reflection.[4] This is still a land where one redeems the value of life through 'good works,' even if it is no longer done for a Puritan or Quaker deity. 'Practical' books on management are expected to offer a checklist, five things you can do tomorrow, a blueprint for transforming the organization by next Tuesday. This is not that sort of book, yet its intent is every bit as practical.

This is not a history written to reclaim the past. What was the 'real' meaning of the period 1870–1920? Who knows? I accept the Nietzschean dictum that the origin is lost; the meanings of the past cannot be reconstructed. This still allows history a role, however, in interpreting the present. Having forgotten the processes through which the present has been constructed, we can easily take it at face value, placing great weight on superficial relationships, overlooking more substantive ones and taking as inevitable, timeless or universal relationships whose social origins are localized and specific. Like a glacier, all of social life is in slow, steady movement. Standing on a glacier, its path is not evident, but studying where it has come from helps one to better understand where it is heading. This

and aggressively pursued. It is therefore experienced as autonomy rather than helplessness' (1986: 451). Citing work such as Chodorow (1978) and Gilligan (1982), Bordo argues that this historical view does not naturalize masculinity and femininity. Rather, it 'helps to underscore that the embodiment of these gender-related perspectives in actual men and women is a cultural, not a biological, phenomenon' (1986: 455).

4 Two insightful analyses of these American qualities are Hofstader (1963) and Wachhorst (1981).

history is written to show some of the patterns made by the present as it kaleidoscopes into the immediate future. It does not yield to prediction, but seeks to throw into relief the fault lines and points of leverage marking the points at which intentional action is most likely to have results. This is, then, literally a practical book because it seeks to change work practices by changing the way we think about what can be changed, what should be changed and what possibilities exist for those involved in change.

Foucault spoke of his analyses as histories of the present. This book is offered in the same spirit. Its intent is not to clarify thinking about the last century, but the next. The story of industrialization is told in order to illustrate the traces of industrial thinking embedded in 'post-industrial' rhetoric. The cultural origins of the employee are searched so that one might better critique the nineteenth-century Federalist values shaping the logic of 'managing for the twenty-first century.' The story of the employee's emergence as a construction, a complex intersection of intentional actions and changing social forces, is told with the hope that it will change the way you view the issues, options, and strategies for dealing with the problems of network organizations, knowledge work, hypercompetition and other problems of today – and tomorrow.

Histories of Organizational Science: Managerialist, Critical, Discursive

Managerialist histories

Open any introductory American text in organization studies and, if it contains a history of management thought, the story will almost certainly be linear, progressive, teleological and truth-centered. It is *linear* in that management is presented as a continuous thread running through civiliz-ation; 'Would you believe that organization theory issues were addressed in the Bible? Well they were!' (Robbins, 1990: 36). It is *progressive* in that management knowledge is portrayed as becoming increasingly perfect over time. Pre-industrial societies may have been 'largely biased against the concept of managing organizations effectively and efficiently' (Bowditch and Buono, 1994: 7), but knowledge has 'evolved' from that primitive point. The term 'evolution' appears almost universally in these stories, but not in a sense strictly in accord with Darwin or current biology. Rather, it has what is called a *teleological* connotation, the idea that knowledge is not just adapting but improving relative to a final goal. The goal in this case is a paradigmatic science of behavior in organizations. Were this day to arrive, behavior in organizations could be assessed with reference to rules of interaction analogous to the periodic table of chemistry or the gas laws of physics. In this sense, such histories are *truth-centered*.

History has a very subordinate role in such inquiry because it is merely a record of the progress made toward discovery of the immutable, underlying rules of human behavior. Were this day to arrive, it would quite literally be the 'end of history.' When science can predict and control, history is simply the story of the reduction over time of erroneous thinking. 'Knowledge' is embodied in testable propositions whose story is irrelevant. In organizational studies, histories of this form can be summed up with reference to the five themes around which they are usually structured: *First there was Taylor who applied science to work; then there was Hawthorne who discovered the informal organization; Weber reintroduced structural considerations; today we have sophisticated models which integrate these perspectives (and implicitly) we are close to a paradigmatic science of behavior in organizations.*

Critical histories

If one has encountered an alternative to such histories, it is likely to be based on critical/Marxist interpretations. Where managerialist histories portray change as the result of a changing 'environment' which is benign (or at least inevitable), critical histories are more likely to emphasize the role of human agency as a form of self-interested power to explain these same phenomena. Managerialist stories tend to seek explanations for differences of organizational role, authority or reward in quasi-natural objective forces such as 'the market,' 'the environment,' or the 'evolution' of systems. Critical histories are more likely to treat the development of present work relationships as stemming from the efforts of a hegemonic class which has collectively created a social system structured to its advantage. Despite this central difference, however, critical histories emerge from a context no less linear, progressive, teleological and truth-centered.[5] In a sense, managerialist and critical stories are like sports teams. They oppose each other, but within a common framework regarding rules, game time, stadium location and structure. They are each integral parts of the same story.

Discursive histories

The discursive story in this book will be based on attempts to look at this industrial perspective itself. This does not mean that I present my story as superior or these others as 'incorrect.' These stories are not incorrect, but they are context-specific. They systematically stress some elements and omit others. They place interpretations upon evidence in accordance with the norms of a particular cultural group and historical period. Any statement they make relies for meaning upon a framework of basic assumptions about reality, truth, values and the nature of knowledge which are, by definition, not *testable*. Competing assumptions are, however, *con*testable.[6] They can

5 Alvesson and Wilmott (1992b) discuss some of the issues raised for the critical theorist by the assumptions of poststructuralist discursive analysis.
6 Cf., Burrell and Morgan (1979).

be discussed, their points of similarity and conflict assessed, their implications weighed. While reading this book, please bear in mind that I have
chosen a discursive approach because it provides a perspective from which
to study the social context *from which* managerialist and critical histories
have emerged. The same context specificity applies, of course, to my story.
It reflects certain values; it is bound to a time and a culture. I do not offer it as
more *true* than these other stories; I offer it as more *useful* for analysis of
certain problems. Central to these is the present 'truth-trap' of organizational science.

The Truth-trap in Organizational Knowledge

What is truth? At the height of nineteenth-century positivism, one might
have responded that truth is accurate knowledge of reality. Based upon this
positivistic worldview, the ideal system of inquiry would make it possible to
collect data free of contamination by social values and belief. Data could be
accumulated into facts, facts into theories, theories into laws. In principle, a
single, unified system of knowledge reliably predicting all physical, animal
and human interaction would be achievable. The language of this worldview
would be mathematics, the ultimate system of universal, logical abstraction.
Thus, measurement would have primacy over other forms of information. In
some domains, this approach has been highly successful. In physics, for
instance, the day-to-day world of mechanical and electrical phenomena is so
thoroughly mapped that for several decades most news has been in the areas
of subatomic or cosmic phenomena. Not so the human sciences, including
organizational studies.

In recent years, unity in organizational inquiry has been decreasing. One
aspect of this splintering has been the appearance of competing 'paradigms'
of knowledge: interpretive, critical, and post-analytic perspectives on
meaning. Another has been the growing prominence of demographic
diversity with the appearance of new 'voices'[7] based on gender, race, sexual
identity and so forth. Yet another source of difference has been the
multi-national locus of problems. In the US, the overwhelming response to
these new issues and voices has been retrenchment, reliance on more data,
more sophisticated computer models and 'meta-paradigmatic' frameworks
for reuniting divergent schools of thought within a single body of assumptions about the value, purpose and means of acquiring knowledge.
Ironically, some of the staunchest advocates of this strategy, such as
Webster and Starbuck (1988) and Pfeffer (1993) are also among those most
vocal in detailing the steady erosion of success along this path for the last two
or three decades.

In the field of knowledge in general, this reliance on data to produce truth
has been eroding since the turn of the century. In the last century,

7 The metaphor of 'voice' in this sense was popularized with Gilligan (1982).

non-Euclidean geometries, such as those of Lobachevskiy and Riemann, cast doubt on the objectivity of physical time and space itself. This was given practical application by Einstein, whose work undercut the presumed boundary between matter and energy. In 1932 Kurt Gödel proved mathematically that a mathematical system cannot show the sufficiency of its own knowledge – a fatal refutation to the Logical Positivist tradition from Comte to Russell and Whitehead. The two World Wars devastatingly indicted the linear argument of Western progress. In 1962 Thomas Kuhn argued persuasively that 'paradigms' – frameworks of basic assumptions in science – do not 'emerge' from data, but reflect the values, beliefs and central problems of the community of knowers producing them. In recent years, a number of competing worldviews – most prominently feminist epistemology, post-analytic[8] philosophy, and post-colonialism – have presented massive evidence that the core values of science correspond more closely to the core values of white, Western males of a certain historical period than they do to other people and other times. Science may be objective, but 'objective' does not equate to 'value free'. Data may be statistically unbiased, but this says nothing of the social bias it may contain.[9]

These considerations suggest that scientific knowledge is context-specific, but they are not inherently *anti*-scientific – unless one holds an outdated nineteenth-century view of scientific inquiry as a machine capable of generating objective truth. This is the 'truth-trap' of organization studies. Many organizational researchers would dispute this allegation, claiming that they do not universalize, that they now seek 'meso' or 'mid-range' rather than grand theories, that they understand that correlation is not causation. This is irrelevant. What creates the truth-trap is that organizational science continues to be governed by rules of inquiry which operate *as if* they produced the Truth. Sealing the truth-trap is a method of education for teachers and researchers which stresses hypothesis-testing methodology to the near exclusion of the history and sociology of knowledge. Within this method-driven community of knowers, 'research' means 'data,' which is easily confused with 'meaning.' Attempts to contextualize the role of empirical inquiry are mistakenly seen as attacks on empiricism. The metanarrative within which knowledge to date has been produced cannot be examined because it is believed to be a transparent framework, not an expression of values. Examination of this metanarrative is a key goal of this book.

Were scientific knowledge satisfying the needs of the members of the organizational science community, one might dismiss these philosophical

---

8 By 'post-analytic' I mean primarily poststructuralist and postmodern positions. I am reluctant to use the term 'postmodern,' because it is a term thrown about in so many inconsistent and heavily value-laden ways. Additionally, as this term becomes more popular in the US it is coming to signify a form of, not a break with, emancipatory humanism (e.g., Boje and Dennehy, 1993). The Boje and Dennehy text has much to offer, but its assumptions are not those to be found in this book.

9 Cf., Shipman (1994).

considerations, but such is not the case. Those in organizations are increasingly critical of organizational theorizing as esoterica produced for tenure and promotion rather than for organizational benefit. Eminent researchers lament the absence of new theories, the continuing small 'effect sizes,' the splintering and stagnation of research streams. Students routinely note the lack of correspondence between textbook themes and current issues in the business and popular press. But, having construed accumulated knowledge as truth (or as if it were truth, which amounts to the same thing in this instance) organizational science faces a dilemma. To hold on to this knowledge very likely involves the expense of decreasing relevance to its applied domain. To jettison it will call into question the degree to which the field was ever a science to begin with.

Does this mean that science is a barrier to understanding? No. It means that the cultural context within which science operates must also become a subject of study. As the lives of Gregor Mendel, Barbara McClintock, Einstein and others have illustrated,[10] exemplars of scientific thinking are far more problem-driven than technique-driven. 'Science' is not a method; it is a form of wonder, starting from and returning frequently to a rich world of metaphor, passing only secondarily and temporarily through the world of technique and method. The truth-trap of science is created by a methodology that has become disconnected from wonder, that is no longer problem-driven. Instead of asking science to deliver *true* knowledge about *reality*, it is entirely possible to envision a science asked to produce *useful* knowledge about *current problems*.[11] But, what is useful? What is a current problem? There are no clean and easy answers to these questions, but a discursive perspective on inquiry can be of invaluable assistance in creating the possibility of dialogue about these issues.

Discursive Inquiry: Study *of* the Truth-trap

This book affirms the need for a community of specialists whose goal is to better understand interaction in organizations and to communicate that knowledge. It does not, however, presuppose the necessity for any particular norms of organizing that community, any specific methods of inquiry or any necessary core values. In this book I hope to provide a basis for students, practitioners and academics to more openly discuss the norms and forms of organizational inquiry appropriate to the problems and interests of today and the upcoming years. What these problems may be is still highly debatable. Perhaps we are in the throes of a revolution, but we should remind ourselves that it appears to be a condition of modernity for

10 On Mendel, see Foucault (1972b); for McClintock, Keller (1983); for Einstein, Pais (1982).
11 Haraway (1988), a primatologist, provides an excellent summary argument and references for a feminist 'successor science' that would be an example of this point.

every generation to believe it is in the midst of revolutionary change. What we can observe with somewhat greater certainty is the increasingly strained correspondence between a system of knowledge formed during the last century and the problems and issues of the present day.

Unlike both managerialist and critical histories, which attempt to tell the truth about organizations, this story documents the development, not of organizations, but of knowledge *about* organizations. It is an attempt to trace the construction of organizational knowledge in order to make connections between the form this knowledge took and the broader social currents within which it formed. My discursive position developed from the archaeological/genealogical approach of Foucault, but this is not the place for a detailed explanation of his poststructuralist position. Besides, I believe that carrying on in the spirit of Foucault is better done by freely appropriating and embroidering upon his work – 'making it groan' – than by using his writings as a rigid system, a fate he bemoaned regarding Freud and Marx.

How should one understand the term 'discursive?' The term has a relatively precise meaning grounded in Saussurian linguistics[12] to which I have attempted to remain faithful, but a relatively usable lay understanding of discourse might be 'what *can* be said,' in the following sense:

> 'Discourse' might be interpreted to mean 'what can be said.' This differs from focusing on what *is* said. While the *site* of discursive analysis is language, discourse is a relationship between bodies, meanings, power and language. Through the process of discursive relationships, material events are related to the words through which they attain meaning. (Jacques, 1992a: 87)[13]

For instance, in a group of sales people who are sports enthusiasts, business propositions might have to be framed in sports metaphors in order to be taken seriously. That requirement is a discursive boundary. Not only does this norm affect how information can be represented, it limits what can be said to phenomena representable in this language and imbues whatever is said with the values of sports-talk. In organizational science, knowledge presented as the result of measurement and hypothesis testing has higher status than 'anecdotal' knowledge. Pronouncements of experts are valued above the 'naive' interpretations of workers. These are also discursive boundaries. In general, one might ask 'in order for an observation to be heard as sensible, what form must it be in?', 'What discursive boundaries must it observe?', 'Which must it avoid?'

Knowledge about organizations has not always been put into the form it is today. My hope is that tracing the discursive construction of the truth-trap will make possible another way of dealing with the dilemma it presents. Instead of constructing the available alternatives dichotomously as truth or

12 Culler (1986) has written an excellent short introduction to Saussure; one fairly short source on the meaning of discourse is Foucault (1972b).

13 The reader new to discursive analysis might find Harré and Gillett (1994), which compares behaviorist, cognitive and discursive paradigms in psychology, informative.

falsity, I would like to show the possibility of thinking in terms of multiple ways of telling the truth, none more 'correct' than the others, but each useful in different ways, for different purposes; each having different implications for who will have voice, who will receive benefits, who will be overlooked. As the empiricist philosopher Willard Van Orman Quine (1953) has argued, one cannot show 'Homer's gods' to be less real than 'brick houses on Elm Street,' but one can choose between them based on the pragmatic criterion of how well each belief system contributes to solving the problems at hand.

'The problems at hand' will, of course, vary from one community of knowers to another. The community I wish to address in this book is those who are seeking new perspectives for relating accumulated organizational knowledge with present organizational problems. If one were to read the history of this period for other purposes, perhaps other 'truths' (other evidence, connections, interpretations) would be appropriate. This contextualizing of truth is not relativism. One can establish to most people's satisfaction that Freeman Hunt did or did not say thus-and-so on page 221 of *Worth and Wealth*. The initial capitalization of US Steel is a matter of record, not speculation. While my values and interpretations pervade this text, they do not appear in a vacuum. This argument is a construction and, like a physical construction, you the reader can assess its logic, its internal proportions, its aesthetics and solidity. Most important, I ask you to submit each point as well as the overall work to this criterion: 'If I accept this argument, how does it help me to see new opportunities for creating, interpreting and applying knowledge about people in organizations?'

3

Federalist Reality – the Pre-history of Management

'It's Not the Same America' proclaims a 1994 article in *Inc.* magazine. According to this article:

> America has always been, above all else, the land of opportunity, a country where those at the bottom can work their way up the ladder to succeed. But now that ideal is endangered – the bottom rung is broken. For some surprising reasons, the American Dream is being destroyed where it's needed most. (Welles, 1994: 82)

Welles echoes Bardwick's (1991: 7) claim that 'the American Dream is based on a contract that says, "if you work hard, you are going to be more successful than your parents were."' It is not surprising that Newman (1988) entitled her study of 'downward mobility in the American Middle Class' as a fall 'from grace.' Many areas of the world have distinct national or ethnic identities, hopes and aspirations, but it makes no sense to speak of the 'French Dream' or the 'Iranian Dream.' The American Dream is a peculiarly specific ideology combining belief in god-given rights and escape from the tyranny of limits. Only in America can the average person be above average. Yet, today's American Dream has not 'always been;' as Welles assumes, the dream of the founding colonists was for a very different form of society. Until the end of the last century, there was no 'ladder' to work one's way 'up.' Like the successive cities of Troy, built one on another, today's American Dream is built upon the foundations of previous dreams. If it is indeed being 'destroyed,' this is not the first time. One must understand this dream to understand the cultural products of the US – including management knowledge. This is both because the US has a strong ideology and because a tenet of the ideology is that the US is not ideological. The present American Dream is largely a product of the nineteenth century.

The US is a nineteenth-century country.[1] At the dawn of that century, the US was a new republic imagining itself an achieved Utopia of yeoman farmers and small merchants. By the end of the century, today's corporate-capitalist social order was substantially in place. The American Dream had left the farm and entered the factory, reshaping itself along the way into a radically different vision, yet one operating within the same Puritan/Quaker framework. Standing at the beginning of that century, Benjamin Franklin

---

1 I have in mind a 'long' nineteenth century, *c.* 1785–1900, loosely analogous to and witnessing some of the same transformations as England's 'long eighteenth century' between the Restoration and the death of George III.

stood in the shadow of Cotton Mather and the founding spirit of the Massachusetts Bay Colony Puritans. Facing the end of the century, Frederick Taylor, Katherine Blackford and Elbert Gary cast shadows into and beyond the present day. To understand US management knowledge, one must understand the radical restructuring of social reality that divides the nineteenth century.

This chapter will sketch some aspects of social relationships in the US in the approximate period 1790–1870. This period, which I refer to as 'Federalist reality,' was a product of eighteenth-century changes symbolized and set loose by the revolution from Britain. As a mode of life, it ended with industrialization. Three aspects of this world are especially significant to the story of management's emergence; these are the *frontier*, *community*, and *character*. One must understand the role these ideas once played in binding together US social and economic life if one is to understand how management as it is understood today emerged from the world marked by their demise.

The Federalist[2] World, Frontier and Community

One must not imagine eras to be too neatly divided from each other. Eras are analytical constructions, not empirical realities. The colonial world flowed gradually into Federalist society, and much of the Federalist colors present-day American life. That said, the years 1790–1870 bracket a relatively distinct chapter in the successive forms taken by the American Dream over three and a half centuries. The American revolution released into the nineteenth century a democratic populism far more radical than the colonial spirit of the eighteenth. This is the spirit that springs from the pages of De Tocqueville (1835/1956). Similarly, historians approach unanimity in pronouncing the decade of the 1870s a time of transformational change as industrialization swept through US society.[3]

To a great extent, the present mythos of America is an idealized vision of the reality of Federalist society. The local community was the dominant social entity. Such communities could be fairly said to be constituted as the voluntary association of free, self-determining citizens (at least among native-born, white families). The nation as a unified republic was still far in the future. As the title of D.W. Griffith's classic film about the Civil War indicates, the 'Birth of a *Nation*' was not a *fait accompli* until late in the

2 The term 'republican' might be a more appropriate label for this time. I am reluctant to use this term because this is not a book for experts in political science and it might be ideologically confusing to use the name of an extant political party to describe nineteenth-century society. I also believe the idea of (a very loose) federation rather than that of republic captures the popular spirit of a time when, for the average person, the 'republic' was little more than a central office for customs collections and diplomatic relations.

3 Cf., DeBrizzi (1983), Dorfman (1969), Foner (1962), Hays (1957), Porter (1973), Smith (1984), Wiebe (1967).

century (*c.* 1865). Despite these limitations, one can consider the early nineteenth century to have been marked by a distinct ethos, a 'common sense.' It is impossible now to represent what this ethos meant to the Federalist citizen, but it is possible to see how Federalist common sense was not the common sense of today. As one comes to better understand the social origin of present US assumptions about the way things 'naturally' are, one comes to better understand the industrial common sense by which thinking about 'management' is (anachronistically) bounded. First, it is important to look at what lay beyond the Federalist community – the frontier.

The frontier

Whatever diverse visions colonizers brought to the Western hemisphere, a prominent feature of their American Dream was the sense of escaping beyond the boundaries of society into a world without limits, a world of unbounded potential. The frontier was not a place beyond limits, however. It was the meeting place of the unknown and the colonizing world. The North American frontier was the outer boundary of old Europe. Pioneering was an activity *within*, not beyond, the culture of old Europe. This ambivalence – imagining oneself a rebel, a trailblazer, a self-determining free spirit, while depending for support on that from which one imagines oneself escaping – is an ambivalence that is still at the core of American inconsistencies about the meaning of the person in relation to social institutions.

'The New World,' writes Wachhorst (1981: 105–6), 'became the magic kingdom in a large literature of utopias' fueling 'the spirit of the Enlightenment, with its faith in the rational perfectibility of man and his environment.' Adam Smith (1776/1937: 69) recognized the role of the frontier in the rapid growth of the North American colonies. Noting that 'England is certainly, in the present times, a much richer country,' he points to the colonies' higher wages, needed to secure a labor force free to quit and start anew on the frontier. At the end of the last century, this was restated in Frederick Jackson Turner's famous 'frontier hypothesis.'

> Whenever social conditions tended to crystallize in the East, whenever capital tended to press upon labor . . . there was this gate of escape. . . . Men would not accept inferior wages and a permanent position of social subordination when this promised land of freedom and equality was theirs for the taking. (Turner, 1893/1956: 28)

Where farmland can be had for the taking, a worker need not enter permanent 'wage slavery.' Business need not worry about depletion or efficient use of resources when there is an infinite West. Communities can expel their undesired elements, human and material, into a void. Whatever tensions exist today, one can imagine they will be solved tomorrow, through growth or through starting over. The 'good life' need not be gained by subjugating one's fellows; it can be built through honest toil by the average, competent citizen. This Dream persists to the present day. Seventy years after Turner noted the official closing of the frontier as documented by the Census of 1890, John Kennedy promised Americans a 'New Frontier,' Alaska; then space travel became the 'last frontier.' Harvard economist and Clinton cabinet member, Robert Reich, has labeled the post-industrial future *The Next American Frontier* (1983). Always looking forward, contemporary America endlessly re-enacts the defining act of 'westering' without which it is lost, like the old wagon master in John Steinbeck's short story 'The Leader of the People.'

> It was westering and westering. Every man wanted something for himself, but the big beast that was all of them wanted only westering. . . . We carried life out here and set it down the way those ants carry eggs. And I was the leader. The westering was as big as God, and the slow steps that made the movement piled up until the continent was crossed. . . . Then we came down to the sea and it was done. . . . There's no place to go. . . . There's a line of old men along the shore hating the ocean because it stopped them. (Steinbeck, 1938: 302)

Over time, this vision has achieved something like the status of divine covenant, a perquisite of citizenship.[4] Is it surprising to find 'entitled' workers in a land whose founding documents contain a 'bill of entitlements' and constitutionally guarantee one's right to happiness?[5] America *means* escape from the limits of zero-sum; on the frontier, everyone can have more than their share.

The community

While a frontier vision could only look forward, the American community backed into the future. There were three forms of relationship between community and frontier. First, there were the scavengers, who through plunder, trade and trapping simply sought to find items of value to repatriate. Sometimes this took the form of imposing a social order, as in the Spanish and Portuguese Americas, or of trapping and trading in the manner of the semi-legendary Davy Crockett and Daniel Boone. Scavenging had little effect on the social structures of the industrializing US (but this might be important for understanding other countries' stories as they are told in other studies). Second, there were the manorial settlements which recreated a feudal order based on a landed aristocracy. In Anglo North America, this social order once stretched from the Hudson River's patroons of New York state southward to the boundaries of Latin America. These societies

---

4 Bellah et al. (1985), Madden (1970), McCaffrey (1964), Newman (1988), Slotkin (1992), Wachhorst (1981) are among the many who have written on this subject.

5 The Bill of Rights, the first eleven amendments to the US constitution, is a list of benefits to which people are entitled simply by virtue of being citizens. There is no *quid pro quo*. Happiness is enshrined as a central cultural value in the famous phrase from the Declaration of Independence asserting that 'life, liberty and the pursuit of happiness' are 'self-evident' and 'unalienable.' I was made aware of the cultural specificity of this value at a recent discussion panel when a UK immigrant observed that he had always found this odd about the US.

declined in importance as Anglo North America industrialized and were decisively eliminated by the defeat of the feudal South by the industrializing North in the 'industrial revolution' known as the American Civil War. The third form of colonization was most central to the story told in this book. It was the attempt to create a 'New' England within the beliefs and precepts of Puritan and Quaker Protestantism. These colonies grew to dominate the business culture of the United States which, in turn, now exports this culture to the world.

The Federalist citizen was largely a legacy of this third group. In the Federalist period, the theocratic founding vision had slowly given way to a secular, more outer-directed, worldview, but no hierarchical institution had yet emerged to replace the institutions of the small community as the primary locus of social control. State governance was loose; federal government was largely hypothetical. The public role of the church had been steadily slipping for over a century. The Revolution had resulted in the marginalization of the pre-revolutionary elite, many of whom had lost at least their status, if not their fortunes or lives, supporting the losing Tories. Among those who were counted (white, male citizens), differences of wealth were relatively modest. George Washington, the richest man in America[6] at the time of the Revolution, could, with some stretching, be thought of as a farmer much like any other, differing in degree, but not in kind, from other citizens. As late as 1850,[7] as many as nine in ten white, male citizens worked for themselves as farmers, merchants or craftsmen. Even 'manufactures,' as the census labeled them, averaged only three to four workers each.[8] Thus, work was organized through interactions between the self-employed. There was little interaction beyond the community. Typical work relationships were face-to-face interactions with those one knew personally over a long period of time. Much 'business' did not take place in places of business, but was externalized as community activity. One's place in the community was an integral part of one's place in business.

These community-based relations imposed certain limits on the pursuit of profit. Wealth *per se* had not been despised, even by the first generation of Puritans,[9] but within a network of personal relationships, self-aggrandizement was checked by responsibilities to those among whom one lived. De Tocqueville (1835/1956: 256) writes of, 'the rarity of lofty ambition to be observed in the midst of the universally ambitious stir of society.' This is not to say that the Federalist citizen was less avaricious than today's

6 Ironically, wealth achieved by marriage to a large landholder.

7 Inferred from the US census of 1850.

8 The Census of 1850, Vol. 1, Table L, lists 73,504 men (the census surveyed males only) as manufacturers. Appended to this table is a list of 265,196 men employed in manufacturing establishments with an annual product exceeding $500 (about two years' average wages).

9 The Plymouth Puritans were generally middle-class and a few were fairly wealthy. The communal holdings at Plymouth were divided into individual plots within a few years. John Winthrop, the first leader of the Massachusetts Bay (Boston) Puritans, preached that there would always be the wealthy and the poor in society.

business person. Rather, the opportunity structure of work in such a society was constrained by different relationships. First, one did not 'get ahead' beyond the community; one had to succeed *within* the community. Second, Federalist success was broadly inclusive. Few today can dream of becoming Anita Roddick or Bill Gates, but virtually every grocery clerk in 1850 could dream of opening a store after working a few years for someone else. Independent prosperity within the community represented an achievable dream for a substantial majority of workers.[10] Third, the Federalist dream of success had a point of arrival because a single community could sustain only so much individual aggrandizement. Federalist merchants were already producing for an international market economy, but the business activities controlling such production operated through community-based norms and sanctions within which the central measure of a person's worth as a supplier, contractor or source of credit was that person's 'character.' This is more than a theme. The Federalist 'discourse of character' was the central axis around which business relations revolved and its legacy shapes organizational thinking to the present day.

The Federalist Merchant, A 'Man of Character'

Character as a social 'language'

If a present-day management student were to pick up Freeman Hunt's book *Worth and Wealth: Maxims for Merchants and Men of Business* (1857), s/he might note the absence of anything presently known as management knowledge. Yet, Hunt was a good reflection of the business 'common sense' of his time. He was the publisher and editor of *Merchants' Magazine*, a leading mercantile journal[11] (Stringer & Townshend publishers thought it worthwhile to publish *Worth and Wealth* at $1.25 when the average daily wage was approximately one dollar).[12] Hunt is consistent with a genre dating from Benjamin Franklin into the latter 1800s.[13] In *Maxims for Merchants* one is not supposed to find encyclopedic advice on topics as diverse as bookkeeping and site selection, but a present-day reader might wonder at the emphasis on 'the conduct of an upright man of business' (1857: 28). The code of this conduct is indicated in Hunt's essay titles, including:

10 There were, of course, large differences in wealth and achieving an independent income was a function of gender and race. In addition, membership in a community was more complicated than simply moving in. Immigrants have been unwelcome since the first years of the Plymouth colony (Bradford, 1856/1981; Takaki, 1993).

11 This is the assessment of Hofstadter (1963), who discusses Hunt on pp. 245–7.

12 Source, *Historical Abstracts of the U.S., Pt. 1*, Bureau of the Census, Washington DC, Tables 167–73.

13 Cf., Goodman (1945), Terry (1869). In *The Protestant Ethic and the Spirit of Capitalism* (1904/1958), Weber does a surprisingly thorough analysis of Franklin.

Morality of Insurance
Peter C. Brooks, The Wise Merchant and Upright Man
Self-Reliance, The Main Spring of Success
Don't Leave a Legitimate Business for Financiering
Honor of an Honest Man
A Benevolent Quaker Merchant
Never Make a Promise That You Can't Keep
Success in Life Depends on Perseverance
Honestly Acquired Wealth
Sacredness of Debts
Wish for No Man's Wealth
Character and Capital
Integrity, the Basis of Credit

It is easy to dismiss these claims as mere self-congratulation, since the sanctity of business has been regularly espoused by wealthy business people. What is interesting in Hunt's topics is not that he flatters the character of the merchant, but the manner in which he does so. From our present vantage point, Hunt's vision of success lies on the other side of a late-nineteenth-century 'industrialization' of values. Somewhere between the 1857 publication of *Maxims for Merchants* and the 1913 publication of Andrew Carnegie's *The Empire of Business*, a new reality emerged, a new industrial common sense replaced Hunt's reality, erased any popular awareness that it had ever existed and placed its logic in the realm of the nonsensible.

The following exchange between J.P. Morgan and Samuel Untermeyer during a 1912 hearing of the US House Banking and Currency Committee helps to illustrate this point. Morgan was perhaps the most influential banking figure of US industrialization. Untermeyer was a Senator and member of the committee:

Untermeyer: Is not commercial credit based primarily on money or property?
Morgan: No, sir, the first thing is character.
Untermeyer: Before money or property?
Morgan: Before money or anything else. Money cannot buy it. . . . Because a man I do not trust could not get money from me on all the bonds in Christendom.[14]

Chernow (1990: 154) writes that financiers cheered the testimony because, 'Pierpont [Morgan] had ennobled banking in an unexpected way,' but that 'to outsiders the statements sounded like cant preached to dupes.' In Morgan's weak defense he notes that 'early merchant bankers used character and class as crude forms of credit.' This exchange illustrates several things. First, it shows the survival into the twentieth century of what I term the 'discourse of character.' Second, it shows that such a worldview was

---

14 This exchange is discussed in a similar manner by both Hoyt (1966) and Chernow (1990).

already passé, being understood in terms of personal goodness or lack thereof ('ennobled,' 'cant') rather than in terms of societal relationships. Finally, the manner of its portrayal by Chernow shows that the very *existence* of the discourse of character has been forgotten.

What this means for understanding present-day work issues is shown by Stephen Covey's (1990b) treatment of this period in the best-selling *The 7 Habits of Highly Effective People*.[15] Covey notes that until the mid-1800s the US literature on self-improvement focused on what he terms the 'Character Ethic.' From about 1920, he observes a change, the emergence of the 'Personality Ethic.' Covey bemoans what he sees as a decline from an ethos that taught the integration of 'basic principles of effective living' into one's 'basic character' into a more superficial emphasis on 'attitudes and behaviors, skills and techniques, that lubricate the processes of human interaction (1990b: 16, 17). What Covey fails to consider is that this transformation in the self-improvement literature reflects a transformation of society. Each 'ethic' is a response to the dominant social reality of its time. When business ceased to be conducted within the discourse of character, the role of self-improvement in society changed. One cannot even speak meaningfully of *a* self-improvement literature between these two times. From Benjamin Franklin to Freeman Hunt, the 'self-improvement' literature *was* the business literature. Today, the former is peripheral to the latter. What survives is a vague notion that the values of Protestant perfectionism are the moral foundations upon which to build business relations. Again, Covey illustrates this point. He is a devout Mormon whose work is integrally connected to his religious belief.[16,17] Those who share that belief may find 7 *Habits* a useful way of bringing their spirituality into the workplace and I do not criticize this (provided it is recognized as such). For others, however, one might question the efficacy of advocating the *values* of Freeman Hunt when it is impossible to re-establish the *world* which produced those values. Exhorting the worker to greater moral fortitude is a universally available excuse to forego analysis of social systems, their failings and inequities. Such moralizing can be expedient for those with decision-making power (and those marketing to them), but is it effective for dealing with the problems of organizing? The practical problem of confusing a moral ideology with human nature is that it leads to the presentation of moral aphorisms (for example, 'Real leadership power comes from an honorable character' (Covey, 1990a: 101)) as if they constituted analytical scrutiny.

15 More than four years on the *New York Times* best seller list. More than five million copies sold – over a million of these exported to other countries of the world (Smith, 1994).

16 Cf., Smith (1994).

17 This is not to equate Mormonism and Protestantism. However, The spirit of Protestant perfectionism has strongly colored Mormon belief. The point is that Covey's prescriptions are not presented as religious teachings, but as secular prescriptions for anyone engaging in business. The secular consumer not committed to propagating the specific tenets of this faith should be given the opportunity to assess the degree to which these 'highly effective people' are not people in general, but people of a specific faith and/or culture.

It is a mistake to idealize (or vilify) the nineteenth-century discourse of character as a collection of personal traits. 'Character' was not so much a superior (or inferior) morality as it was a different *language* within which was enacted the entire range of more and less virtuous human qualities. Character was simultaneously the religious credo John D. Rockefeller worshipped on Sunday and the club he wielded in the workplace on Monday. In this book, I attempt to describe character as the language of a social system rather than as a personal attribute in order to direct analysis away from the individual and toward the organizations of the society of which s/he is a part.

Outlining the features of the discourse of character

Within Federalist society, one's social position was based upon the assessment of many personal/interpersonal qualities valued by that society as reflections of 'character.' This was not a 'crude form of credit,' but a completely different system of social control. The 'man [*sic*] of character' was one whose practices were governed by honest dealings and acceptance of reciprocal responsibility between the individual, business contacts, and the community as a whole. Viewed as a set of *social practices*, rather than as a form of *moral goodness*, maintenance of 'character' not only involved timely payment of debts, it went far beyond financial obligations to assessment of one's overall effect on the community. Today's 'objective' credit data could as well be described as 'a crude indication of character.'

First and foremost, the discourse of character emerged from and in turn supported a society of relatively equal freeholders, a society not unlike an idealized version of an early-modern English village.[18] As a freeholder, the Federalist citizen is not in thrall to a seigniorial lord, but neither does s/he enter 'wage slavery.' Nordhoff (1875/1962: 12–13) speaks of trade unions as 'mischievous and hateful,' specifically because they encourage the worker to accept being a 'hireling for life.' Terry (1869) is at pains to explain to merchants that they must expect their clerks to leave after a few years and start up their own businesses. To settle for a clerk who will settle for wage labor, is, for Terry, a bad bargain, since any worker worth anything will obviously be looking toward self-employment within a few years.

In this relatively closed universe, the 'omnicompetence of the common man', to use Hofstadter's phrase, was a basic, and not unrealistic, assumption: '[i]t was believed that he could, without much special preparation, pursue the professions and run the government' (1963: 34). The Federalist citizen was the antithesis of the industrial expert. Compared to the industrial subject, the Federalist citizen was a highly unified self. An active participant in community self-governance, this citizen preceded the split between the business person and the professional politician. On the family farm or in a home-based craft, the citizen's public and private roles

18 As described, for instance, by Tate (1967).

were substantially integrated. For women, this did not mean equality with men, but 'managing' the domestic sphere involved control of a vital dimension of production. The roles of producer and consumer were not yet separated, as they would soon become.

Although the norms structuring the discourse of character were predominantly determined by relationships between men, the Federalist order can be understood as metaphorically feminized relative to the norms of late-twentieth-century US society in that emphasis on relationship maintenance and community responsibility – practices presently coded as 'feminine' and work coded as 'women's work' – were integral to the public sphere of business. Later chapters will elaborate this point. This is important to bear in mind because, just as the pre-industrial order required business people with greater relational skills, so too may the emerging post-industrial order. Managers today, we increasingly hear, must be listeners, facilitators, coaches and so forth. To ask for these qualities without questioning how their expression is suppressed by industrial practices that have been sedimenting into common sense for a century is naive and probably futile. This is one of the ways 'pragmatic' post-industrial managing will require philosophizing. Only by questioning common sense can the pragmatist loosen the shackles of industrial habit. This will be easier if some attention is given to the medium through which the discourse of character operated. This medium, Protestant perfectionism, was simultaneously a religion, a political ideology and a guide to business.

Perfectionism and the Discourse of Character

The 'American' Dream: the first 2000 years

'America' – the ideological mythos of the US – is descended from two ancestral families. One, the Greco-Roman world, is accorded a place of honor. The other, three millennia of Northern European civilization, has been banished.[19] This is unfortunate because the American Dream, in most forms, is a dream of escape from, not participation in, the standardized and hierarchized society that characterizes the Greco-Roman legacy. Cut off from this past, the nineteenth-century American Dream of a republic of yeoman farmers can appear to have sprung *de novo* from the soil of New England. But could that be?

Was there a spiritual kinship between the 'pioneer colonists' (Morgan, 1988: 63) who left Jutland and the Low Countries to settle in the wild west of southern England fifteen hundred years ago and their descendants who

---

19 Those who wonder whether the present time might represent a transition from modernity into some postmodern future might look toward reconstructing this silenced voice of Northern European history. It may be a vehicle for destabilizing the canonical story of Western civilization as a linear development from Greco-Roman roots to the present day.

sailed to the wild west of Boston in the 1600s? Would it be inappropriate to speak of the American Dream of the seventh-century British society of *ceorls* (free peasant farmers)? This 'American' ideal was expressed in England as an early argument against the enclosure of common lands: '[In the Tudor period and up to the sixteenth century] the yeomanry . . . were, apart from the navy, the backbone of national defence. . . . Moreover, men fought all the better for having a stake in the country they were defending' (Tate, 1967: 121).[20] Thomas Jefferson would have agreed emphatically.[21]

One should ask where the idea developed of civil society as the product and servant of the free, individual citizen. This was not a Roman inheritance. Moreover, Macfarlane (1978) has traced this 'modern' belief back into at least twelfth-century England. According to Cantor (1993), the Anglo-Saxon invasion of Britain brought with it the custom of election by the folk (*gefolge*): '[B]ecause England, even in the High Middle Ages, remained relatively untouched by Roman law . . . England alone preserved the early Germanic idea that law resides in the folk, rather than in the will of the king' (1993: 98–9). One might push this line of thought a bit further. According to Michel Rouche (1987), the early medieval Frankish society, closely related to the tribes which colonized England, placed a high value on property over life, believed that 'wild nature could be subdued only by violence' (1987: 487) and embodied a principle not unlike that of endless corporate growth; the leader (*heer-könig*) was 'condemned to conquer in order to maintain his authority.'

My suspicion – admittedly highly conjectural – is that the American Dream is the silenced portion of 2000 years of Western European history. 'America' is meaningless as a geographical entity or if it is looked for only from the time European colonization began. For two millennia, there was an 'American' dream which crossed the Atlantic only as the European continent ran out of frontier. This dream consists of opposition to the increasing hierarchization and regularization of society with a vision of a society constituted by a voluntary association of free yeomen. That this dream of escape today forms the cultural mythos of a US that simultaneously imagines itself to be the product of that dream of escape while constituting the largest economic empire on the planet is a dangerous irony deserving of study. Today's 'rebel' *represents* the empire (see Chapter 1). This convolution of ideologies has produced a highly contradictory picture of the 'individual' in a society of organizations. Paul Veyne may be correct when he says that, '[a] culture is a tissue of exceptions, whose incoherence goes unnoticed by those involved in it' (1987: 202), but to the degree that this incoherence will go unnoticed, so too will its role in shaping work knowledge and practices.

---

20 Machiavelli (1537/1952: Chapter XII) notes the deference given to soldiers of the Swiss Confederation, attributing their reputed invincibility to the fact that they were a freeholder army rather than conscripts or mercenaries. Was the Swiss Federation an 'American Dream'?
21 Cf., Boorstein (1960).

I do not yet know what to make of this 'prehistory' of the employee, but I can see enough plausible connections to be fairly confident that there is more to be made of this. These connections are very speculative; hopefully others will see this as an opportunity for further study. In terms of the story this book tells, I wish merely to establish that the roots of Federalist reality run deep, that many pieces of the puzzle are missing, and that the more we understand of this history, the more we can understand 'the employee' in American management thought.[22]

American Dreamers: Puritans and Quakers

The New England colonies were born during a time of transition in Europe. Theistic thinking was giving way to secular humanism, aristocracies to representative-bureaucratic institutions, and tradition to an idea of progress.[23] Individualism and personal freedom were emerging as social issues. But modernity in Europe developed slowly, over centuries. It was neither a homogeneous nor a steady process. Consistent with its birth in this context, the vision of New England looked back into the middle ages as well as forward into a corporate-capitalist future.[24]

At the heart of the Puritan/Quaker vision was belief in the perfectibility of personal character, the belief that the average individual, through proper practice, could experience knowledge of God and ultimate Truth. In early modern Europe, this theology was of major secular importance. If the individual could know God without the mediation of another, the entire Catholic church hierarchy, the anchor of the feudal social order, would be made superfluous. If the duty of the faithful was to do God's works on Earth, rather than to accept suffering penitentially while awaiting salvation in the next life, 'busyness' becomes a sacrament rather than a necessary evil. This vision remained theistic in that the secular order of things was shaped by belief in an all-knowing God, but it is no longer a God revealed through a hierarchical great chain of being. The source of knowledge and of right conduct became personal in that any person can look within to learn the universal Truth. But this knowledge was only available to those who cultivated their ability to know through contemplation and practice, those who developed their *character*.

---

22 My primary background sources for this section have been Braudel (1981, 1982, 1984, 1986), Cantor (1993), Duby (1988), Herm (1976), Tate (1967), Tuchman (1978) and Veyne (1987).

23 An excellent popular discussion of the development of the idea of progress is contained in Burke (1985). Habermas (1987) provides a more scholarly view. Foucault (1984b) discusses some key points.

24 Bear in mind, the early settlement of New England in 1620 preceded Descartes's *cogito ergo sum*, his central philosophical insight which was published in 1637. If Cartesian thought was an expression of emerging modernism that was secular and abstract, the Protestant settlement of New England was another expression of this spirit, one that was religious and concrete.

This tension between belief in the immediacy of divine knowledge and the need for the average person to have such knowledge mediated through a hierarchy of experts, a clergy, was not a new tension. Johnson (1976) traces this theme through Christianity's history. Such theological points have regularly had important political effects. In the seventh century, an Irish monastic tradition representing belief in self-knowledge of the Divine colonized Europe, contesting with the established Benedictine tradition, originating from Naples, which ordered both heaven and Earth on a Romanesque hierarchical vision. In sixteenth-century England, this tension erupted as a series of politico-religious schisms. The founding of the Anglican church in the 1530s was based less on spiritual purification than on the political goal of removing the Papacy as a foreign colonizing power from an England which was just developing sufficient national identity and strength to succeed in this effort. The resulting Anglican church looked much like Catholicism if one substituted for the Pope the Crown of England. Over the next several decades, a profusion of sects[25] arose with the goal of purifying the Anglican church. This culminated in the 1640 overthrow of Charles I by Cromwell's coalition of 'Puritans.' Once in power, the Puritans found themselves the target of further purifying schisms. Prominent among these were the Quakers.

It was during the generation preceding the overthrow of Charles I, when Presbyterians were a marginal but vocal group, that the Massachusetts colonies were founded. West Jersey and Pennsylvania were founded a half-century later by Quakers, driven by conflict with Puritan and Anglican authorities at home and drawn by the promise of creating a model society on the 'frontier.' What was new to the Puritans and Quakers of the seventeenth century was that this debate occurred within a capitalist merchant society whose outer reaches encompassed what was literally termed a new 'world' – the Western hemisphere. This produced a laboratory within which believers in individual perfectibility could band together to create the perfect society.

The Puritan and Quaker nonconformists whose influence dominated these colonies were engaging in 'a deliberate and self-conscious act of Church-state perfectionism' (Johnson, 1976: 421). Johnson emphasizes the medieval roots of this vision to create an Augustinian 'city upon a hill.'[26] Johnson compares the Puritan colonies to the eighth-century Franks; 'like the Carolingians,' Johnson observes, 'they were seeking to create a total Christian society.' Consistent with this neomedieval vision, the 'American

25 Including but not limited to the Anabaptists, Familists, Muggletonians, General Baptists, Diggers and Levellers.

26 The city-on-a-hill imagery has not yet passed into history. Dr Peter Pflaum (personal communication) traces the recent survival of this image from a speech at the 1964 Republican convention, through corporate publicity work done by Ronald Reagan, to William Bennett's current proselytizing about 'traditional' American values. Ironically, this is an image of a society whose passing was bemoaned by Cotton Mather in 1700, so what 'tradition' it might represent is not entirely clear. Such is 'common sense' that when one speaks from within it, this three-hundred-year anachronism conveniently disappears.

Dream' of the Puritans was less a dream of conquest than of fortification. As Sheehan has written of *ancien régime* Europe:

> The principal purpose of traditional institutions was to help people . . . survive in a hostile, unpredictable, largely unmanageable universe. People did not expect the social order to make them healthy, happy, and successful; such expectations are distinctly modern, the products of eighteenth-century ideas and nineteenth-century institutions. In traditional Europe, people were content if the social order could shield them from disaster, or at least soften its inevitable blow and provide consolation after it had struck. Institutions, therefore, were supposed to protect their members, by erecting real or symbolic walls between them and those outside. In this context, *liberties* were not general rights to engage the outside world as one might wish; they were restricted rights to enjoy the privileges and protection within a particular community. These liberties – to gather wood in a certain part of the forest, to farm a particular piece of land, to make shoes for a town or music for a prince – were necessarily limited to a specific group; they had no meaning if they belonged to everyone. (Sheehan, 1989: 79; emphasis in the original).

The groups colonizing New England were not believers in radical democracy. The Puritans had been anti-monarchy, but Cromwell's Puritan commonwealth was hardly an example of 'participatory management.' The Quakers had been active in the anti-tithe movement which weakened the financial structure of the established churches (Catholic and Anglican), but the Quaker faith, in both Europe and America, rapidly developed an identifiable hierarchy dominated by economically prominent families.[27] In today's terms, we might say the colonizers supported a 'flat organization' of society. Rather than removing status differences, the vision of these empirical Utopians was a society without the extremes of aristocratic privilege or subproletarian poverty. In place of a ruling aristocracy, authority and responsibility were to be concentrated in the hands of 'gentlemen' of 'middling means' whose legitimacy was grounded, not in heredity, but in achievement; not in a life of leisure, but in the performance of works; not in social status alone, but social status in a society where earned wealth is understood as a measure of the success of one's practice, one's character. In place of the great chain of being, these reformers substituted a vision in which status difference reflected differences of *earned* merit. This difference aside, the vision was basically medieval, a protected haven in a static, theocratic world.

On the other hand, New England was also, from the start, a corporate state. The early settlers may have been motivated by religious factors, but they were supported by corporate investors. These 'adventurers' were profit-motivated capitalist speculators who remained in England; only their capital went on the 'adventure.' The Plymouth colonists signed an agreement to divide the fruits of the venture after seven years, with those who had labored seven years on the 'plantation' receiving proceeds equivalent to

27 Frost (1973), Holder (1913), Reay (1985). In terms of following the dynamic relationship between the domestic sphere and that of formal organizations, one might say that the colonial 'business school' was in the private sphere of the prosperous family and its relations with the community. The externalization of 'management' knowledge from the eighteenth to twentieth centuries is a subject that would constitute another profitable study.

those who remained in England and invested £10 of initial capital. In its early years, the colony survived by supplying beaver pelts for the growing market economy of Europe. Within a generation, supplying the livestock markets of the old country led to the charter of new towns, such as Duxbury and Marshfield (one could literally say that these Atlantic seaboard towns were then a 'wild West' populated by 'cowboys'). The debt on the Plymouth colony was paid at rates as high as 50 per cent per annum. As early as 1641, the colony experienced difficulty meeting its debt commitments because of a fall in the 'stock'[28] markets when the value of cattle plummeted by about 80 per cent.[29] It is important to realize that the *founding condition* of these colonies was a *corporate* form actively connected with and made possible by an expanding European capitalist market economy.

Johnson (1976: 422) writes that the uniqueness of the American experiment was that: 'America was born Protestant and did not have to become so through revolt and struggle. It was not built on the remains of a Catholic Church, or an Establishment.' Johnson describes this as, 'a traditionless tradition, starting afresh with a set of Protestant assumptions, taken for granted, self-evident, as the basis for a common national creed.' He might have said the same about the new colonies' corporate character. Unlike the 'free cities' of Europe, America was, from the first, corporatist and did not have to fight against an aristocracy, a church or a standing military in order to establish the primacy of a social order governed by market relationships. Moreover, the religious and the corporatist spirit were not in conflict, nor even entirely distinct; because 'the beliefs and objects of the two were necessarily identical . . . [there could be] no jealous juxtaposition and confrontation of a secular and ecclesiastical world' (1976: 422).

Puritan character: the 'spirit of capitalism?'

Max Weber (1904/1958) attempted to describe something very close to character, as a specific *ethos*. Disclaiming the 'foolish and doctrinaire thesis'[30] that this spirit 'could only have arisen as a result of certain effects of

28 This is not a pun. It was capital exchanges organized for the literal exchange of animal and grain stocks which became the exchanges for today's paper or electronic 'stocks.' One fascinating picture of this development in Europe is presented in Braudel (1982).

29 A first-hand picture of the corporate adventures and tribulations of the Plymouth Puritans is readily available today in the diary of one of the founders, William Bradford (1856/1981).

30 This disclaimer appears to have been lost on those one regularly hears stating as fact the idea that Weber's thesis 'has now been largely discredited' (e.g., Drucker, 1993: 26). Such a view appears to be based on the questionable proposition that Weber's complex analysis of the mutual influence between developing European capitalism and the secular effects of Protestantism can be formulated as a testable hypothesis and subjected to measurable data. This, in turn, is based on what I believe are erroneous readings of Weber which interpret his position to be that Protestantism *caused* capitalism and that capitalism is a form of organization unique to Western Europe and America. Using the same questionable logic, one would have to argue that the growth of the Methodist faith in Korea discredits the idea that the origins of Methodism in England can be understood as a product of British culture in that period. Before deciding on this issue, I urge the reader to at least browse *The Protestant Ethic and the Spirit of Capitalism*, judging Weber's arguments on their merits.

the Reformation,' or that 'capitalism . . . is a creation of the reformation,' Weber attempted 'to ascertain whether and to what extent religious forces have taken part in the qualitative formation and the quantitative expansion of that spirit over the world' (1904/1958: 91). Several observations supported the importance of this question. First, based on his extensive historical knowledge Weber observed that only in the modern 'Occident' has capitalism based on 'the rational capitalistic organization of (formally) free labor' (1904/1958: 21) appeared. Secondly, 'capitalism existed in China, India, Babylon, in the classic world, and in the middle ages,' but in none of these contexts did an 'ethos' exist to make capitalism the central institution of society. What, then, was distinctive about the ethos of European, and especially American, capitalism in modern times?

Weber is clear that greed is not a critical factor; 'The impulse to acquisition . . . has in itself nothing to do with capitalism. . . . Capitalism *may* even be identical with restraint' (1904/1958: 17). He also distinguishes between a *spirit* of capitalism and the *institutions* of capitalism. In the English putting-out system[31] of protoindustrial times, Weber notes, 'The form of organization was in every sense capitalistic. . . . But it was traditionalistic business, if one considers the spirit which animated the entrepreneur' (1904/1958: 67). In contrast, Weber cites Benjamin Franklin's writings as exemplary of the capitalist ethos, even though, 'in the country of Benjamin Franklin's birth (Massachusetts), the spirit of capitalism . . . was present before the capitalistic order' (1904/1958: 55). Weber notes the irony that this spirit was more developed in Massachusetts than in neighboring Southern colonies, 'in spite of the fact that these latter were founded by large capitalists for business motives, while the New England colonies were founded by preachers . . . for religious reasons' (1904/1958: 55–6). This is crucial. It provides strong support for Weber's claim that the driving force of the modern capitalist order 'was not generally in such cases a stream of new money invested in the industry, – in other words, capital*ism* cannot be explained simply with reference to capital structures. Neither can one look for a cause to the capital*ist*, since 'the bourgeois as a class existed prior to the development of the peculiar modern form of capitalism' (1904/1958: 56).

At some point, notes Weber, an ethos is present in European capitalism in which 'activity, which was at best ethically tolerated' (1904/1958: 74), had come to be understood instead as a 'calling,' a duty to God. The worker's goal of reaching a fixed income with a minimum of work was replaced by the goal of achieving an increasing income through increasingly hard work; 'some participated and came to the top because they did not wish to consume but to earn' (1904/1958: 68). This cannot be explained as an 'industrial' spirit or a 'Protestant' spirit because industrialism and this form of Protestantism were produced *within* a world where this ethos was already established, a world in which the normative citizen was governed by '*a systematic*

---

31 A system in which the capitalist supplied materials and picked up finished goods from workers working in the home, under their own direction, and paid based on output.

self-control which at every moment stands before the inexorable alternative, chosen or damned' [my emphasis]. Where the Catholic cycle of sin and redemption led through one's life only to a 'succession of individual acts' (1904/1958: 116), good or bad, the subject of this ethos sought

> a life of good works combined into a unified system. . . . The moral conduct of the average man was thus deprived of its planless and unsystematic character and subjected to a consistent method for conduct as a whole. It is no accident that the name of Methodists stuck to the participants in the last great revival of Puritan ideas in the eighteenth century. (Weber, 1904/1958: 117)

This required, in Weber's words, 'a life guided by constant thought. . . . Descartes' *cogito ergo sum* was taken over by the contemporary Puritans with this ethical reinterpretation' (1904/1958: 118). The capitalist ethos, then, preceded capitalism and industrialism, both of which were unforeseen products of a particular mode of rationality. *Before capitalist institutions or industrial practices had structured society, the subject of the Protestant ethos had learned to live a life within which one capitalized time, capitalized good works and – only secondarily – capitalized goods. 'Character' was a mode of 'capitalizing' one's life.*

Rather than 'testing' Weber's views as a 'hypothesis' one could treat his essay as an early attempt to contextualize a particular mode of common sense, a way of looking at the world that is increasingly referred to as Modernity. Beginning in the Western Europe of the fourteenth to sixteenth centuries, one finds the growth of a mode of consciousness that contrasts with that of previous European culture, with other cultures of the day, and with most cultures since. One can trace the spread of this way of seeing over the globe through the subsequent centuries. This mode of consciousness has a 'mechanical' orientation to it, emphasizing instrumentality, emotionlessness, accumulation, skepticism, individual consciousness, standardization and objectification. It is also from within this mode of consciousness that the particular form of production and exchange currently dominant worldwide has emerged. Might it not be informative, as a means of getting perspective on the assumptions underlying present management thought, to ask how this body of cultural values structures one's way of understanding the Modern market-capitalist world? If one accepts that this ethos is not inherently tied to industrialism, one should not expect the advent of the post-industrial to necessarily signal an end to their influence.

Secular perfectionism: from theocratic to Federalist order

Between the Calvinist seventeenth century and the Federalist nineteenth century, the dream of social perfectionism underwent an extroversion. Liberty no longer meant the freedom to perfect an enclosed city protected from the world. It was redirected as the freedom to conquer and order that *outer* world. Progress no longer meant movement toward a finite goal, but infinite expansion into a limitless universe. The contract with God shifted by degrees from the city on a hill to a 'manifest destiny.' One excellent analysis of this new formation of character is Boorstein's in *The Lost World of Thomas Jefferson* (1960).

> By indefinitely improving the condition of man [*sic*] in America, and thereby vindicating the human species, the [mid-eighteenth-century] Jeffersonian sought to satisfy his need for a divinely appointed mission. . . . He was unwilling to chart his course by looking backward. . . . He was earnest and convinced that for him destiny should supplant tradition. (Boorstein, 1960: 233)

This Jeffersonian view redirects Perfectionism toward science in a way that presages late nineteenth-century Social Darwinism to a greater degree than is commonly acknowledged. The Jeffersonian already viewed humanity as one species competing with others, a significant departure from humanity's status above the 'beasts' in medieval great-chain-of-being cosmology. Social Darwinism, according to Boorstein, 'became preoccupied with man's struggle against other creatures of his own species. . . . Social Darwinism was a significant variant on the Jeffersonian naturalism, but was still only a variant' (1960: 241). This is significant because organizational histories generally present Social Darwinism as a brief aberration in thinking peculiar to the late nineteenth century. A more complete history would start before Darwin and continue through present-day 'ecological' metaphors in organizational theorizing.[32]

This new embodiment of character continued to be expressed through action rather than reflection. Boorstein writes 'Philosophy was to be a by-product of right and fruitful activity' (1960: 237). As today, the Jeffersonian was 'largely unconscious of the philosophy [s/he] has adopted,' leading to 'the dangerous assumption that a plan of action is the same as a philosophy' (1960: 8) – an assumption that today reinforces the 'truth-trap' of organizational knowledge as 'practical' people seek answers in reorganization plans rather than reflection on the broader issues facing business and society. In this world, perfectionism and corporatism were not competing tensions: 'To enrich one's neighbor was to improve America and to enhance a corporation in which every settler was a shareholder. . . . He was earnest and convinced that for him destiny should supplant tradition. . . . The Jeffersonians had a sense of living at the beginning of history' (1960: 7, 233, 237–8).[33]

---

32 Another study waiting to be done. Systems theory, contingency theory, cognitive science, population ecology models are all pervaded with evolutionary assumptions that remain largely unexamined. As in the biology program in which I earned my undergraduate degree, evolution is called a theory, but operates as a law. If it is a theory, discussion should take place regarding its appropriateness and limits.

33 It is more than ironic that the Jeffersonian 'beginning of history' is virtually synchronous with the Hegelian 'end of history' (1807). The early 1800s were the high-water days of the corporate-bureaucratic German *Beamtenstaat* (Sheehan, 1989) whose institutions analogize in many respects – and indeed contributed – to the US social order *c*. 1900. Much of this book will be concerned with the ways the US moved from buoyant pursuit of pioneering a presumed-infinite continent to more sanguine acceptance of a thoroughly contradictory industrial reality. The beginning/end contrast excellently symbolizes this shift.

As one example of this new attitude, consider the changing basis for legitimating racial inequalities. For the Puritan, the indigenous North Americans were (to quote Cotton Mather *c.* 1693) 'forlorn *Pagans*, to whom the Devil is a leader.'[34] In the static terms of the Puritans' Calvinist theology, the native American belonged to the damned; the Puritans (at least potentially) to the elect. By the time of Thomas Jefferson, this racism had taken a new form. While the values, beliefs and practices of indigenous people were no more highly prized, the differential status of North America's red and white peoples was expressed as a reflection of differential progress. Where 'opponents of human equality had simply asserted that the Indian had been created a species inferior to the European,' Jefferson emphasized the effect of what today we would call the 'environment.' For instance, 'In the Indian the faculties employed in tracking down an enemy or a wild beast were extraordinarily well developed. . . . Jefferson had no hesitation in asserting the Indian in body and mind equal to the white man' (Boorstein, 1960: 85). Thus, the individual native American could conceivably 'progress' to the social level of the white.[35] With this background in mind, it is now possible to sketch the Federalist world of Freeman Hunt.

Contextualizing the Federalist World

Freeman Hunt, then, exemplifies a worldview that was not simply a naive or partially formed view of managing in business. It was a well-formed and sophisticated response to the social relations and physical/technical constraints (what Braudel termed 'conditions of possibility') of a particular time. It was the heir to a very specific cultural legacy which placed particular interpretations on core values of individuality, freedom, and progress (personal and social). The 'common sense' of this time reflects an historical period whose roots are still nourished by sixteenth-century English Protestantism, while its branches are twining toward Social Darwinism and – as will be seen in later chapters – the present day.

In its incarnation of roughly 1790–1870, this US discourse of character embodied the following key elements: (1) *Progress* – The American Dream was no longer of a haven in a dangerous world, but of the conquest and ordering of the world itself; (2) *'Omnicompetence* – the average citizen with no special training had the knowledge to effectively deal with the problems of society; (3) *Action* – far more than even the colonizing Puritans, the American was now a 'man of action' for whom deeds substituted for philosophy and for reflection, both of which were tainted by negative association with European upper classes; (4) *'Middle-class' mentality* – in

---

34 This epithet is from Mather's *The Wonders of the Invisible World*, reprinted in 1991 (1692/1991: 43). Mather represents the end of an era, but an excellent example of that era. Mather's text fairly crawls with similar vilification of the indigenous people.

35 Takaki (1993) has much to say on this as well.

this republic of the self-employed, to be poor is a sign of inferior 'character' (note that the Calvinist distinction between the 'worthy' and the 'unworthy' poor plays a prominent part in US distinctions of public assistance to this day); [36] to be rich is a sign of service to the community; to be an aristocrat is impossible because society lacks the hierarchy to support it. The person of 'middling means' is the social ideal; (5) *Mutual interest* – in this republic of 'average men,' as in Adam Smith's hypothetical republic of butchers, bakers and brewers, there is no conflict between self-interest and the social good; both individual self-interest and the institutional self-interest of God (Protestantism), prosperity (business) and democracy (politics) are treated as socially desirable. More generally, *one's 'capital' in business is largely in the form of the assessment made by others of one's 'character,' based on long-term relationships within a community governed by interpersonal relationships*.

What I call Federalist reality, Hofstadter (1963: 253) calls the 'mercantile ideal.' Laurie (1989: 52) terms the great religious revivals in the 1820s and 1830s a 'shopkeeper's millennium,' condemning as evil, 'libertine habits rooted in preindustrial times and antithetical to the exigencies of the market revolution' (1989: 53). Still dominant in the US of 1850, this mercantile ideal in many ways invokes the British 'nation of shopkeepers' of the previous century (the incubator of *Wealth of Nations*). One can see Protestant perfectionism adapting to the times; the subject of self-control in the development of character is less the general citizen of the community than the particular role of the person of business. A similar connection between market needs and the ethos of Protestant perfectionism is analyzed by Langton (1984) in the relationship between the British pottery manufacturer (and father-in-law to Charles Darwin), Josiah Wedgwood, and the Methodist preacher, John Wesley, a participant in what Weber (1904/1958: 117) called the 'last great revival of Puritan ideas.' Note, however, that by the 1760s in Britain perfectionism is interacting with an emerging industrial order, while nearly a century later in the US these forces are peripheral to a mercantile social order. One must be careful when periodizing or drawing conclusions across cultures.

One must resist thinking of Federalist reality as a rough draft of later, industrialized social relationships. Such thinking reflects that Jeffersonian view of social 'progress.' The Federalist mercantile order was more than a dress rehearsal for the twentieth century. It was as complete with reference to its world as today's society is to ours. A central argument of this book is

36 Yet another hindrance to society as a whole and, increasingly, even to the self-serving interests of business. The US is a society of large-organization members whose ideology is that we are free individuals. The morality supporting this view constructs the poor as meriting their fate. Whether this is correct or not, it prevents facing the social fact that in such a closed system, those who are not integrated into the system as productive members remain in the system anyway, becoming a problem in terms of skilled labor shortages, crime, health care expenses and so forth. The present-day US consistently confuses Calvinist morality with effective social policy regarding this issue.

that it is *not* useful to study this time with reference to linear, progressive history. Rather, one must attempt to see this as a world within which social relationships were configured along lines unsuspected, and barely imaginable today. If we can imagine this world as a different reality and get some sense of the logic by which it operated, we can much better appreciate that our present 'reality' operates within a culturally and historically specific logic. We study Freeman Hunt not to learn the truth of his world, but to learn to question the truths of our own.

To speak of a society governed by a discourse of character is not to imply that Federalist reality was some Golden Age. It had benefits relative to the society that followed it and it had drawbacks. Certainly differences of power and status existed. People might be venal, ambitious and cruel as well as generous and community-minded. This world cannot be judged overall to be better or worse than the present one, but one can recognize that justice and injustice, inclusion and exclusion, reward and punishment operated through different social relationships and were judged according to different ways of seeing than today.[37] To ask 'how did this society come to an end' is to ask 'how was the world we now know produced?' That is the subject of the following chapter.

37 As Ulla Johansson, of the University of Lund, pointed out to me on this topic, the pre-industrial worker could be 'oppressed, but not alienated.' Alienation required an industrial system of relations in order to become meaningful.

4

The Demise of Federalist Reality – 'the Birth of a Nation'

Even as Freeman Hunt was writing *Worth and Wealth*, the work, the worker and the world it reflected were heading into perdition. Five years after its publication a civil war engulfed the nation. This war is usually represented as either a contest between state and national authority or as a fight to end slavery.[1] It was, in part, both of these things, but it could more appropriately be termed the country's 'Industrial Revolution.' By 1865, the industrializing Northeast of the US had politically demolished the feudal economy of the manorial South. The war concentrated capital. Railroad and telegraph construction had created a vastly more national transportation and communication infrastructure. The devastated South and the 'virgin' West presented vast markets for industrial products. The society transported to North America by the Puritans and Quakers – and modified over time – rapidly colonized the remainder of the country.[2,3] This chapter will trace the emergence during the post-Civil War era of social forces which marked the demise of Federalist reality and created the 'conditions of possibility' for the emergence of contemporary organization and management knowledge.

My reference to the US Civil War as an 'Industrial Revolution' is tongue-in-cheek, but I find this a useful metaphor as well. The emergence of Federalist reality coincides with the growing dominance of mercantile interests in the structuring of US society. The War of Independence from Britain was so focused on issues of trade that it might be called the US 'Mercantile Revolution.' With the significant exception of some Virginia planters such as Washington and Jefferson, the upper classes in that

1 The widespread scorn of abolitionists in the North and the tardy abolition of slavery in the Emancipation Proclamation of 1863 (two years into the war) aptly illustrate the secondary status of the slavery issue.

2 In considering the role of the colonies centered on Boston and those centered on Philadelphia, an obvious omission has been that of New York and I have asked myself whether omitting its influence was simply for my own conceptual convenience. Difficult as it may be to imagine today, however, I believe New York's influence before the late nineteenth century was minimal. Perhaps this was because the feudal/manorial patroon system established by the Dutch lasted until the 1840s, making old New York – amazingly – a closer relative to the Southern plantation system than to the mercantile/small-farm Northeast. As it exploded in the late nineteenth century, New York City appears to have begun reflecting forces that began in the Quaker/Puritan colonies. Elaborating this role would be a fruitful topic for further investigation.

3 Andreano (1962), Porter (1973), Smith (1984), Wiebe (1967).

revolution largely supported George III. The majority of the poor, scattered throughout a vast area, sought – fairly successfully – to avoid subjection to any central authority, foreign or domestic. Those with the most to win or lose – and most active in carrying on the conflict – were the emerging elite of the urban/mercantile class such as the Adamses, Franklin, Hancock, Revere and so forth. In this sense, the US revolution of 1776–84 reflected tensions similar to those leading to the English Civil War and Commonwealth of 1648–60 or rebellions in France as early as the fourteenth century[4] (and preceding the French 'industrial revolution' of 1789). One could draw cautious parallels to later civil wars such as the Bolshevik Revolution of 1917 in Russia and the Meiji Restoration of 1868 in Japan.[5]

At the end of this industrial revolution in 1865, one could not justifiably say the country had industrialized. Federalist reality was still dominant, but the forces that would bring about its decline had been set in motion. In addition to centralizing regional power, nationalizing markets and boosting the industrial base, the war had created changes in the social infrastructure of the US as well. Both the Union and the Confederacy discharged an army of men accustomed to the hierarchical mobilization of great numbers of workers to serve the complex needs of a large organization. The wage worker appeared for the first time as a visible group in a heretofore self-employed society. 'The Civil War had abolished the system by which the master hunted down the slave. Those who had fought that war returned home to find a society, one of whose striking features was a body of workers hunting for masters' (Simons, 1912: 312). Hidden in this army, as yet unnoticed, is the character who will emerge to dominate organizational discourse of the next century, the employee. Before speaking of the employee, however, it is important to understand three major 'questions' reflecting the spirit of the times and structuring what was said about work. The 'labor question' asked whether workers, concentrated in large numbers and resistant to acceptance of industrial terms of work, might overrun society. The 'works management question' asked how, after building huge mass production facilities ('the works'), one could make them functional. The 'trust question' asked if the builders of the great oligopolistic combinations of companies, the 'trusts,' might not be as much of a danger to society as the 'labor question.'

4 For instance, the role played by mercantile interests in the bourgeois uprising in Paris in 1355 (Tuchman, 1978: chapter seven).

5 It would be interesting and useful, in the spirit of Chandler (1990), to study the different effects on the development of industrial capitalism between countries whose wars of industrialization have been civil wars resulting from the build-up of internal tensions, those countries which have experienced industrialization as a result of wars of colonization, and those which have experienced post-colonial wars of industrialization (e.g., nominally civil wars influenced by a legacy of colonial influence).

The Rise of the 'Labor Question'

Today, the division *manager/employee* is habitually used to distinguish the primary boundary between organization members. This would have been a meaningless division within Federalist reality. One would have referred to *owner/worker*, which are not analogous. Neither can one move directly from the Federalist to the industrial pairings. Between them lies an unbridgeable gulf created during a time when a society fell apart and was recreated, not from scratch,[6] but along radically different lines. The pairing more representative of that period is *capital/labor*. It appears in US discourse to signify a problem: the labor question.

'Labor' and 'capital' had not yet come to represent threatening groups. 'Labor' was merely a verb; 'capital' merely a material resource. Leaders of this period 'did not habitually post a dichotomy between the interests of business and those of the American people; these were seen to go hand in hand' (McCraw, 1984: 41). Federalist society still reflected the founding realities of Puritan/Quaker communities in which one's work simultaneously served self-interest, the common wealth,[7] the church and the civil state – whose boundaries blurred indistinctly one into another. Even in the decade or so following the Civil War, the increasing concentration of industrial power did not interfere with the public ideal of work as a relationship between small owners and independent workers. Complaints against 'the modern spirit of competition,' inducing 'an *appearance* of business' (Hunt, 1857: 117; emphasis in the original) or against 'this incessant business' (Thoreau, 1863: 356; in both quotes, read 'busy-ness') were sporadic and minor – at least while wages and material standards of living rose.

After 1868, however, wages for employed industrial workers dropped every year save one until 1879, resulting in a total wage reduction of 25 per cent.[8] In this decade union membership expanded geometrically.[9] Confrontations with employers became larger in scope and more threatening in tone. At this point, the benign individual worker begins to be replaced in public accounts with a hostile, aggregate class, as writers begin to refer to 'labor.' By the 1870s, it was becoming clear that the US was not simply a nation of

6 Continuity of the American Dream themes, even as their specific meanings changed dramatically, is as important to note as are the points of rupture between Federalist and industrial realities.

7 While little more than a symbol today, Massachusetts is still incorporated as a commonwealth, a direct reference to the communitarian spirit of the English commonwealth of 1648–60.

8 Source: *Historical Statistics of the United States, Pt. 1*, (1975) Bureau of the Census, Washington DC. Overall cost of living dropped a similar amount, but where the cost of living drop was shared by all of society, the drop in wages was borne entirely by the minority in industrial employment, which must have produced a significant relative disadvantage.

9 Foner (1962).

yeoman farmers, self-employed craftspeople and merchants. E.W. Martin's book following the labor riots of 1877 regularly decries

> [t]he worst elements of the Old World, that had been driven out of Europe, suddenly appeared in our midst, and proclaiming their terrible doctrines of destruction and rapine, endeavored to revive in our prosperous and peaceful land the horrors of the Parisian Commune. (Martin, 1877/1971: 4)

By the time Taylor's famous article on piece rates appeared in 1895, the reference in its title to 'the labor problem' invoked a major theme of the preceding decade. 'Anarchism,' 'syndicalism,' and 'communism,'[10] had become stock epithets, reflecting both indignant denial that class enmity was entering the social order and fear that class war was imminent.

The coming of the organization of scale

The labor question was not simply produced by the appearance of large organizations, nor was size automatically linked to regimentation, deskilling and alienation of the work force. Available statistics suggest a more nuanced explanation is required. During this period industrial work grew more prominent, but industrial workers only increased from 14 per cent to 19 per cent of the work force between 1860 and 1890.[11] Even at the turn of the century, the agricultural sector alone occupied more of the labor force than all other concerns combined. Large-organization employment was hardly the reality of the average citizen.

The increasing average size of firms is also less dramatic than might be supposed. Between 1869 and 1899 the average number of workers employed per 'manufactory' increased only from 7.8 to 10.4. In 'blast furnaces' (iron producers), one of the most concentrated industries, the average producer

---

10 Ironically, the values espoused by Marx were quite close in many ways to Federalist common sense. One must be careful not to assume that the meanings of nineteenth-century communism can be understood with reference to the twentieth-century planned economies which have called themselves communist. Both corporatist and communist ideologies share a common institutional root, the medieval free city which was *both* a corporation *and* a commune. Venice still reflects this origin in its official name, *Commune de Venizia*. To discredit 'communism' *per se* is to simultaneously discredit Federalist values. Young Karl Marx and Freeman Hunt would have found many common values if they had ever set out to hunt together in the morning, fish in the afternoon, rear cattle in the evening and criticize after dinner. It would make a fascinating study to trace how, from a common starting point, communist and corporatist threads have woven through industrial societies, sometimes reinforcing, sometimes opposing each other and how, as Davis (1905/1961) observes, the capitalist corporation slowly came to be treated less as a subdivision of the state and more as an aggregation of individuals. Rather than reinforcing the limiting dichotomy of communism/capitalism – a product of Cold War politics more than of relationships within work organizations – one might tell the complex, intertwined history of these economic cousins, offering new insights and possibilities for imagining a post-Cold War world order.

11 Source: *Historical Statistics of the United States, Vol. 1*, (1975) Series D–152–166, Bureau of the Census, Washington, DC.

increased only about 2.5 times, to 176 employees per works.[12] The percentage increase is dramatic, but shops of 176 workers did not represent unprecedented problems of administration. One could borrow this from more than a century's experience from continental European manufactories, through the mills of Manchester to the organizational experiments of the Boston Company in Lowell and Lawrence, Massachusetts.

The transformative change at this time was a transition from industrial size based on *scope* to size based on *scale*.[13] Before the turn of the century, railroad administration experts were already speaking in a sophisticated way about the relationships of departmental *versus* divisional structures subject to varying 'contingencies'[14] of technology, and business volume. The argument for divisional management was that it reproduced a small company within the large company, preserving work relationships based on face-to-face contact. In textiles, the oldest concentrated industry, scope, not scale, had been the driving principle. Theoretically, there is no limit to the size an organization of scope can attain; it grows like a tapeworm by reproducing semi-autonomous segments. But within this 'large' organization, work relations and work processes mimic the established relationships found in small shops. The need for the functions thought of today as management did not exist. Present-day accounts are likely to present this as ignorance or inefficiency on the part of employers, but if one considers the context, one might conclude otherwise.

For instance, in 1886 the Whitin Machine Works was a large, prosperous, machine tool producer, the dominant employer in the company town of Whitinsville, Massachusetts. Beneath this appearance of size, however, '[t]he Whitin Machine Works was not just one unit, but a dozen or more small enterprises housed under one roof.' The foremen heading these units were subject to little central coordination, but 'production flowed with almost autokinetic ease. Administrative red tape was kept at a minimum, and so-called indirect labor was all but unknown.' After thirty years in business, for instance, the entire financial function had been handled as a part-time duty of the owner without even one full-time bookkeeper (Navin, 1950: 139, 142).

Through most of the nineteenth century, divisional organization allowed owners of large firms to reap financial benefits of large size without entering the *terra incognita* of organizing large departments. The demands of fixed

---

12 Litterer (1959/1986: 308, 311).

13 My thinking on the qualitative differences between scope and scale was triggered by the title of Chandler (1990). However, while benefiting from Chandler's treatment of scale and scope in US, British and German industry, I did not find Chandler raising the points I bring out in this book.

14 Dewsnup (1906), Fagan (1909), Morris (1920), Perkins (1885). To call these writers contingency theorists would be to impose meanings from the twentieth century on experiences of the nineteenth century, but to find such theorists speaking in terms compatible with a contingency framework should lead one to question the linear, evolutionary story of business history that has become the standard narrative in organization studies.

capital were relatively less critical to employers than the rhythms of business cyclicality and environmental seasonality. Many workers entered industry during the agricultural off-season. Industrial enterprises were heavily dependent on the seasons; for instance, water-powered sawmills were often iced over during winters. Markets were local, transportation slow, and inventory carrying capacity limited by the owner's personal finances. This led employers to exert caution both in their commitment to fixed capital and in their willingness to assume full responsibility for the worker's earning capacity and, thus, his/her social welfare.

As the nineteenth century passed, however, the risk structure for employers changed dramatically due to the appearance of mass production technologies. The McCormick reaper in agriculture, the automated meat-packing line at Armour, mechanical grain transportation centrally owned by the Chicago commodity merchants, the Bessemer converter at the Carnegie mills, the cigarette rolling machines of American Tobacco – all offered massive production increases, but only if problems of scale were addressed. It is here that statistics show the *environment* of work to have been changing more dramatically than the raw *size* of the industrial work force or of manufactories themselves. Industry after industry was centralized and transformed as the potential rewards for implementing large-scale systems grew. Between 1879 and 1899 capital per miner invested in mining increased more than eight-fold. During this brief period, total capital invested in manufacturing tripled from 2.7 to 8.2 billion dollars.[15]

Social effects of scale production

Early industrialization had not been an urbanizing force. Dependent upon falling water for power, this period dispersed people in semi-rural towns along rivers. Only in the late 1800s did the US enter the steam-driven period that had begun in Britain nearly a century earlier. Steam could be utilized almost anywhere, and permitted centralization around markets (which were still predominantly local) and sources of labor, 'reversing the antebellum tendency of industrial dispersal' (Laurie, 1989: 115). This centralization supported and was supported by a period of massive immigration. From 1840 to 1900, the size of urban centers increased almost twenty-fold.[16] This development was a double-edged sword for employers. Immigrants were desperate for work and did not have to abandon a Yankee ideology of self-sufficiency before entering 'wage slavery,' as it might be known to the Yankee worker. Few had the means to leave urban areas for pioneering on the frontier. But, the background of these new Americans also gave them a

15 Calculated from or cited in Foner (1962), Bureau of the Census (1975), Reich (1983) and Litterer (1959/1986).

16 Chandler (1962: 23) cites an increase in urban population during this period from 11 per cent to 40 per cent. The Bureau of the Census (1975) cites an increase in the total work force from 5.4 to 29 million.

higher degree of class consciousness and experience in industrial conflict. Centralization facilitated group solidarity. Increasingly dependent on wage employment, urban workers were less dependent on any single employer and could more feasibly consider collective action.

'Wages' and 'jobs'

The labor question was also related to radical changes in the relationships defined by wages and jobs. Beginning around 1880, the convergence of scale technologies, urban concentration and the closing of the frontier produced for the first time in the US a significant group of citizens[17] for whom the Federalist discourse of self-sufficiency was irrelevant. In 1875, Charles Nordhoff, who was generally sympathetic to the situation of workers, wrote:

> For the character and conduct of our own population in the United States show conclusively that nothing so stimulates intelligence in the poor, and at the same time nothing so well enables them to bear the inconveniences of their lot, as a reasonable prospect that with industry and economy they may raise themselves out of the condition of hired laborers into that of independent employers of their own labor. . . . Hitherto, in the United States, our cheap and fertile lands have acted as an important safety-valve for the enterprise and discontent of our non-capitalist population. . . . The spirit of the Trades-Union and International Societies appears to me peculiarly mischievous and hateful, because . . . [t]he member of a Trades-Union is taught to regard himself, and to act toward society, as a hireling for life. (Nordhoff, 1875/1962: 11–13)

Note the disreputability of being a 'hireling for life.' In Federalist reality, the primary long-term employment relationship was that of the owner to customer. The employment relationship was ideally limited to a few years, not to a life's work. S.H. Terry, a contemporary of Freeman Hunt, criticizes the 'false notion' among retailers that training a clerk entitles them to 'a continuance of his services.' After all, observes Terry, 'The young man having thoroughly learned his business, naturally is desirous of forwarding himself in the world' (Terry, 1869: 127–8). The average small size of mercantile businesses made the ideal of eventual self-employment workable. The more complex organizations of industry made the goal of owning fixed capital more elusive. Nonetheless, a form of industrial 'free agency' was maintained through the system of 'job' payment.

Today, one is likely to think of a 'job' as a position of relatively permanent wage work within a large organization. This is a reflection of a common sense specific to industrial realities. The term originally meant a small, definite portion of something, a cartload.[18] For centuries, one's 'job' was

---

17 It is also important to remember that not all who worked were free citizens. Slaves, native Americans and Asians were excluded from freely seeking work (cf., Takaki, 1993). In the present century, however, these problems have come to be contested within a framework of work relationships formed around the nominally free citizens of late nineteenth-century America.

18 *Oxford English Dictionary.*

done with every batch of work completed; taking the next batch was a matter to be negotiated between worker and employer. One should not idealize this system; negotiations did not necessarily occur on a level playing field. What is important is to recognize that the expectation of permanency in the employment relationship was low on both sides. This was the norm until well into the present century (Navin, 1950).

Until this time *both* employers and workers had resisted wage systems (i.e. payment by the hour for regular hours of work). Employers had shied away from committing to payroll that did not vary with business volume. They sought to make labor a flexible cost, introducing payment by day, by month, by trip, by mileage and by business volume.[19] For their part, workers 'for several decades adopted programs through which they hoped to destroy or to escape from the wage system' (Hays, 1957: 32–3). Retaining the link between payment and output through job-lot rates gave workers more negotiating strength than a system in which they merely sold their time. In addition, like British workers of the previous century, US workers recognized that

> [t]he imposition of an exclusively monetary form of wage payment marked a fundamental change in employers' attitudes to property and labour. . . . Whether financially compensated or not, workers bitterly resented the enforcement of this new money-wage discipline which denied them their traditional rights and perquisites. . . . What was at stake for workers was not simply a traditional source of 'extra' income, but the maintenance of some independence at the workplace, some control over the product and the labour process. (Belchem, 1990: 14–15)

None of the elements of 'the labor question' were new to society in this decade. Trade unions had existed since the previous century. By the 1820s, US armories for weapons manufacture and the Boston Company's experiments in textile manufacturing at Lowell and Andover presented the problem of 'large' organizations.[20] The labor question was a largely unforeseen consequence of the unplanned convergence of several factors which precipitated a qualitative change in social relations. The change took common sense by surprise. 'The sharp contrast between the realities of social tension and inherited ideals of a classless society [resulted in a] sense of shock . . . only slowly did Americans seek to understand and come to terms effectively with their new experience' (Hays, 1957: 38).

The labor question indirectly posed a question to which the answer would be 'management.' As more and more workers sold their *time* rather than *products*, the connection was severed which had connected work, quality and output. With the mass-production technologies then becoming available, this same shift created heretofore unimaginable profit potential for employers who could fix wages based on time and still deal with the problems of alienation such wage systems created. One might say there were two 'labor questions.' One was the outright fear of class war: would labor

19 Healy (1940).
20 Hoskin and Macve (1988), Prude (1983).

revolt? The other was more mundane, but no less relevant to the emergence of management thought: how does one motivate labor severed from output?

The Rise of the 'Works Management' Question

What does it cost? How is it made? The coming of scale production presented employers with problems of 'works management' so basic we tend to overlook them today. Litterer (1959/1986) documents the existence of a generally overlooked school of management thought from the period 1870–1900 which called itself Systematic Management. This school was most concerned with three problems of works management. The first is development of cost accounting, a then-radical innovation. A second challenge was production control; what Taylor (1911) called the 'task management' concept required a new way of thinking for employers accustomed to semi-autonomous work gangs. A third area of concern was wage systems. If payment was not based on output, who should get how much?; when, if ever, should this rate change?; by what criteria should change be governed? Every detail of today's compensation systems was a dramatically new insight to employers at its point of emergence.

As it reached the question of wage systems, the 'works management movement' (Jenks, 1960) dovetailed with the labor question. The works management movement of the late 1800s encountered a difference in kind from the problems of the past. Work gangs had been held together by foremen who could 'knock down a man now and then as a lesson' (Carnegie, 1920:174). These foremen,[21] autonomous and paid by the 'job,' were a self-monitoring source of order and authority in the works. In the scale organization, with authority centralized and payment routinized, this fundamental organizing force was eviscerated. Work lost the 'autokinetic ease' characterizing job work.

For owners, conditioned by habit to consider profit a function of paying the lowest labor rate possible, lower wages for less work seemed nothing but 'common sense,' creating a vicious cycle of labor less and less willing to work and employers offering less and less for the work that was done. As Weber notes, traditional work relationships were based on the presumption of a relatively static society in which one did not 'get ahead;' – one 'got by.' If wages were raised, a worker was likely to do less work, stopping after earning what s/he would have under the lower wage scheme. However, this, coupled with the 'superficial' belief that money paid out in wages lowers profits by that amount, had sedimented over centuries into 'an article of faith, that low wages were productive' (Weber, 1904/1958: 60).

21 Were this a discussion of current events, I would prefer to use the term 'foreperson,' but the sexist usage is a better reflection of both the unreflectively masculinist thinking of the time and the biased practices which resulted in forepersons who were, indeed, almost always fore*men* – even when the workers were female.

Perhaps the key insight of Scientific Management was its explicit connection of the works management problem and the labor question. Towne (1886), Partridge (1887), Taylor (1895) and others argued that the cheapest cost per unit was achieved with 'high-priced labor' coupled with efficient systems for maximizing output. However, this radical view was vehemently opposed for a number of years.[22] I have found in the *Transactions of the ASME* – the *avant garde* of this developing school of thought – only nine articles on this subject between 1880 and the turn of the century. Works management was not yet seen as a mechanism for 'engineering' an answer to the labor question except by a dissident few.

Competing sources of authority in the works

Mid-nineteenth-century large organizations of *scope* may have represented a shift in the relative power of certain organizational stakeholders as the ownership role split more and more distinctively into the providers of capital and the providers of operational control. But the *form* of this relationship was no newer than the Hudson's Bay Company or the Massachusetts Bay Colony. The Lowell mills, the early railroads, the iron works making steel by 'puddling'[23] did not require new ways of understanding organizing. Except in a financial sense, they were not so much large organizations as clusters of small organizations. On the other hand, the organization of *scale* created fundamental problems of authority and legitimation. I would like to discuss three aspects of this problem: (1) The changing role of the foreman; (2) The decline of owners as operators; and (3) Tensions between *occupational* and *organizational* control of work.

Changing role of the foreman To appreciate the role of the nineteenth-century foreman it may help to imagine business during this time as being conducted through a process of co-entrepreneurship. A 'capital entrepreneur' provided a physical plant, technology and materials, assuming the market risk of selling the finished product. A 'labor entrepreneur' contracted to produce a 'job' lot of a product, providing labor of the appropriate amount and skill mix and assuming the production risk related to producing a specified product for a specified fee. This is an idealized model, subjected to infinite variation in actual practice, but it fits reasonably well into accounts such as Stone's (1974) analysis of the steel industry or Navin's (1950) case study of a machine tool works. An enabling feature of this model is that the effort of everyone from owner to laborer is engaged by an interest in the final

---

22 Urwick (1956).
23 For a perspective on the work relations of steel puddling compared to later processes, see Stone (1974).

product.[24] One could almost say present-day Employee Stock Ownership Plans (ESOPs) are a timid return to this way of understanding the sharing of risk and remuneration.

That Carnegie's ideal foreman could 'knock down a man now and then' suggests that this system of motivation did not ensure spontaneous cooperation, but it also shows that the process of raising the recalcitrant worker's consciousness was simple, direct and in the hands of the foreman. It required no 'management' experts. In addition, the foremen

> hired their own men, trained them, determined their rate of pay, set their jobs, and had the power to fire them or transfer them to another department. . . . Since a supervisor's workers were literally 'his' employees, the supervisor also kept track of his workers' time. . . . In addition, each supervisor acted as his own production manager. (Navin, 1950: 140)

Within the work gang, the foreman organized workers with different kinds and levels of skill. He was paid in a lump sum for the job and took responsibility for the distribution of both tasks and payments among workers. In short, the foreman assumed responsibility for the entire 'human side of enterprise.' Owners of capital had only to hire and fire foremen as needed. This would explain why Freeman Hunt's advice to men of business barely mentions the interpersonal aspects of organizing.

With the demise of the foreman as the central authority in the works, an increasingly complex space grew up between the production worker and the ever-more-diffuse forces directing the organization. In 1886, when 'Marston Whiting set about breaking down the independence of his department supervisors . . . [and] transferred to the superintendent's office many of their former responsibilities,' he reflected the spirit of his times. To effect this transfer of authority, 'he had to convert the superintendency from a one-man job to an office organization' (Navin, 1950: 140). As the 'office organization' began to appear, functions which were formerly the private domain of the foreman were externalized, routinized and placed in the hands of experts. Paradoxically, this decline of power on the part of the foreman – the labor entrepreneur – did not translate directly into more direct control on the part of the capital entrepreneur. The role of the owner-operator in running the organization was also in decline.

The decline of owner-operators   Control of Federalist business had been predominantly in the hands of a working proprietor, the sole owner of the establishment. In the late nineteenth century, the owner-operator became constrained in two directions. Operationally, every responsibility removed

---

24 A detailed account of this system of 'motivation' in another industry is represented in Herman Melville's *Moby Dick*. Ishmail recounts the bartering he and Queequeg conduct with the (not coincidentally) Quaker owners regarding what 'lay' (i.e., portion of the proceeds) they would receive in return for sailing. As in the colonial ventures, providers of labor and providers of capital are paid according to the same system. There is no wage labor on the *Pequod*, even in the least remunerative, least skilled job.

from the foreman resulted in an expansion of the office staff and the bureaucratization of practices.[25] The proliferation of externalized rules created a new source of power that was not resident in any particular person. Weber (in translation) called this 'the files.' Who would control this new source of power? It is simplistic to view these new developments simply as tools for capitalist control. They also took on a life of their own. In addition, once a rule was made explicit, it reduced the arbitrary power of the owner to make situational decisions. 'The organization' as a thing in itself began to be discernible as more than a simple extension of the person of the owner.

In a second direction, financial ownership became increasingly diffuse as an increasing portion of capital was supplied by people who thought of themselves as investors, not business people. In extreme cases, such as that of the Erie Railroad,[26] operation of a business concern was an almost incidental adjunct to stock market manipulation. But even where the investors' goal was long-term business growth, absentee ownership was a new, and not entirely benign, development[27] – but more of that below.

Organizational versus occupational control of work   In a co-entrepreneurial situation, some aspects of work were controlled by the *organization*. These included overall responsibility for the capital goods, relationships with suppliers and with customers. Other aspects were controlled by *occupations*. Key elements of the work process, technologies and tools used, numbers of workers and their roles relative to each other, were largely determined by occupational groups of steel puddlers, coopers, tinkers, tanners, and so forth, without whose knowledge production was impossible. Federalist social structure limited the degree to which either organizational or occupational forces could dominate work in the large organization. This relative equilibrium ended with the coming of the organization of scale.

Work process mechanization moved under organizational (capital) control an area that had traditionally been the domain of the occupation (craft, union, guild). During the most violent and bloody period in US industrial relations, roughly 1870–1900, the issues contested were not wages, hours and benefits – those were the terms of a later form of relationship. During 1870–1900 labor and capital were fighting a total war to determine which party would control the technology, training and personal relationships of the labor process itself. As we will see, with industrialization the organizational/occupational conflict moved from a war of attrition

---

25 Cyril Parkinson's (1957) famous essay on the growth of administrative systems, while presented tongue-in-cheek, can also be read as a plausible account of the historical development of 'the office.'

26 Gordon (1988).

27 Veblen (1923).

between owners and crafts to a mere tension between 'management,' 'employees' and 'professionals.'[28]

In sum, the large 'works' of the late 1800s was a new world to workers and society. The marginalization of the owner-operator, disempowerment of the foremen and open conflict between occupational and organizational stakeholders severely hampered internal operations and raised questions about the social legitimacy of large capital as an institution.[29] The early *combinations*, creating large financial structures which were little more than a collection of individual small shops, were manageable. But, as mass technology made it feasible to 'rationalize' entire industries into *consolidations* – Standard Oil, American Tobacco, US Steel – works management became a critical issue. At this point, the problems of labor and works management intersected with the 'trust question.'

The Rise of the 'Trust Question'

> *Corporate Trusts* – As popularly understood, a trust means a consolidation, combine, pool, or agreement of two or more naturally competing concerns, which establishes a limited monopoly with power to fix the prices or rates in any industry or group of industries. (*International Correspondence Schools*, 1901)

How big should an organization be? By the 1890s, this third general question pervaded thought about organizing. Traditionally, monopoly was not a business problem. Monopolies, such as the Hudson's Bay Company, were deliberately created, explicitly restricted arms of the state. Until the late 1800s, this was reflected in the fact that each new incorporation in any state required a special act of the legislature. The first general act permitting incorporation 'for any lawful purpose' did not appear until 1837 in Connecticut, and restrictions on incorporation were to be the norm throughout the nineteenth century (Berle and Means, 1932: 136).[30] Only in the closing decades of that century did monopoly, formed as an aggregation of individuals (as opposed to a specialization of the state or crown), become a possibility.

'Financiering'

One must struggle today to appreciate the low regard the Federalist citizen had for 'financiering.' From the heart of Federalist reality, Freeman Hunt

---

28 To briefly explain a point that will be made later, the apparent asymmetry of the terms used in this sentence is not accidental. As industrial relationships developed, the *bodies* of craft workers analogized to the bodies of employees dealt with through systems of industrial relations. The *knowledge* that had been held by crafts – to the extent that it was retained by workers and did not become the property of the organization – passed largely into professional occupational groups. This will be clarified in subsequent chapters.

29 Brown (1927), Carpenter (1921), George (1905), Vail (1907)

30 Davis (1905/1961).

castigated as 'evil' the move away from 'legitimate business' toward 'schemes of speculation.' Acknowledging that 'financiering has its place in legitimate business,' Hunt also deplores that 'the calamity of a great city is, that everyone who gains a little money takes to financiering.' Hunt is not opposed to 'investments in stocks as property,' but to 'the spirit of speculation' through which 'Wall Street, the focus of financiering, gives a tone to the whole business community.' More important than losing one's capital, to Hunt, is the potential loss of one's 'character' (which was, for the Federalist, the source of capital). Hunt's advice to the aspiring business person is 'Keep, therefore, to honest toil in a legitimate business, and do not aspire to become a *financier*' (1857: 72–3; emphasis in original).

Much later, Henry Ford still reflected the ideals of this era, arguing that 'the place to finance a manufacturing business is in the shop, and not the bank.' Like Hunt, Ford admitted the necessity of banking, but abhorred 'the kind of banker who regards a business as a melon to be cut.' Of the days when Ford Motor Company had been controlled by bank receivers,[31] Ford notes that 'the financiers proposed to cure by lending money and not by bettering methods. They did not suggest putting in an engineer; they wanted to put in a treasurer.' Looking backward on a lifetime journey from Federalist to industrial reality, Ford notes the 'great reaching out by bankers in the last fifteen or twenty years.' 'It was not the industrial acumen of the bankers,' Ford asserts, 'that brought them into the management of industry. . . . They were pushed there, willy-nilly, by the system itself' (Ford, 1922: 156–7, 176–7). Indeed, sometime about 1880, the public role of 'financiering' underwent major change. Hoyt (1966: 170) cites Cornelius Vanderbilt's 1879 divestment of his private railroad holdings as marking 'an entirely new direction and consideration in the matter of railroad and other corporate finance, where ownership would be spread widely and bankers would become managers as well as financiers of railroads and other businesses.'

Monopolies of scale/monopolies of scope

What was this 'system' to which Ford attributes such power? For Chandler (1962) this system can be described as successive waves of 'rationalization' of resources. For many living through the events of 1870–1900, another term might have been 'Morganization.' J. Pierpont Morgan was a sixth-generation descendant of Miles Morgan who had left Wales in 1630 to pioneer the 'wild west' of Springfield, Massachusetts. The Morgan dynasty was a mirror of the growing country itself as successive generations moved from farming to gentleman farming to business and eventually to banking. Raised in London, J.P. Morgan inherited a banking empire that was the largest conduit between

---

31 One indication of the depth of Ford's disdain is that once he had regained control of Ford Motor Company, it remained in family control for nearly forty years, going public with a stock offering only in 1956.

British capital (then the world's largest financial hub) and US business. In Pierpont, one finds an excellent example of the transition made by the US during this period from a capitalism of *scale* to one of *scope*.

It was largely capitalism of scope which made the term 'trust' a synonym for evil with the US public. One excellent example is the formation of John D. Rockefeller's Standard Oil Company in the 1870s.[32] Before it became an integrated organization, Standard Oil had grown very large as a loose agglomeration of formerly independent businesses, many still run by their former owner-operators who were now Standard Oil employees and stockholders. Indeed, it remains an open question whether the company's formation was due more to market and managerial advantage or to the ruthless manipulation of railroad rates against competitors. This was the monopoly of scope, whose primary purpose was to dominate a market.

The monopoly of scale was not simply large; it was integrated in a manner producing a qualitatively new organizational form. The novel aspect of this form is succinctly summed up by the key business principles of J.P. Morgan,[33] principles of organizing which became known at the time as 'Morganization.' First, reorganize the operation to put it on 'a paying basis.' Second consolidate the industry and create a community of interest among participants so that all major players work cooperatively. Third, secure financial control through voting trusts, stock purchases and interlocking directorates.[34] While this scenario is easily explained by invoking the stereotype of 'robber baron,' such a pat answer covers up the differences between the monopolist of scale and the monopolist of scope. The former advocated *laissez-faire* economic warfare and understood wealth as the legitimate spoils of war. The latter were self-interested enough, but theirs was an interest in which the achievement of wealth was a byproduct of other activity: 'rationalizing' markets to prevent 'destructive competition.'

This change was not unrecognized at the time. In 1890, Abraham Hewitt, an experienced steel man and an advisor to J.P. Morgan, noted that 'Most of the writers of the day have failed to comprehend the significance of the great movement toward concentration of management, accompanied by diffusion of ownership' (Tarbell, 1925: 163). While concentration created organizations of unprecedented size, diffusion of ownership and control vested in professional managers created a new structure of self-interest for those governing these new forms. Profit *maximization* was less important in the long run than *steady* profitability. Federalist business had accommodated itself to fluctuations of markets and seasons, but had dramatically changed two factors. First, business cycles were relatively tolerable in an agrarian

---

32 Tarbell (1902).

33 Both Hoyt (1966) and Chernow (1990) give similar accounts of these principles.

34 Chernow (1990) credits Jay Gould, the prominent Wall Street speculator, with creation of the voting trust, in which outside interests would purchase stock and delegate their voting rights to a financial trustee. Interlocking directorates are discussed in detail by Berle and Means (1932), who show how a relatively small percentage of a company's total stock can be 'pyramided' to yield control by having one company purchase the stock of another. This gives the purchasing company a seat, or seats, on the board of the other.

order to which industry was a supplemental activity; they became destructive when people's overall welfare came to depend on industrial employment and its products. Second, in industrial competition between firms where a great deal of the cost is fixed, competition easily drives prices into the area where they are more than paying for the variable cost of production, but are not profitable overall. This has been amply illustrated by the US airline industry since its deregulation in the late 1970s.[35] In the late 1800s, industry regularly oversaturated the new and highly volatile national markets resulting in a situation where sales at virtually any price were preferable to sitting on produced goods or stopping production.

Out of this desire to regulate business, came informal groups of producers and financiers who agreed to 'trust' each other to maintain relatively steady production levels and prices. In 1879 J.P. Morgan called a meeting at his home

> to which were invited all the major bankers who participated in railroad finance and all the heads of the Eastern railroads. . . . The result of it was the formation of various regional railroad associations. . . . The associations that were formed out of these meetings were trusts, combinations of corporations agreeing to cooperate and not to compete. . . . [And again later] Pierpont managed to persuade all the important railroads of the country and the important railroad bankers to come to his house in January 1889 in order to secure agreement among the roads that they would not cut rates, not build unnecessary lines, not engage in ruthless and wasteful competition. (Hoyt, 1966: 172–3).

Judge Gary of US Steel, who was closely associated with Morgan, organized regular dinners where similar issues were discussed relative to the steel industry (remember, such meetings were, at the time, quite legal). At one of these 'Gary dinners,' Charles Schwab praised Gary for bringing 'a new and successful principle' into the steel industry. That principle was the understanding that cooperation was more critical than competition (Tarbell, 1925: 217). These meetings were self-interested, but one can see self-interest beginning to take a different form; it is no longer served through *laissez-faire* competition. While Judge Gary advocated control of the steel industry by what amounted to collusion, he also testified publicly in 1911 'that cooperation is bound to take the place of competition and that cooperation requires strict governmental supervision' (Tarbell, 1925: 232). Hewitt went so far as to suggest that this emerging order could be a *cure* for destructive monopoly rather than a symptom of its triumph; through public scrutiny and diffusion of stock ownership, 'the harmony of capital and labor will be brought about by joint ownership in the instruments of production, and what are called "trusts" merely afford the machinery by which such ownership can be distributed among the workmen' (Tarbell, 1925: 163). This argument is not unlike that expressed by Carnegie (1913, 1920) or Taylor (1911).

---

35 Suppose the variable cost of a flight is $50 per passenger, but the overall cost, including fixed assets, requires a fare of $300 per passenger to break even. If competition drives the fare to $200, the airline loses $100 per passenger if it flies, but $250 if it does not.

The monopolist of scope: a 'man of character'

Where the monopolist of scale had invoked *laissez-faire* to legitimate his/her enterprise, the monopolist of scale invoked *noblesse oblige*.[36] There is no better illustration of this than J.P. Morgan himself. Hoyt argues that Morgan's concern in creating the railroad trust (he was also instrumental in creating the steel and other trusts) was 'not control for its own sake, or power for its own sake . . . he wanted to bring order to an American business scene that suffered from disorder' (Hoyt, 1966: 186). Morgan's proposed mechanism for bringing order was the 'exercise of economic power in the hands of responsible gentlemen whose word could be trusted and who sought only what was best, in their minds, for all the nation' (Hoyt, 1966: 186). Chernow also emphasizes that for Morgan, 'a gentleman wasn't a rich man but a member of a social caste. . . . The Morgans would always be strong believers in the work ethic and the duties of the rich' (Chernow, 1990: 48). 'It simply never occurred to him, says Hoyt, 'to believe that what was best for business could possibly be inimical to the interests of the public at large' (1966: 172).

Here, one sees self-interest in a particular shape, one distinct to the times, but simultaneously indebted to three centuries of Christian perfectionism. Concern for order; emphasis on work as an 'ethic;' rule by 'elders;' self-control; the belief that business simultaneously served God and the community – in these elements, the 'robber baron' ethos[37] shares a Utopian dream nourished by the same roots as the anti-industrial communistic experiments of the day (for example, Amanas, Shakers).[38] Today, it is easy to imagine J.P. Morgan's extensive involvement with Episcopal church governance, or John D. Rockefeller's work in his Baptist parish as impression management. In so doing, we short-change ourselves. Only if we take seriously the possibility that these men participated in a discourse which allowed them to be *both* ruthless predators *and* 'good' citizens can we begin

36 This is an admittedly murky distinction. Carnegie, for instance, was both to a significant degree, although not simultaneously. I am attempting to distinguish those who merely built business empires (e.g., Cornelius Vanderbilt) from those who effected the great consolidations and sought to have a prominent role in constructing a new society of oligopolistic business regulated by government and public scrutiny (foremost among these being Elbert Gary and J.P. Morgan).

37 Another interesting study would be to clarify the varying discursive roles played by those usually lumped together as 'robber barons.' Some, such as Cornelius Vanderbilt and Andrew Carnegie, built businesses as entrepreneurs. Only a few, such as Jay Gould, Jim Fisk and perhaps Hetty Green, plundered companies for speculation. J.P. Morgan represented a different form of financial domination, actively consolidating entire industries, intervening in management with the goal of long-term growth rather than speculative profit (what Tarbell (1925: 147) was trying to distinguish between 'a banker's idea and a stockbroker's idea' of running a company). John D. Rockefeller's background as an accountant, not an 'oil man', presaged the coming dominance of finance over production; it was followed by the first professional managers such as Elbert Gary and Alfred Sloan, whose emergence signified the transition to a modern managerial order of business.

38 Nordhoff (1875/1962).

to appreciate the world constructed during this period. Ironically, the death of the Federalist order was presided over by men whose 'character' was thoroughly Federalist.

The importance of 'the trust question' for this book is only secondarily related to size, monopoly power or inequality of wealth. The emergence of the trusts signified a new *way* of becoming a large business, represented new *relationships* through which monopolies or oligopolies of scale were legitimated and exemplified new *qualities* that would henceforth constitute the business leader. The merchant had already been displaced by the industrialist.[39] Now the industrialist, whose reality was the shop floor, was already being replaced by the financier whose reality was the record book; 'Most of the conquering types in the coming order were to be men trained early in life in the calculations of the bookkeeper' (Josephson, 1934/ 1962: 47). It is to these times that we must look to understand the 'managerial mystique' Zaleznik (1989) criticizes today.

The American 'Reign of Terror': Meanings Unbundled from Practices

Taken together, 'the trust question', 'the labor question' and the 'works management question' mark the entry of the US into its own 'reign of terror' – a crumbling of the social order. Christian perfectionism, the frontier and community had intertwined to provide a functional reality governing the first centuries of Anglo colonization of America, but the laws, norms and institutions of this reality depended upon 'a community of manageable size in which most persons would be known to the majority' (Watkins, 1927: 20). These institutions proved completely inadequate as a means for understanding or controlling capital or labor as they became national entities. Unlike Europe which had experienced industrialization within an old culture with established institutions,[40] when 'big business' appeared in the US 'no countervailing force existed to soften its impact: no aristocracy, no mandarin class, no guild tradition, no labor movement, no established church' (McCraw, 1984: 42–3). By the turn of the century one institution alone pervaded social life: '[In America] everything, even the churches, is conducted on business lines. There is no institution, local or national, which is not imbued with a commercial spirit' (Lawson, 1903: 3). Even in law enforcement, the Pinkertons, a private business and 'the largest provider of investigative and protective services in the United States between 1858 and

39 Holbrook estimates that the first US millionaire was not created before 1830. His candidate is Israel Thorndyke who, 'typical of the change from seaborne to industrial fortunes . . . began to make money as captain of a privateer,' moving only later into 'the still new and risky manufacturing ventures of Massachusetts and New Hampshire' (1953/1985: 11).

40 See Sheehan's (1989) excellent account of the slow and complex growth of the nineteenth-century German *Beamtenstaat*, or civil state; and Braudel's magnificent three-volume history of European capitalism (1981, 1982, 1984).

1898,' were 'the only instrument of police power to function throughout the nation' (Slotkin, 1992: 139). Community-based institutions of social control (law, religion, militia, markets, credit) were helpless against nationally and internationally based corporations and fearful of newly emerging national labor organizations such as the Knights of Labor and the American Federation of Labor.

As Federalist reality passed into history between about 1880 and 1900, Smith (1984) provides a detailed account of a society with a deteriorating family structure, an increasing mass of the destitute, political institutions dominated by patronage and business, industrialization of farming, proliferating radical and reform movements, anti-immigration sentiment and a pervasive sense of doom (yes, in the 1890s, not the 1990s); 'revolution was in the air' (Smith, 1984: 483).

> The half century roughly bounded by the close of the Civil War and the commencement of the Great War was characterized by a quite unprecedented disintegration of 'the settled use and wont' of the people. It was a period of extraordinary change. Institutions of every sort were dissolving and reforming with bewildering rapidity. Evolution, electricity, and education were overhauling all the established habits of thought and action which so pervasively curb and guide human conduct. (Watkins, 1927: 19)

Managerialist business history is likely to reduce the breakdown of the Federalist social order to something like 'the extraordinary mobility of America's capital and labor,' permitting 'productive resources to be mobilized' (Reich, 1983: 31–2) efficiently and productively. As these changes were occurring, contemporary accounts of 'mobilization' were more likely to refer to armed troops being called out against their own people. According to Laurie (1989: 136), '[a] government study showed that state troops were called out to calm unrest nearly 500 times between 1875 and 1910.' This figure does not include private mercenaries, such as the Pinkertons. The reigning mood during this period was one of *terror*. Whatever faults characterized Federalist reality, its boundaries were known. The rights, obligations, freedoms and constraints of citizenship were, if not just, at least relatively explicit and stable. As business activity overflowed the levees of social control, it washed away the channels through which meaning had flowed in comprehensible rhythms. Industrial reality began as a shapeless terror drowning the known world of Federalist reality.

One can easily forget that society was not divided neatly into capital and labor, since that conflict so dominates accounts of business activity in this period. *Both* groups were minorities and widely seen as threats. Outside of the union halls and the board rooms lay an agrarian and middle-class majority rooted in Federalist common sense, for whom labor represented the evils of oppressed European peasantry, while capital invoked the equally unthinkable reality of aristocracy. It is difficult today to adequately convey the depth to which these two forces shook, and ultimately dismantled, the Federalist sense of order. No longer free from history and no longer imagining themselves its master, Federalist citizens faced the unthinkable possibility of having recreated the European society America was supposed to have transcended. Two millennia of 'westering' ended at the factory gates of the new industrial order.

This was a period in which social meanings became increasingly unbundled from practices; Federalist interpretations did not fit industrial social relations. The demise of Federalism left no authority to limit vested interest. In the emerging order, a discourse of objectivity, pronounced by university-certified 'experts' and grounded in ideally value-free science, would provide a new basis for order. As organizing becomes scientific, '[w]hat constitutes a fair day's work will be a question for scientific investigation, instead of a subject to be bargained and haggled over' (Taylor, 1911: 142–3). But, legitimating the new corporate order was a task still to be accomplished. The emergence of this new reality begins another chapter in the history of work, one requiring a new 'common sense,' and new subjects: the *manager*, the *employee*, the *professional*, and the *consumer*. The following chapter traces the way these changes coalesced into a new social contract which, for the first time in history, created the conditions of possibility for what is today known as 'management.'

5

A New Social Contract – Industrial Reality, a Problem to Manage

The terror of the 1880s and 1890s was symbolized by the clash of capital and labor, but it did not necessarily result from the malevolence of individual workers or capitalists. It was far deeper, more extensive and structural. The key axis of conflict was not capital against labor, but industrialism – symbolized by capital *and* labor[1] – against Federalist society. Capitalist work relations had grown up outside of communitarian society and played by a different set of social rules.[2] While beholden to international capitalist relationships, Federalist America had been able to treat them as peripheral. America could be imagined as the land of escape from resource limits, class stratification and the state-level power of civil society or crown. In the early nineteenth century this view was not seriously at odds with the lived experience of the Federalist citizen. But, as the century progressed, and 'big business'[3] appeared, it appeared in a social vacuum; no other institutions of national scale existed. As with the Terror following the French 'industrial' revolution of 1789, any horror seemed possible because the institutions of society were demonstrably inadequate to control emerging social practices. An accumulation of incremental changes had eventually created a seismic shift in the social order. As this shift occurs, the final conditions of possibility for management as it is known today finally coalesce.

One change was the dominance of the organization of scale, which reordered work and ownership relationships. Truly national markets, developing technology and the appearance of marketing created for the first time early in the twentieth century a climate in which the logic of the scale organization could be expressed to its full extent. Another change was the atrophy of the foreman's role; the 'co-entrepreneur' was eventually reduced to little more than liaison between workers and the developing 'office.' The

---

1 Capital and labor could be enemies, but they could not threaten each other's existence because each had come into existence through opposition to the other. Without capital, labor would not be labor, and vice versa. The struggles of capital/labor were internecine (if bitter) fighting within an order, industrial capitalism, that was itself not yet integrated into the order of things.

2 This development parallels the European shift from a feudal to a mercantile order in the thirteenth to eighteenth centuries (Braudel, 1982; Galbraith, 1983; Marx, 1947; Toffler, 1980).

3 Porter (1973) is an excellent short summary of what was distinctive about 'big business' in the late nineteenth-century US.

permanent, full-time work relationship meant that workers had to accept the previously despised position of wage-worker for life; it meant that employers would alternately seek and be expected to assume greater responsibility for the non-work life of those employed. Increasingly concentrated, deskilled and organized workers were a source of fear for society and a visible refutation of the Federalist version of the American Dream. As financial control grew more distant from the workplace, more extensive and more sophisticated, the US moved from being a 'frontier' society to being an integral part of an international industrial order. The staple roles of Federalist work – owner-operators and workers – were disappearing. New roles appeared – managers, employees and capitalists – which could not be understood in Federalist terms. In this turbulent and unfamiliar world, finding effective means of social control meant striking deals with the devils of 'big government,' 'big capital' and 'big labor.'

Big government

Baudrillard has astutely described America as 'a Utopia which has behaved from the very beginning as though it were already achieved' (1989: 28). This comment captures an ironic and important conservative subtext to the more overt ideology of America as a radical social experiment. Croly (1909) observes that the popular belief regarding the institutions of the new republic *c.* 1800 was that

> [w]hen Jefferson and the Republicans rallied to the Union and to the existing Federalist organization, the fabric of traditional American democracy was almost completely woven. Thereafter the American people had only to wear it and keep it in repair. The policy announced in Jefferson's first inaugural [1801] was in all important respects merely a policy of conservatism. The American people were possessed of a set of political institutions, which deprived them of any legitimate grievances and supplied them with every reasonable opportunity; and their political duty was confined to the administration of these institutions in a faithful spirit and their preservation from harm. . . . Misgovernment was a greater danger than good government was a benefit, because good government, particularly on the part of Federal officials consisted, apart from routine business, in letting things alone. (1909: 47–9)

For the Federalist, this was a sort of Lockean political Utopia. For Locke (1632–1704), humanity was not inherently social. Rather, 'man' (that is, the individual) in the 'state of nature' was 'absolute Lord of his person and possessions.' The only justification for civil society to infringe on this freedom was 'mutual *Preservation*' of '*Property*.'[4] Thomas Jefferson (the primary intellectual exponent of the Federalist political views) was indebted to Locke to such an extent that the formation of the US government might be thought of as an experiment in applied Lockean philosophy. As Locke represented the mercantile/democratic spirit of the English Civil War and

---

4 *Second Treatise on Government,* Chapter IX, lines 2–19 (1703/1960: 395).

the Glorious Revolution (which, remember, had produced the Puritan and Quaker colonies in America), Jefferson represented the flourishing of that spirit in the US a century later. The average American probably knew little of Jefferson's writings, let alone those of Locke, but s/he had absorbed as fundamental truth two principles: (1) *The natural state of humanity is the free individual; civil institutions are, at best, a necessary evil*; (2) *Government is legitimate only when it is the voluntary association of free individuals.*

Through the Federalist period, the federal government's main role was regulation of international trade. It had little domestic infrastructure to maintain and no responsibilities for social welfare. Internationally, the geography of the US made a standing army unnecessary and regional attitudes made its support next to impossible. This changed radically during the US Civil War of 1861–5, but industry outgrew government. Business policy and corporate law were state affairs and large organizations were practically capable of purchasing the relevant state legislators.[5] Agrarian/middle-class society was caught between its Federalist suspicion of big government and the need for such institutions as a countervailing force.[6]

Big capital

As defenseless as US society was to industrial corporate-capitalist[7] transformation, capitalists could not rest easy. Increasingly, they sought social legitimation to prevent nationalization or dismemberment. This is reflected in 'the railroad question' present in every discussion of that industry from the late 1800s into the twentieth century.[8] Social backlash was evident in the 1880s with the court break-up of the Standard Oil Trust and the passage of

5 Gordon (1988) and Riordan (1963) provide entertaining popular accounts of the purchase and sale of legislation at this time.

6 Also discussed in McCraw (1984).

7 This is a bulky term and space does not permit a detailed discussion here, but one must distinguish between 'industrial,' 'corporate' and 'capitalist.' Soviet industry developed in a context that was neither corporate nor capitalist. Corporations preceded industry or capitalism and for centuries were more closely allied with the state than with capital. Capitalism has existed in pre-industrial economies and was primarily non-corporate until the last century or so (cf., Braudel, 1982; Davis, 1905/1961). Appreciation of these differences helps one to see that the post-industrial is not necessarily post-corporate or post-capitalist. On the other hand, the advent of post-industrial relationships should lead to questions about whether and to what degree this is changing corporate and capitalist relationships.

8 Byers (1908), Dewsnup (1906), Fagan (1909), Haines (1919), Healy (1940), Hogg (1906), Morris (1920), Reece (1895) and others. Hogg, who boasts of having sold more than 100,000 copies of *The Railroad in Education*, begins his book with the announcement that while its original purpose had been 'To give the evolution of steam, to chronicle the great engineering feats, to show what science and skill have done for the world . . . to make known that these gifts have been in the line of an advanced civilization,' that the purpose of the fifteenth edition would be 'To bring about a better understanding between labor and capital – to demonstrate that the very vastness of our territory suggests the necessity of aggregations of capital – corporations; that without these it would be impossible to have so great a country, so enlightened a people' (1906: 3).

the Sherman Antitrust Act. However ineffective they may have been, these measures served as a warning that the corporation must present itself to society as a participant in 'the long march upward' (Carnegie, 1913) toward a better life. Both sides felt threatened; both sought a stable basis upon which to negotiate a relationship.

Big labor

For labor, a bargaining relationship with capital appeared more and more as the alternative to a bloody revolution in which the odds for victory were remote. This led to a shift of emphasis. Prior to this time, labor had not fought primarily for wages, but for control of the work process and for 'job'-based compensation related to output. Only as this vision was beaten back by adverse legislation, media and public hostility, organized employers and pro-employer mercenaries and soldiers did a 'new' labor movement arise that sought to work *within* the wage system.[9] This was associated with a shift from *craft* unionism, organized by occupation, to *industrial* unionism, which attempted to forge fraternal bonds between all industrial workers, focusing not on the various tasks they performed, but on their common employment relationship with the organization. When not omitted entirely from managerialist histories, the 'evolution'[10] of labor unions is presented as a quasi-natural process of development. By considering the changing structures of work, one can see that a craft-organized fight to control the labor process was not merely an early stage of 'mature' unionism, it was a form of organizing appropriate to Federalist work relationships. The eventual development of industrial unionism was a response to the changed work relationships of industrial reality.

Not all favored this change. Three general visions were held by labor in this period. First, craft unionism and craft control of the labor process were the traditional view, declining along with Federalist reality. Second, a socialist vision combining industry-wide organizing and control of the labor process existed.[11] Increasingly toward the turn of the century, the main stream of labor organizing lay with a third vision, that of a labor bureaucracy working within the industrial system as a legitimate opponent to the developing management bureaucracy. Samuel Gompers, for instance, sought to legitimate the American Federation of Labor by presenting it to

9 Cf., Foner (1962), Kaufman (1986).

10 This argument could be explained using an evolutionist approach if one does not confuse evolution (adaptation to an environment through a selection process) with progress (movement toward a goal). In biology, the idea that evolution has a direction or a goal is dismissed as *teleological* error (cf., Chapter 2). It is this teleology in current historical accounts that is inappropriate. By what criteria? By its own. To do science teleologically is to base that science on extra-scientific (quasi-religious) assumptions.

11 This movement probably crested with the rise and fall of the Independent Workers of the World, the 'Wobblies,' c. 1905–20.

society as a countervailing power to the trusts.[12] This was new middle ground. For his approach, Gompers has been called both the '"clarion consciousness" of craft unionism' and a '"class collaborator."' Even today, 'Gompers' name is as likely to evoke the name of a labor bureaucrat as it is that of a working-class hero' (Kaufman, 1986: xv).

One lesson in these events of post-industrial theorizing is that unions did not begin with an interest in restricting production. Rigid job descriptions, strikes, 'work to rule,'[13] and increasing wages for decreased work are not techniques inherent to unionizing. Only after being disenfranchised as a legitimate partner in the control of work did labor resort to reliance on restricting managerial prerogative *within* the industrial system. Industrial union practices may be a barrier to the creation of organizations appropriately designed to reflect post-industrial needs and relationships – but no more or less so than industrial management itself. Both are products of the same, passing era.

The New Social Contract and '*L'employé*'

The image of Gompers as a labor bureaucrat is an apt representation of the new order coalescing around the forces of capital and labor. In a 1902 dissertation (published in 1907), Margaret Schaffner proposed that the possibility of a stable industrial order was brought about only when strikes, lockouts, work stoppages and other industrial strife 'brought the contending parties to the point where sheer exhaustion compelled them to meet each other in a business-like way . . . where they were able slightly to appreciate each other's view point' (Schaffner, 1907: 51). Before negotiation could become possible, she argues, a new 'social contract' had to be forged. Note that Schaffner refers to a *social*, not a legal, contract. The change she is suggesting is nothing less than a shift in a society's 'common sense' regarding the relationship of the individual to the institutions of society. This new 'contract' was not a victory for capitalists or for workers, but for industrial-*ism* over Federalism as a new way of understanding work, the worker and the world. The emerging industrial order may have been inimical to the deskilled, alienated shop worker, but it was no less alien to Cornelius Vanderbilt, J.P. Morgan or Freeman Hunt. There was privilege in the new order, and misery, but its distribution followed different rules. Those

---

12 Cf., Ozanne (1979).

13 Less known in the US, 'work to rule' is popular in Britain, Canada and other countries. Instead of striking, union members enforce every applicable policy and regulation in the performance of their jobs. The result, of course, is that the organization becomes almost totally inoperable. The very fact that it can be effective is a strong comment on the 'rationality' of bureaucratic organizations. It is hard to deny the cultural aspect of organizational activity when, in order to work effectively, the organization requires tacit knowledge of where to follow, go beyond or ignore nominally applicable rules.

included and excluded were different social groupings than before. It was largely a new reality.

Most critical accounts present this shift as a victory of capital over labor. Most managerialist accounts describe it as some combination of the victory of capitalist productivity benefiting everyone and/or as a necessary 'evolution' in response to environmental necessity. These perspectives were and continue to be appropriate for debating problems *within* industrial reality, but if one is to begin thinking about the possibility of a *post*-industrial reality, it is necessary to ask: how did industrial thinking *itself* become possible? How can one trace the formation of a specific complex of social relationships and meanings about work in a manner that will show how these meanings today limit the range of thinking one can bring to bear on problems of post-industrial organizing?

The 'new social contract' Schaffner saw coalescing did not answer the labor question, the works management question or the trust question. However, it did remap knowledge about work life in a new way that offered new possibilities for dealing with these questions. In this process, an entirely new vocabulary of objects and concepts for speaking about work was produced and a new chapter in the history of the worker was begun. These changes produced the possibility of 'management.' They also produced new subjects to manage. The profusion of Federalist workers – the merchant, clerk, craftsperson and so forth – were replaced by a universal worker. In the emergence of this new way of understanding work, one finds the first references to the '*employé*.'

The Appearance of *L'employé*

Today, the term 'employee' is so common that it is difficult to look at it with fresh eyes as signifying a specific form of work relationship, an industrial 'product.' To speak of the employee as a social production will sound strange to many readers, especially in the US, where individuals are treated as self-producing. That is, if one exhibits a certain behavior, it is because one has decided to do so. My perspective, similar to that expressed by Foucault in *The Order of Things*, recognizes this intentional aspect to human interaction, but emphasizes the effect of social structures in shaping that interaction. This is partially a value position related to my assumptions about reality; it is also a useful perspective for the analysis this book conducts because it focuses one on social systems, their effects and – hopefully – on prospective areas for influencing their construction and reconstruction.

A discursive approach to the study of social reality focuses on knowledge and language. What can be said is both an indication of social values and a powerful shaper of social action. Experience that does not reflect the values embedded in discourse may as well not exist because it has no social effect. Thus, when Foucault (1973b: 128) states that for eighteenth-century science 'life itself did not exist,' he is not claiming that living beings originated after that time. Rather, he is tracing the development of a shift from 'natural history' to 'biology,' a shift that was marked in part by the appearance of 'life' as an organizing concept for a science of the animate world.

Similarly, before the late nineteenth century in the US, there were workers, but the employee did not exist. 'Employé' appears in the French language in the seventeenth century,[14] already as a worker in a large organization, *un bureau, un administration*, a *chemin de fer* (railway). It seems to have entered English usage as a term for the railway worker. Thoreau (1854) is one of the first to use the term in the US referring to the Fitchburg Railroad workers who 'take me for an employee'[15] (the spelling 'employé' was the norm until well into the 1900s). Through the 1880s, the term referred almost exclusively to railroad workers. It appears in mining and steel at least as early as 1877[16] and first appears as a general, if minuscule, category in the US Census of 1870. Documents cited by Martin (1877/1971) show the term, rare a decade earlier, to be appearing casually in government reports, personal correspondence and the press by this time. Still, it was sufficiently novel in 1875 that Nordhoff, writing of 'hired laborers,' adds parenthetically, 'or, as it has absurdly become the fashion to say, employés' (1875/1962: 11). In other words, there was nothing 'natural' about the word a century ago; its appearance may be a flag indicating a site of social change[17]. The desire of large employers to create a new worker was discussed quite frankly in the literature of railway management at this time. The following passage was first published in 1910:

> In young countries it is difficult to find men to perform routine service. . . . In an older state, however, there grows up a class of men who are less sanguine as to their own earning power, since they are sons and grandsons and great-grandsons of men who have spent their lives in subordinate positions. A man of this habit of mind makes a far better railroad employee. . . . [There is currently] a trend toward the condition found throughout the older countries of Europe, where there is a clear distinction between the class of people in the community who are rising and progressive and the class of people who are satisfied, on the whole, with subordinate posts. . . . *The theoretical equality of all free citizens, which used to trouble men's minds so much in the earlier days of the Republic, is now recognized to mean little except equality of opportunity*. Really safe railroad operation in the United States needs greatly a class of men like that from which the railroad servants in England, France, and Germany are recruited, and there is reason to believe that in comparatively few years, perhaps in another generation, this condition will be realized. (Morris, 1920: 264–5; emphasis added)

14 Littré (1966).

15 Probably 'employé' in the first edition; I have been unable to verify this.

16 Martin (1877/1971: 195, 202).

17 As an example of such a flag, the word 'wife' (*wyf*) in Old English meant simply a female human being. During Middle English times, 'woman' (*wyf-man*) appeared and 'wife' came to mean a female person contracted to a man through marriage. The change from one word roughly equivalent in status to 'man,' to two words defined in relationship to men can be used 'archaeologically' as evidence marking the changing social status of women.

As an analytical tool, one might think of this emerging worker as an individual: *l'employé*. This worker existed within a society which presumed certain things about his/her abilities, motivations, rights and duties. It produced popular and scientific literatures whose spaces constituted the boundaries of the social space s/he could occupy. Eventually, as we have become 'the sons and grandsons [daughters and granddaughters]' of those 'who have spent their lives in subordinate positions,' this space even conditions the perceptions, expectations and self-image of *l'employé*. To study the discourse that grew up around *l'employé* is to learn the boundaries that today determine what can and cannot be said – and thus done – to understand and influence post-industrial society.

Federalist 'Citizen' to Industrial 'Employé'

In the mercantile world of Freeman Hunt, there was no uniform discourse about work. Most such knowledge was confined to groups within industries or occupations. Much more was hoarded as a trade secret by individuals. A term equating the clerk, the tinsmith and the iron puddler did not exist, nor was it needed. If all free workers[18] shared an identity (idealized, of course), it was that of the 'citizen,' the landowning and/or self-employed Lockean who participated in society as a peer to all. It was the rights, duties and values of this 'citizen' which dominated the structure of Federalist business discourse.

What identity dominates today? Pick up a management text at random and look for workers. Chances are the text is written *to* 'managers,' or those who identify with that role. It is written *about* 'employees,' who are the object of research and theorizing. Passing attention may be given to the employed 'professional,' or to 'knowledge workers' (who are usually treated as a subcategory of professional). Occupational labels are incidental. If I study nurses, for instance, it is presumed that it is to learn something about 'employees.' Knowledge in the management disciplines is not organized by craft or skill. To enter management discourse, one must enter as a manager, employee or professional. But wait, *managers and employed professionals are also employees*. Management discourse is a discourse about 'the employee.'

Who Was *L'employé?*

L'employé appears simultaneously with new boundaries around work and the worker. In contrast to both the Federalist citizen and to non-employees,

---

18 This excludes slaves, for instance. In addition, the Naturalization Act of 1790 explicitly restricted citizenship to 'whites,' excluding Asians, native Americans and others. It was not repealed until the McCarran-Walter Act of 1952 (Takaki, 1993: 9, 79, 400).

Table 5.1   *Industrial employé and Federalist citizen*

L'employé was . . .	*The Federalist* . . .
The good worker	. . . expected to control the work process, not 'serve' a master ('boss,' from the Dutch *baas*, literally means master).
The permanent worker	. . . either entered wage work as a supplement to other income earning and home-based production or as a temporary state permitting one to learn a skill and save the capital necessary to start up on one's own business.
The organization's worker	. . . worker considered dependence on the organization a debased state; employers did not yet seek the direct control of the worker which would later lead them to assume commitment for worker welfare.
The sub-ordinate	. . . believed sub-ordination to be un-American, one of the ills of aristocratic Europe.
The task worker	. . . followed the work process through to a completed product.
The wage worker	. . . was paid for out*comes*, saleable goods or services.
The typologized worker	. . . believed in the 'omnicompetence' of the average person to farm, support oneself, acquire a variety of skills and participate in the governance of society.
The ignorant, childlike, encoded self	. . . considered it a perquisite and basic criterion of adult participation in society to speak one's truth knowledgeably, without accepting the higher judgment of business superiors, the state (except by the common will) or 'experts.'
The divided self	. . . unified the roles of business person and politician, domestic and paid worker, producer and consumer.

l'employé is a subject characterized by a number of specific practices, all alien to the reality of the Federalist citizen. These are listed in Table 5.1.

The good worker

According to a Baltimore newspaper's account of an incident in the great strike of 1877, '[t]he number of railroad employés engaged in the rioting here has from the first not exceeded 150; but at the outset of the affair they were joined by thousands of laborers and mechanics' (Martin, 1877/1971: 61). In another incident on the Ohio and Mississippi railroad, '[a]rmed employés were placed on each train' (Martin, 1877/1971: 354). Throughout these accounts, *l'employé* is loyal to the organization, avoiding or even resisting the 'tough,' the 'foreigner,' the 'mechanic,' and so forth. One might also note that unions have chosen to call themselves workingmen, workers, laborers, crafts or tradespeople – but seldom employees. The employee is not part of labor, even if s/he is a laborer. Labor is a threat, *l'employé* an ally, to employers.

The permanent worker

As recently as 1923, Scott and Clothier claim that '[t]he company which, to maintain a work force of 1,000 persons engages 1,000 new employees in a year's time, is neither above nor below the average' (1923: 450). Until about the time of the First World War, payrolls were largely composed of 'boomers,' 'floaters' or 'five-day men,' likely to quit after any pay day. The very profusion of names for this relationship attests to its centrality in work relations. *L'employé*, however, had an ideally career-long[19] relationship to the organization. Routine today, this continuing relationship was then the exception to the norm. Only as it began to sediment into 'common sense' could topics such as 'turnover' and 'absenteeism' become meaningful subjects of analysis.

The organization's worker

In his account of the Ohio and Mississippi railroad strike, Martin uses a telling phrase when he mentions that the railroad 'officers' (not yet managers), 'armed their employés with revolvers and coupling pins' (1877/1971: 354). *Their* employees? At what point did the worker become the property of the employer? Freeman Hunt's Federalist was his own person. In the organization of scope, the foreman might see members of the work gang as 'his' as is reflected in Navin's (1950: 140) language, but prior to this time neither employers nor workers would have wanted the organization to 'own' employees. If the employee could be viewed as a free Federalist citizen, only supplementing his/her basic subsistence with part-time or temporary wage work, this did not create the expectation that the employer would assume responsibility for the worker's social welfare. This was supported by the historical structure of the wage-labor market. This is a passage from the diary of Thomas B. Hazard, a nineteenth-century 'mechanic' (that is, a skilled factory worker) known as 'Nailer Tom.'

> Making bridle bits, worked a garden, dug a woodchuck out of a hole, made stone wall for cousin, planted corn, cleaned cellar, made hoe handle of bass wood, sold a kettle, brought Sister Tanner in a fishboat, made hay, went for coal, made nails at night, went huckleberrying, raked oats, plowed turnip lot, went to monthly meeting and carried Sister Tanner behind me, bought a goose, went to see *** in town, put on new shoes, made a shingle nail tool, helped George mend a spindle for the mill, went to harbor mouth gunning, killed a Rover, hooped tubs, caught a

---

19 Note the roughly simultaneous transformation of the word 'career' from a verb meaning to gallop or drive out of control to a noun indicating an orderly progression through a work life. I thank Dr Pushkala Prasad of the University of Calgary for this observation.

weasel, made nails, made a shovel, went swimming, staid [*sic*] at home, made rudder irons, went eeling. (Borsodi, 1929: 138)

The reader of *The Principles of Scientific Management* will find that even the famous 'Schmidt'[20] of Taylor's early experiments, although allegedly 'a man of the mentally sluggish type' according to the text, was also building his own house before and after work (1911: 44–6). How many of today's 'knowledge workers' possess the skills to accomplish this feat? Like the pre-industrial European peasantry, the Federalist worker, however poor, was not a proletarian. 'The peasant survived . . . thanks to plying a hundred extra trades: crafts . . . wine-making . . . haulage . . . working as miners, quarrymen or iron workers . . . sailors . . . weaving . . . peddlars and carriers . . . day-laborers . . . borrowers and lenders of money . . . herdsmen' – as well as farming for both subsistence and the market (Braudel, 1982: 255–6). Indeed, the origin of 'freedom' as a social value is associated with the period between the demise of the 'old' feudal order of seignorial obligation, *noblesse oblige*, and the 'new feudalism' of industrial order. This was not simply the *freedom-to-act* of the citizen, but *freedom-from-responsibility* of the lord or employer. As the century passed, the tension between this ideal and material conditions grew. Even before the Civil War, the South had argued that wage slavery in the North was more cruel than slavery in the South because the Southern planter had to assume responsibility for the slaves' well-being, at least to the degree of keeping them fit and willing to work; the Northern employer need not care who was starving and freezing as long as a sufficient number showed up at the factory gates. This observation was not entirely unfounded.

With the coming of the organization of scale, the economic value of a stable work force grew by orders of magnitude. Increasingly, employers were willing to risk the commitment implied in claiming the workers as 'theirs.' Backward integration into markets of physical inputs was matched by a form of backward integration into workers' lives. Only as this becomes the case (the process is described further in Chapter 6) does it come to make sense to speak of workers as 'resources' analogous to coal or iron. Unlike her/his predecessors in the history of work, *l'employé* is a 'human resource.' Capitalization of time and knowledge had a long history within Federalist values, but the combination of a long-term employment relationship and increasing authority of 'the organization' exacerbated the contest for ownership of this human capital.

The sub-ordinate

In a society of equals, how does one legitimate difference? Federalist differences of wealth could be thought of as differences of magnitude, not of kind. The existence of a gentry did not challenge this ideology. If some were

---

20 A pseudonym.

wealthier than their peers they were simply *primus inter pares* (first among equals). Their success could be viewed as signifying their greater contribution to the 'common wealth' and as an example to others of the possibilities available for a 'man of character.' Where Federalist differences of kind did exist, they did not require a common basis for comparison. Between the tinsmith and the farmer, between the ship's chandler and the oculist, there was no need for a common measure of authority or responsibility relative to work. Each operated in their own, relatively autonomous sphere. But as the organization of scope grew into the organization of scale, it could no longer be rationalized within this belief system. The 'theoretical equality of all free citizens' could not be reconciled to a permanent class of 'men who have spent their lives in subordinate positions.' Expediently, at this point one finds 'service' entering public discourse about work.

In the history of America as an ideal, one can broadly outline three successive norms regarding service: service to God, service to community and service to the organization. These intertwine in a complex way, but each has a fairly distinct period of predominance. Service to God was the central principle legitimating Puritan and Quaker colonial settlement. In these particular sects, where action in the world was valued as the path to salvation, service to God easily translated into service to community. By the 1700s, while religion remained a strong force, community as a secular value had become dominant. Except for the trailblazer, the American ideal of independence was one of independence within community. Both forms of service emphasized *self*-control through Christian perfectionism within a *laissez-faire* business community. Like the Roman patrician class, one chose to enter a group of nominally equal and free citizens who jointly ran society.[21] While individual freedom was bounded by community responsibility, this could be viewed as the *noblesse oblige* of the free citizen; a person could still claim to be in the service of no*body*. The Federalist citizen did not *serve*; to do so was *servile*. Accordingly, *service* was looked down upon. Those 'in service' were those who worked as domestics.

This is the social tradition into which the organization of scale emerged. For the first time on a large scale, free citizens were grouped in a social structure characterized simultaneously by differences which were ordered horizontally and vertically on a common grid of value specifying both qualitative and quantitative differences regarding one's privilege, responsibility and, implicitly, one's value to the institution. In order for the organization of scale to operate, hundreds or thousands of people had to participate in a single plan of action; a system of subordinates and superordinates ('superiors') was coalescing. But, in the American tradition, there was no source of legitimacy for subordinating one free citizen to

---

21 An excellent description of these relationships in the Roman world, contrasting them with the hierarchical relationships characterizing feudal European society, is presented in the contributions by Paul Veyne and by Michel Rouche in Ariès and Duby (1987).

another. Remember Nordhoff's (1875/1962) and Hunt's (1857) scorn of the 'wage-worker for life.'

Railroads were the first to encounter this problem on a large scale. Expanding after the Civil War, they adopted the tactic of appropriating the spirit of wartime service to country – even today, entering the military is often spoken of as going into 'the service.' As late as 1906, Dewsnup refers to 'our railway lieutenants, captains, colonels and generals of tomorrow' (1906: vi). In his *Memoirs*, General Grenville Dodge, a railroad executive drawn from the military, wrote

> The organization for the construction of the Union Pacific Railway was purely upon a military basis. Nearly every man working upon it had been in the Civil War; the heads of most of the engineering parties and all of the construction forces were officers in the Civil War; the chief of the track-laying force, General Casement, had been a division commander in the Civil War; and at any moment I could call into the field a thousand men, well officered, ready to meet any crisis or any emergency. (Morris, 1920: 2)

This basic distinction between 'officers' and 'men' created a new boundary through the organization. It would have made no sense in the co-entrepreneurial foreman system of the organization of scope, but it is the antecedent of the now-basic distinction manager/employee. Also appearing at this point are contemporary-sounding distinctions between 'staff officers and line officers,' between 'headquarters staff' and 'field staff' (Morris, 1920: 23). The military provided business with then-radical concepts including unity of command, a shift from personal authority to positional authority, concepts of information and authority 'flows,' divisional and departmental forms of organizing.

It would be tempting to see this form as the parent of today's organization, but that would be to overlook a disjunction introduced by the organization of scope. By the turn of the century, Morris (first published 1910) clearly sees that military organizing is most applicable only to 'divisional' organization (scope); 'a railroad managed on the departmental plan [scale], however, is not comparable to an army.' The military metaphor, then, was useful as a transitional ordering principle, primarily within the organization of scope. Its limits were quickly reached. By Taylor's time, use of the term 'soldiering' as a term for working as little as possible indicates that, even at this early date, command-and-control operation left something to be desired.

Here one sees the entry of 'the environment' as a factor in thinking about work. How can the person born into a society where wage work is neither a temporary condition nor a debased state feel a level of commitment to 'the organization' proceeding from moral obligation and innate quality of character rather than from any quid pro quo? More durable than the adoption of military norms was yet another transformation underway in the 'man of character.' For those who labor, 'character' will come to be expressed as acceptance of organizational subordination in the war of society against 'scarcity.' The spirit of Calvin is easily discerned in the ordering principle of modern economics, which 'designates in labor, and in the very hardship of that labor, the only means of overcoming the fundamental insufficiency of nature and of triumphing for an instant over death'[22] (Foucault, 1973b: 257). This 'discovery' of late eighteenth-century Europe became a discovery of late nineteenth-century America. This is ironic since, after millennia of humans living on the margin of subsistence, a culture with the highest level of material production in history makes the *scarcity* of goods its central principle for analyzing production and distribution. One may understand this in part as reflecting a shift from a mercantile business/economic discourse centered on *exchange* to an industrial discourse centered on *production*. The man of character would now be a soldier in the war on scarcity. One role of 'service' was to legitimate the organization's ownership of 'human capital.'

The task worker

Until this time in US history, social division of labor had been organized primarily around *products*. Society was complex – there are 324 basic occupational categories for white male citizens even in the census of 1850 – but most workers followed a work process from start to finish. Among other things, this meant that most work required skilled workers. Within the organization of scale, few workers followed a complete process resulting in a finished product. *Organizational* division of labor was added to *social* division of labor. That is, specialization occurred within, as well as between, organizations. Increasingly, this specialized task was highly mechanized and/or routinized.[23] Workers became more or less commodities in the sense that one was about as desirable as the next. One hired a person only because that was how workers were packaged; one needed only to hire a 'hand.' The employé lacked the occupationally based skills, social unity and resulting power of the craftsperson. Even if s/he did acquire specialized skills, they were those which could be utilized only *within* the large organization. The Federalist blacksmith could set up shop anywhere as the vendor of a finished product. The industrial lathe operator could apply metal-working skills only within the task-specialized environment of the factory. Today, as the task-centered worker becomes a problem in more and more work situations, it would help to bear in mind that this orientation is not a 'natural' attribute

22 Foucault places Adam Smith at the end of the 'Classical' period (*c.* 1650–1790) in Europe and looks to David Ricardo for the first articulation of economics reflecting modern assumptions (Foucault, 1973b: Part II, Section 8).

23 This feature was common to two forms of industrial organizing. The high fixed-capital factory, of course, is the model for highly divided task work. The same principles, however, were also applied to 'sweated labor.' In 'sweat shops,' such as the cigar-rolling and garment-sewing industries, capital requirements were low, work was organized along task rather than craft principles. This suggests that the appearance of this system cannot be attributed solely to the requirements of scale technologies.

of the worker. It is a characteristic of *l'employé*, a particular worker whose construction took a good half-century.

The wage worker

Broadly speaking, if one wishes to purchase the time of another, one can purchase *outcomes*, *outputs* or *inputs*.[24] Traditionally, labor was tied to outcomes. Within seigniorial society, one's own produce and that of the lord's was not distinct until after the harvest. In order to cheat the lord, one had to cheat oneself as well. Within trade, one was likely to pay a fixed price per shipment or a fixed price to hold an office; whatever revenues one could then secure from reselling the goods or the rights of the office was one's own.[25] With compensation dependent upon outcomes, the quantity and quality of work is assured by the system of payment. One need not worry about the producers of shoddy labor; they will be their own punishment.

Wage work shifted the focus of compensation to inputs. The worker was not selling a product, but a *unit of time*. As many of us have learned from working in such situations, self interest now mitigates in the direction of doing as little work as possible within a given unit of time. When one has sold one's employer an hour or a day, the object is to reach the end of that hour or day and leave. A worker may still care about the quantity or quality of his/her work, but only if this stems from factors extraneous to the work process and compensation system such as family, community or religious socialization.[26]

One of the 'radical' compensation schemes proposed in the 1890s by mechanical engineers such as H.R. Towne (1884, 1886) and Frederick Taylor (1895) were piece-rate systems which shifted the focus of compensation from inputs to *outputs* (but still not to outcomes). Piece-rate systems have been widely applied and are often useful, but they also have the tendency to set workers against each other (especially when piece-rate

24 This distinction is based on Ramanathan (1982). Ramanathan ranks five levels of measurement: benefits, outcomes, outputs, inputs and expenditures. For present purposes, the three middle levels are adequate.

25 In developing his theory of bureaucracy, Weber offers an extensive tabulation of pre-bureaucratic arrangements (Gerth and Mills, 1946).

26 There is an irony here that returns to haunt post-industrial managing. For decades, industrial organizing has relied on the home and community to produce a worker who values honesty and hard work. Some occupations, primarily female-dominated ones, have been constituted as workplace manifestations of domestic practices and values – e.g., the secretary as the 'organizational wife;' the nurse who wants to care for the sick. Today, the source of these workplace values, the family, continues to decline as a viable institution. Dual careers, the need to value organizational mobility above attachment to community, the ongoing reduction of the home into little more than a site for consumption, continue to weaken the family as a source of social value production. This trend is sometimes (if insufficiently) recognized as a factor in controlling crime, in the breakdown of the public education system, and in the effects of instability on latchkey children and children of 'broken' homes. It must also be recognized as representing the ongoing reduction of precisely the social skills said to be critical for both the performance and management of knowledge-intensive work.

workers are dependent upon flat-wage workers) and there is still a space between output and outcomes – as the popularity of Deming and Juran methods to managing quality suggests. Paid for putting in time and restricted to tasks which are not in themselves products, *l'employé* is the worker reflected in this interview of an insurance company clerk:

> The other day when I was proofreading endorsements I noticed some guy had insured his store for $165,000 against vandalism and $5,000 against fire. Now that's bound to be a mistake. They probably got it backwards.
> I was just about to show it to Gloria [the supervisor] when I figured 'Wait a minute! I'm not supposed to read these forms. I'm just supposed to check one column against another. And they do check. So it couldn't be counted as my error.'
> Then I thought about this poor guy when his store burns down and they tell him he's only covered for $5,000. But figured the hell with it. It'll get straightened out one way or another. . . . If they're gonna give me a robot's job to do, I'm gonna do it like a robot. (Garson, 1977: xi)

The Federalist worker would have understood the world of Adam Smith, where '[i]t is not from the benevolence of the butcher, the brewer, or the baker, that we expect our dinner, but from their regard to their own interest. . . . Nobody but a beggar chuses [*sic*] to depend chiefly on the benevolence of his fellow citizens' (1776/1937: 14). For *l'employé*, self-interest no longer connects work and reward in any obvious way; s/he is reliant on the 'benevolence' of the employer.

The typologized worker

Taylor, above, refers to Schmidt as being of the mentally sluggish 'type.' This was a new way of thinking about the worker. A Federalist clerk could have been sluggish or stupid, but this was not a 'type.' To say the clerk was sluggish was a description of behavior, not essence; of a person, not a category. Individual sluggishness, understood with reference to Federalist 'character,' was an indication that one should attempt to perfect that aspect of one's personality through self-control. The citizen who would not do this was not worthy to participate in a society of equals. As society became more stratified and equality gave way to 'mere equality of opportunity,' it was simultaneously 'discovered' that people possessed innate differences in the level to which they might develop. In other words, as society hierarchized, a 'natural' hierarchy of personality was discovered which meshed conveniently with the emerging institutional order.[27] This permitted the legitimation of hierarchy within a rhetoric of equality: everyone had an

---

27 A contemporary example of this thinking is offered in exceptionally explicit form in Lichtenstein, Smith and Torbert's (1995) vision of ethics applied to leadership. They propose a hierarchy of individual ethical development and match it to formal hierarchical status in the organization. On the one hand, this can be read as implying that correspondingly higher levels of authority have greater incumbent moral responsibility. On the other, it is easily appropriated to legitimate both the existence of a natural hierarchy and the claim that 'superiors' are morally superior.

equal chance to go as far as his/her abilities would take him/her, but this was not equally far in every case. Hierarchizing workers could be presented as an advantage to them because it facilitated their task of finding the place where they would be most satisfied and best compensated. It also had the reassuring effect of creating a less threatening way of speaking of the worker. As 'labor' the worker was, collectively, a threat to the social order. As 'the employee,' s/he could be fitted, one by one, into an order. True, it was a radically different order, but it was order. This was no small thing to the agrarian and middle-class majority.

What one can see emerging is an assumption that there is a unity of interest between all parties to industrial work. This assumes that: (1) If labor is classified and ordered according to a natural hierarchy of types, this ordering will match the hierarchical structure of the organization of scale; (2) The work to which the worker is best suited is that which will bring her/him the highest level of compensation; (3) The worker will be happiest doing the work suited to her/his 'type;' (4) When everyone has been put into the proper place and the organizational community has been properly set up and governed, profits will be higher, wages will also be higher and, because of increased productivity, prices to the consumer will be lower.

While these assumptions are not simply statements of empirical truth, neither are they wholly without substance. Both those who support them and those who think them a transparent rationalization for capitalist oppression can find examples supporting their position. That aside, a specter is haunting these assumptions, the specter of Perfectionism. George Fox, a founder of the Quakers, or Cotton Mather, the prominent seventeenth-century Boston Puritan, would have been able to see the logic in these assumptions. Through quite an amazing transformation, the Protestant city on a hill has reappeared in the 'American Dream' to legitimate work within the emerging order. One once showed one's character by escaping from wage work; one now showed one's character by approaching wage labor with a good 'work ethic.' Is it fanciful to hold Cotton Mather accountable for the mode of US industrialization? In 1989 one of the premier empirical management research journals published an article advancing differences in 'work ethic' as an explanation for differences in absenteeism among employees.[28]

The ignorant, childlike (and encoded) self

Down-east humor is a regional form of US humor from coastal Maine. The quintessential protagonist of this humor is an old Yankee. The butt of the joke is often somebody 'from away,' perhaps a city person from neighboring Massachusetts or New Hampshire. Classic examples of down-east exchanges include:

28 Hackett et al.(1989).

'Does this road go to Bangor?'
'Nope, just lies there.'

'Does it matter which way I go at this fork in the road?'
'Not to me it doesn't.'

'OK, Seth, now I was born in New Hampshire and didn't move here until I was eight months old. Even though I've lived eighty years in Maine, you wouldn't call me a native. But my kids were born in this town and lived here all their lives. Surely they're natives?'
'Maybe, but if my cat crawled into the oven and had kittens, I wouldn't necessarily call them biscuits.'

In down-east humor, one finds the Federalist citizen confronting the industrial subject, but from a Federalist point of view. One invariant feature of this humor is that, unlike the industrialized subject from the city, the Yankee apprehends what's really going on. The industrial subject doesn't even know if a road goes to Bangor or just lies there. Where this Yankee 'omnicompetence' was a fundamental tenet of Federalist belief, the modern American, noted Hofstadter, 'cannot even make his breakfast without using devices, more or less mysterious to him' (1963: 34). As the social order grew rapidly more complex and the domain of most workers' knowledge grew more specific, the growing ignorance of the subject was a matter of daily 'discovery.' Lamented Borsodi in 1929:

> We buy our music today; we do not produce it ourselves. Perhaps the time will come when it can neither be produced or enjoyed by us. . . . We now have maternity hospitals, nurseries, and nursery schools, sanitariums and even funeral churches, all of them efficient – and hard. The modern mother is merely maternity case number 8,434; her infant after being finger and foot printed, becomes infant number 8,003. By virtue of the same mania for system, a modern corpse becomes number 2,432; while a modern funeral becomes one of a series scheduled for parlor 4B for a certain day at a certain hour, with preacher number fourteen, singer number 87, rendering music number 174, and flowers and decorations class B. Thus the factory system begins and finishes the citizen of the factory-dominated world. It introduces him to his world in a systematized hospital, furnishes a standardized education, supports him in a scientifically managed factory, and finishes him off with a final factory flourish, by giving him a perfectly efficient funeral and a perfectly scientific entrance into the regions of eternal bliss. (Borsodi, 1929: 193, 198–9)

Merely to live, the modern subject had come to need an army of experts. In contrast with the down-east Yankee, we find Taylor's Schultz who, simply to carry pig iron, must accept the instructions of an 'inspector,' 'gang boss,' 'speed boss,' 'repair boss,' 'time clerk,' 'route clerk' and 'disciplinarian;' 'It was not due to this man's initiative or originality that he did his big day's work, but to the knowledge of the "science of pig-iron handling" developed and taught him by some one else' (Taylor, 1911: 124–5). Replacing the omnicompetent Yankee, *l'employé* is ignorant and, not coincidentally, a 'foreigner':[29]

29 In this case, possibly not even foreign-born. Schmidt is described (Taylor, 1911: 43) as a 'Pennsylvania Dutchman,' which would mean a person of German ancestry (*Deutsche* had become corrupted in English to 'Dutch'). This community often resisted assimilation, retaining its Germanic culture. Schmidt may have been a native-born 'foreigner.'

Figure 5.1　*'One Reason for His Embarrassment'*
Source:　*Industrial Psychology* (1926) Vol. 2, No. 1

'Schmidt, are you a high-priced man?'
'Vell, I don't know vat you mean.'
'Oh, come now, you answer my questions. . . . I want to find out whether you want to earn $1.85 a day or whether you are satisfied with $1.15, just the same as all those cheap fellows are getting.'
'Did I vant $1.85 a day? Vas dot a high-priced man? Vell, yes, I vas a high-priced man.' (Taylor, 1911: 44)

That Schmidt was Pennsylvania Dutch facilitated this stereotyping. A century before, Benjamin Franklin had stigmatized the 'Palatine boors' [the Palatinate was a German principality] entering Pennsylvania and worried that they would 'shortly be so numerous as to Germanize us instead of our Anglifying them.' They would no more assimilate into 'white' Anglo-Saxon culture 'any more than they can acquire our complexion' (Goodman, 1945: 335).

Portraying the worker as a well-intentioned buffoon in humor served a deadly serious purpose. Bear in mind that by the turn of the twentieth century, the country had, for a generation, feared class warfare with 'labor' fomenting a revolution. It would be hard to fear the smiling oaf in Figure 5.1. In it labor is not hostile, but merely 'embarrassed.' Workers do not seek to overturn the system, merely to be 'selected' into 'the right job' by the wise and knowing expert. Two themes in this cartoon are worth noting.

First, portraying the 'Other' as childlike fits into a theme reaching back to US colonization. The first slaves brought to Jamestown, native Americans, Asians and a succession of European immigrant groups shared this bond of being infantilized by a society that was at heart Puritan/Quaker.[30] Bear in mind, infantilization was (and is) traditionally the more *progressive* view of difference. Instead of open hatred of Others for what they simply are, the infantilizing view permits the idea that the Other will 'develop' into the mainstream norm. This belief has been applied at both the individual and the social level. The individual, in Lamarckian fashion, 'progresses' through stages from the less to more mature levels. Leaving one's cultural heritage behind and assimilating has consistently been associated with growth to a more 'mature' level. Societies, in a more Darwinian[31] manner, change in response to their environments. Harsher environments produce more complex societies. These, in turn, produce more advanced individuals. Between the late 1800s and the early 1900s, this thinking is pervasive in writing as diverse as that of Thorstein Veblen (1899/1983), Blackford and Newcomb (1914) and Albert Keller (1915/1973). It was not a conservative or liberal position as much as a condition for speaking as an informed individual. It reflects a view alien to Federalist reality, but central to industrial reality: people and society *evolve* in a *progressive* manner. Society is neither static nor changing randomly. Human history has a direction and purpose. Culture mirrors history. The starting point for human conscious-ness is 'darkest Africa,' progresses through Eastern civilizations (stagnant reflections of Ancient glory) to Europe and thence to the 'frontier' of culture and history – America.

A second point embedded in the cartoon of 'embarrassed' labor is that the worker has now become a secret to be decoded. Federalist relations of community and character were *external*; they capitalized time and space in terms of correct practice. Granted, correct practice was attained through the development of character which, as self-knowledge and self-control, were part of the Federalist's interior life. But the domain of character was private. The community rewarded and sanctioned *practices*, not *perceptions*. Individual sense-making, belief, and feeling were irrelevant as long as they led to correct practice. *L'employé* emerged as a subject with an *interior* composed of sentiment, motivations and traits[32] subject to analysis and

30 This emerges gradually, but persuasively, from the panorama of Takaki's (1993) marvelous account of 'multicultural America.'

31 Lamarck believed that adaptation within an individual's lifetime resulted in enhanced traits that it passed on to successive generations. Darwin, reflecting the view generally adapted by modern science, believed that the source of change was random variation; successive generations adapted in the aggregate because those with more advantageous traits were more likely to survive and reproduce, thus passing those traits on to progeny. They were simply the bearers, not the sources, of the changes.

32 'The Hawthorne studies . . . involved a shift from the psycho-physiological model of the worker to a socio-emotional one . . . . I call the subject of this new knowledge the "sentimental worker" because it was at this time that the worker was formally discovered to have sentiments (feelings or emotions as we would call them now).' (Hollway, 1991: 71)

control. The focus of discourse changed from Federalist *what* questions ('what does the subject do?') to industrial *why* questions ('why does the subject do it?'). As this shift occurred, meanings left the surface of social interaction and disappeared into the interior of the subject; they now had to be decoded using knowledge not available to the average person. As will be seen in Chapter 6, this required appropriation of a whole new tradition of more statist, less individualistic, knowledge (German and Russian instead of English). *L'employé*, then, emerged as an ignorant, childlike and encoded self. His/her knowledge, 'development,' and meanings had to be placed in the hands of those who were (at least implicitly) knowledgeable, adult and capable of decoding – managers and professional 'experts.'

The divided self

The Federalist citizen lived in a world which believed, with some reason, in the mutual interest of God, business and government. The world of wage work was only one relatively peripheral role of membership in a community within which most economic activity took place outside the monetary economy (see Nailer Tom, p. 71 above) – the home was a bigger business than 'business.'[33] To be a competent, average adult in this community, one acted as a subject integrating these many roles. The Federalist frowned upon, and was largely capable of avoiding, specialization. *L'employé*'s appearance is marked by the fragmentation of this unity. Croly (1909) argues that the 'dominant note' of the period beginning about 1870 is 'disintegration of this early national consistency.' The first result, 'was to send the man of business, the politician, and the lawyer off on separate tracks' (Croly, 1909: 104). From the Plymouth and Philadelphia colonies until 1870, the ideal of 'admirable manhood' had been that the maker of laws, the executor of law and the man of business would be one and the same person. As the politician and lawyer split off from business, the Federalist took a step toward the reality of *l'employé*.

This ideal, which has now been anachronistic for more than a century, survives in US politics with candidates who win popular support running as 'outsiders'[34] to politics. Although politics has been a full-time specialization since the 1800s, one can still campaign for a job in Washington using one's ignorance of the inner workings of the system as a campaign platform. This is one of many ways that we fail to see post-industrial changes coming. It is not because we wear *industrial* blinders, but because we wear *Federalist* ones. Influence in politics has long been vested in control of 'the files,' as Weber called the medium of bureaucratic power. The candidate who runs as an

33 The predominant occupation was family farming. Add in production of clothing, food preparation from raw materials, care of the young, sick and elderly, as well as a hundred other tasks now part of the market economy, and the domestic sphere of the time dwarfs the business community as an economic producer.

34 This was a theme in the successful campaigns of the last two Democratic Presidents (Carter in 1980, and Clinton in 1992). It also gave H. Ross Perot nearly a quarter of the votes cast in 1992.

outsider is no Cincinnatus,[35] but one who demonstrably lacks knowledge of the dynamics of power. An unexamined Federalist ideology transforms this critical ignorance into a presumed virtue – the outsider will be a positive influence because s/he possesses 'common sense.'

A further division of the self occurred along gender lines. Federalist society had been highly sex-structured and male-centered, but both men and women presided over critical domains of work in which the public intertwined with the private. The center of work life was the family-centered farm or business. With the coming of industrial order, paid work left the household. In addition, more and more household work entered the marketplace (prepared foods, appliances, off-the-rack clothing, healthcare, education; the list is endless).

> The factory system . . . destroys the economic utility of women's work in the home. It cheats the women in the home of opportunity for self-expression in what they do. It deprives them of their husband's assistance in building real homes, because the men are forced to be away most of their days. And at the same time that it thus lessens the significance of all work in the home, it opens innumerable alternative careers for them. (Borsodi, 1929: 167)

Elsewhere, Borsodi defends women's ability to have paid careers; he is speaking against the development of a system in which work in the home is not valued as 'real' work. This issue has remained alive until the present time with advocates of women's rights divided between those for whom gender equality means breaking the 'glass ceiling' in formal organizations and those who seek to question the devaluation of work in the domestic sphere and the values associated with such work.[36] Like the normatively male employee in the factory, the housewife became more and more of a 'hand,' a machine tender. In addition to affecting housewives, this change reduced the status of domestic service. When homes of the wealthy became 'mere show-places,' the servants became 'pure parasites' (Borsodi, 1929: 140), maintained largely as evidence of 'conspicuous consumption' (Veblen, 1899/1983). More and more, the critical skill demanded as the sphere of domestic work atrophied was the ability to knowledgeably *shop*. What is today treated as an eccentricity, perhaps even a 'trait' of women, has its roots in the creation of *l'employé*. The shopper appeared as a subject in society at the same time men's work roles were taking them away from the domestic area and women's roles were normatively restricted to a less self-produced and more prepackaged domestic sphere.

This is yet another split; *l'employé* does not produce his/her needs, but

35 A Roman statesman who left his farm to lead the army against a barbarian invasion, then peacefully returned to farming. The image of George Washington as an American Cincinnatus has had enduring appeal and survives in the belief that politics is a process best engaged in by amateurs.

36 The former is emphasized, for instance, in Powell (1994); the latter in Mills and Tancred (1992) and Smircich and Calás (1990). McQuarrie (1992: 4) points out that 'women in management,' the nominal subject of organizational gender research, constitute a privileged special-interest group constituting 'less than 6% of all American working women.'

gets them as a *consumer*. Here, the division of labor and the construction of the employee as ignorant interact. *L'employé* does not produce for him/herself, nor does wage work involve interaction with the community through the sale of a product. It is a sphere completely divorced from consumption. Simultaneously, consumption moved from simply *satisfying* to actively *creating* needs for consumers whose 'ignorance about the nature and value of foods and textiles is duplicated in almost every class of product which they are called upon to buy' (Borsodi, 1929: 169). Borsodi cites a woman speaking before a dry-goods merchants' convention contrasting consumers of the 1890s and the 1920s. 'The women of the nineties . . . went to the stores with lists of things which they needed, and they bought them as promptly as possible.' In contrast, 'Today . . . the shopping lists are gone. Modern shoppers do not go out to buy what they need – they go out to "shop"' (Borsodi, 1929: 171). Before this time, 'shopping' was a verb only. Only as these changes sediment does being 'a shopper' become an identity.[37] Cushman describes this consumer as the 'empty self.' The empty self experiences itself as lacking meaning and worth. As a result of the 'chronic, undifferentiated emotional hunger' this self experiences, it 'seeks the experience of being continually filled up by consuming.' The primary sources Cushman identifies as filling the empty self – advertising and psychotherapy – are also central to the construction of this self. Thus, selfhood in this context chases an ever-receding horizon of satisfaction (Cushman, 1990: 600)

L'employé, then, does not simply succeed the Federalist citizen as the normative citizen of society. A profound remapping of the boundaries of social life has occurred. The business self is split from 'public' sector activities of laws and governance. The 'public' life of the working 'man' (male or female) is split off from 'private' domestic production and family support activities. *L'employé* the producer is split off from him/herself as consumer. This opposition is manifest in new social tensions between poles that were not distinctly separate in Federalist society: business *versus* the community (do not all business people also live in a community?), church *versus* state (was the state not founded to extend the work of God in the world?), jobs *versus* prices (the same individual who earns wages is the person paying the prices).

One should also consider the tension these changes produced regarding men *versus* women and work *versus* family. When the family was the main productive unit, work could be hard and family life could be cruel, but work

37 Another area for study would be to relate the historical development of advertising as an element of industrial discourse, with the development of the modern subject of organizing – and the consumer (*l'employé* at home). As the 50th anniversary edition of *Printers' Ink*, the trade journal of advertising, notes, these 50 years (1888–1938) span the history of 'machine distribution' analogous to the history of 'machine production' (1938: 4). In this issue, Erbes invokes the frontier metaphor, linking the closing of the physical frontier in 1890 to the opening of one 'not geographic but economic.' These essays present the development of advertising as a complex relationship in the mutual development of printing technologies, public values, and publishers' relationships to advertisers. If one wishes to understand the 'MTV generation,' one must start with the construction of both mass culture and the subject of mass culture.

and family were not antagonistic tradeoffs. Work *was* family and vice versa. The increasingly rigid boundary between home and workplace rigidified boundaries between a masculine domain of production and a feminine domain of consumption. For women in wage work, this has created a Faustian choice. To be valued in society has meant entering the world of men on its own terms, a sort of occupational cross-dressing.[38] By their very existence, these women and women choosing to value traditional domestic work – mothering and housekeeping – have been threats to each other's legitimacy within this system. This can be seen in heightened form in the turbulent history of the relationship between feminists and housewives, or that between nursing and feminism.[39]

Even in a hypothetical, 'androgynous' world where gender disparities between men and women in the workplace were completely remedied, this devaluation of the 'feminine' sphere of domestic labor and relational work would be untouched. In the masculinized workplace of the industrial society, women and men can be equalized *only by giving both the status of men*, that is, of wage earners. This is heard in the plaintive lament of dual-career couples: 'we need a wife!' These couples perhaps say more than they realize. Their statement concisely captures the homosocial cross-dressing which has produced two masculine role players who recognize a missing dimension of their life and express it in sex-role specific terms. They do not say they need specific services, nor even a servant – they need a 'wife.' Today, these divisions: public/private sector, work/family, business/community, church/state, jobs/prices, men/women, are understood through the lens of an industrial common sense. Many have argued against these partitionings on a humanistic basis. My argument reflects a different perspective: as the world continues to change, these partitionings of the self, which are based on an industrial reality, are becoming increasingly at odds with the lived experience of people who must fit into roles of a society other than the one in which they live. Recent conservative recognition of this tension has coalesced in a rhetoric of restoring 'family values' (a particularly virulent expression of which characterized the 1992 US Republican convention). Desire for a lost Federalist world of individual and community does not make it possible to return to one. No ruby slippers will take us back to Kansas. What will become of the industrially divided self in post-industrial societies remains an open, but crucial, question.

'Character' to 'service'

In these changes, one can trace the development of a new set of meanings for personal character. A good 'work ethic' continues to be valued, but the self-knowing, self-governing, self-interested producer of Federalist society is being replaced. A character of *self-control* is being replaced by a character

38 Showalter (1987).
39 Cf., Baer (1991); Vance et al. (1985).

of *service*. The new worker is not born free; s/he is not asked to make her/his way in an undefined world, but to take a place in a predefined order to which s/he is born indebted. How else could it become possible to talk about the 'organizational commitment' *of* the worker apart from organizational commitment *to* the worker? How else could 'work ethic' come to be talked about as an individual *trait* connected to doing neither the work of God nor the work of the community. For *l'employé*, 'wage slavery' has been transformed from a dishonorable state into the arena within which one seeks honor as a member of society. This applies not only to employees who produce goods and services, but the employees 'handling' them – management.

The very term 'office,' derived from the same root as 'officer,' has a two-thousand-year history of denoting service.[40] In Rome, the boundaries between civil, military and religious office were indistinct – one could serve all three at once. Through medieval Europe, office was likely to be church office. Even in the courts of secular kings, the functions of writing and accounting were largely done by clergy (did you ever wonder why it is today called 'clerical' work?). Civil administration was largely in the hands of a hierarchical warrior caste. One might trace the growth of civil office to the *noblesse de la robe* and the free cities of the late middle ages. The transformation from a military governed by 'knights' and one governed by 'officers' reflects a rational bureaucratic shift one might call an 'industrializing' of the military. As the 'officer' enters nineteenth-century US business, this tradition enters also. The manager may be a privileged employee, but s/he is equally an employee in organizational 'service.'

Employees 'Handling' Employees: *Il Maneggio*

While it is defensible to say that labor was transformed into employés, one cannot as neatly say that capital was transformed into management. In Europe, social relations had tended to support a division of operational and financial control in organizations. As power passed from land to industrial capital, the aristocracy was economically pushed to invest, but was socially tainted if it engaged in work. Caste differences tended to separate the holder of capital and the business person. In the US, the small scale of production and the high social value placed on being a 'self-made man' encouraged integration of the financial and operational roles. With the coming of large-scale organizations, a more European division began to arise. It appeared in the earliest railroads,[41] according to Ashton

---

40 *Oxford English Dictionary*.

41 This was the form of the Boston Company, which started large-scale textile production in the US (based on stolen British technical knowledge), creating the cities of Lowell and Lawrence in the process, but that is off the path of this story. The mills, important as they are to industrial history, were an industrial aberration emerging so early that they had to adapt to their still-strong Federalist context. This is radically different from the transformation, half a century later, *of* Federalist society *by* large organizations.

(1906),[42] with a 'principal officer, who was usually the representative of the financial interests,' and 'under him was a Manager or Superintendent' (1906: 142). Consider also the growing complexity of organizing larger and larger enterprises, the removal from the foreman of many now managerial functions and one has the major components of the complex social space into which the manager appears. This role represents a new cluster of social relationships. It cannot be thought of simply as the modification of the Federalist employer, foreman or worker. The manager is a special form of *l'employé*, one formally charged with representing the interests of owner- ship to other employés. His/her most immediate ancestor is the railway 'officer.' The first source of officers was literally the military and the term 'officer' was more common than 'manager' until well after the turn of the century.

A two-tiered system of employment

For the Federalist, only a citizen's militia was in accordance with American principles. A European-style standing army was anathema. But after the Civil War, the Grand Army of the Republic could claim to have saved the nation – history is written by the victors. Borrowing from the army for civilian purposes could be defended as consistent with prevailing social values. In so doing, however, a principle of European social stratification entered Federalist society. In the British army, for instance, the commoner entering the ranks could hope to advance only as far as sergeant-major. Officerships were reserved for and purchased by gentry. Adoption of this model was not accidental. Railway executives were explicit in their vision. In 1919, Haines praised the German model of railroad operation, where 'advancement to lower-grade positions is facilitated by the attention paid to primary education, and the higher grades are as readily filled by graduates from the technical schools.' Haines still values 'the discipline derived from a general military training,' but in looking to a two-tiered school system as the source of a two-tiered work force, he is reflecting the future of US management (Haines, 1919: 481).

A decade earlier, Dewsnup (1906) had praised new programs at the University of Chicago and McGill for training 'our railway lieutenants, captains, colonels and generals of tomorrow' (Dewsnup, 1906: vi). Fagan (1909) approvingly cites a high railway official candidly telling a Harvard audience that, because union loyalty was competing with company loyalty, '[w]e are being gradually compelled to abandon this policy [of internal promotion] and to look elsewhere, particularly to the colleges, for our material' (Fagan, 1909: 62). Note the term 'material,' which would have made no sense a generation before; it was now appropriate to refer to the worker as something capitalizable, a raw material. Frederick Taylor reflects

---

42 General Manager of the Chicago and Northwestern Railway.

the two major forces driving this turn toward the colleges for human 'resources.' Describing his early experience at Midvale Steel in 1878, Taylor says he differed from the other foremen in that he 'happened not to be of working parents.' Because of this, the owners 'believed that he had the interest of the works more at heart than the other workmen' (Taylor, 1911: 50–1). In another context, when emphasizing the scientificity of his studies, Taylor, quite unnecessarily, notes that measurement was being conducted by 'college men' (1911: 55–6). Taylor reflects both the increasing status of technical knowledge and the desire of employers to remedy 'the labor question' by developing an officer corps not sharing the sympathies of the production worker – as, apparently, did the traditional foreman.

Not just a hand

In today's folk wisdom about this time, it is axiomatic that industrialization reduced the worker from possessing a craft to being just a factory 'hand.' Were this the sum of the change, management might not yet exist. Coercive control of generic labor has been practiced successfully for at least several millennia. Physical punishment was not yet dead. Monetary fines for tardiness, carelessness and inappropriate behaviors were common from the earliest industrial environments[43] and are mentioned as a technique by Taylor (1911). Systematic compensation policies did not yet exist to protect workers from income reductions. Firing could be done more or less at will. If all one needed was to boss the factory 'hand,' one did not need a manager.

It is the *insufficiency* of these traditional forms of control that produces the manager. As the basic problems of organizing 'works management' systems became less central at about the turn of the century, a new way of speaking about control in the works began to appear. Unlike the foreman, the overseer, the gang 'boss', the officer in the new industrial 'army' had to become proficient in coaxing and persuading. While the secret to getting this army to perform was still somewhat mysterious, it was clear that the traditional system of physical punishment and coercion was out of place in the new order. One can infer from this shift that, even in the most deskilled production environments, it was recognized that the knowledge and discretion of the worker were critical factors in operating profitably. As the organization of scale proliferated, a new concept appeared, that of 'handling' men.[44] The work of the officer corps gradually changed significantly enough to earn a new name derived from the Italian verb *maneggiare* meaning 'to handle,' especially, to handle horses.[45] *Il maneggio*, the managerial employee, emerges.

---

43 One place these are discussed is Zuboff (1988). There is also, of course, an entire literature on this period in industrial history.
44 For example, Bloomfield (1916), A.W. Shaw Co. (1917).
45 Shaiken (1977: 115).

Professionalizing the Employé – and Vice Versa

So, capital/labor did not exactly become manager/employee. Owner-operator capital became more strictly financial capital,[46] while labor elaborated into *both* manager-employés and production-employés. Another face of *l'employé* emerges at this time – the 'professional.' While the focus of this book is on the professional employed in large organizations, this cannot be separated from the story of the changing role of professions in late-nineteenth century US society.

The 'industrial revolution' in the professions

Unlike the manager and employee, whose names are terms from the last century, the professional may seem to be a thread of continuity, an actor with roots stretching back to the middle ages. This terminological continuity, however, masks the industrialization of 'professional' work. While the three 'learned professions' (law, medicine, clergy) were present in feudal times, the terms 'professional' and 'professionalism' appear in secular usage only in the nineteenth century, with the traditional connotation of divine calling, vocation, already being displaced by the notion of specialized expertise.[47] Elliott (1989) distinguishes a shift with industrialization from traditional 'status professionals' whose authority was derived from social standing, to today's 'technical professionals,' whose authority is grounded in specific occupational knowledge.

There is a loose parallel between the 'industrial revolution' of the traditional professions and the transformation of the railroad officer into the industrial manager. Like the European military officer, the status professional was typically of the gentry. Due to the laws of primogeniture,[48] all sons save the firstborn were landless, yet maintenance of social status demanded that they should not engage in labor or industry. A military commission, a suitably ranked position in the clergy, law and medicine were the primary avenues available. The main requirement of an officer or professional was traditionally behavioral – one must act as a gentleman. The traditional legitimating appeal of the gentry was 'service' to God and the state. The manager and the industrial professional both inherited this aura of 'service' as a privileged position, one of status. But the manager claimed

46 The distinction between capital for production, merchant capital and finance capital is not widely used in the US. I believe this is one of the limits of managerialist theorizing. The systematically different logics of production, exchange and ownership become hopelessly confused if one equates the owner-operator, the trader, the banker and the speculator. The *reductio ad absurdum* of this confusion is the idea that capitalism is itself part of the passing industrial era. Drucker (1993) is only the most extreme example of this confusion. For an antidote, one might consult Braudel (1982).

47 *Oxford English Dictionary*.

48 That is, passing the family lands in their entirety to the firstborn son instead of dividing them.

technical knowledge, not breeding, as a basis of authority. Similarly, the claim to legitimacy of the nineteenth-century status professional rested on expertise, science and education. Professionalism had been industrialized.

'Profession' as a set of discursive relationships

'Profession' is not a universal institution. 'It was within the Anglo-Saxon tradition,' argues Sarfatti Larson, 'that modern ideas of professionalism formed.'[49] The idea of 'profession' encodes a relatively specific set of organizational relationships. One might think of professionalism as a *language*, a system of objects, concepts and normative practices within which occupations and individuals must work if they are to successfully claim professional authority. The main relationships structuring this language are:

- *With science*: Professional knowledge is both theoretical and externalized in rules. These rules are in the form of testable propositions because they are shaped by the central scientific procedure of building knowledge through hypothesis testing.
- *With the university*: The profession is associated with a university discipline, a 'professional school.' This school performs two critical functions: (1) It legitimates the scientific objectivity of the knowledge; and (2) It controls access to the profession through the awarding of degrees.
- *With the law*: Professional knowledge is proprietary. Not only does the profession have the use of this knowledge, but all other occupations are proscribed, through licensing, from using it. Professionals are also held legally liable for executing programs in a standardized manner.
- *With the community*: The profession monitors the relationships the individual professional will have with the community through ethical codes and peer review. Service norms (*pro bono* work) also legitimate the professional as working within the discourse of objectivity rather than for self-interest.
- *With the client*: Professional status is closely linked to performance of work seen as critically important by a constituency capable of supporting that status. For example, medicine has made itself virtually synonymous with health care in the public's eye. Management, to select a more precarious example, has seen its support and status eroding in the last half-dozen years.

'Professional' knowledge has a specific form conditioned by these relationships. It is theoretically explicit (that is, codified in text in the form of testable rules/hypotheses). It is occupationally standardized. It is internally produced and monitored, this occupational self-discipline being a source of

---

49 Sarfatti Larson (1984) contrasts the Liberal-individualist conception of the 'free profession' to the 'civil service' model of continental Europe. Also, see Carr-Saunders and Wilson (1933), Friedson (1983, 1984) and others. In Jacques (1992a), I discuss difficulties in understanding the meanings of 'profession' in greater detail.

work autonomy and occupational status. It is proprietary; the professional shares the *product* of professional knowledge, not the knowledge itself. One might visualize the professional as a gatekeeper who mediates between the locked vault of knowledge and the client. Occupations can form other relationships between work and knowledge, but not as professions. Specifying these relationships is important because certain work is complex and knowledge-intensive, but other than professional. This may include a great deal of what is currently described as knowledge work. If such workers are unreflectively assumed to be technical professionals, any emerging qualities of such work will be hidden behind the industrial assumptions embedded in the concept of the professional.

The 'culture of professionalism'

Bledstein (1976) further distinguishes professions in the US as playing a role specific to the formation of the industrial social order. Bear in mind that at the end of the nineteenth century the US had exhausted the institutions of the Federalist order. Capital and labor appeared to be running rampant over society. In the new, large organizations there was increased need for expertise, but the traditional source of skill was disintegrating, a casualty of the shift from occupational to organizational control of work. 'Apprentice training has collapsed,' announced Charles Steinmetz of General Electric, 'and at the same time the requirements [for knowledge] have been and become more strict, more general, more variegated' (Steinmetz, 1918: 3). In addition, much of the knowledge required (cost accounting, double-entry bookkeeping, statistical interpretation) was not possessed by traditional occupations. With old roles disappearing and new roles still unclear, the entire set of social relations through which knowledge would be developed, communicated, applied, accumulated and owned was up for grabs.

The theme Bledstein identifies as bridging Federalist and industrial institutional orders is the ideal of the middle class. The ideal of America as a land of people of 'middling means' was well established. It appears in De Tocqueville (1835/1956). A half-century earlier, Franklin boasts of a 'general happy mediocrity' (Goodman, 1945: 346). Reay (1985: 20) notes that many seventeenth-century Quakers were known as being of 'the middling sort of people' (as was the dominant element of the Puritans). Even today, many in the US hold to the belief that America is a classless society while identifying themselves as middle class. Professionalism fits into this ideology, offering an employment position in between the aristocracy of the robber barons and the proletariat of the 'wage-worker for life.' To the public, the long association of status professionals with the doctrine of a 'calling,' 'vocation,' or 'service'[50] also fit into a staple tenet of the American Dream, helping to legitimate professions as socially beneficial.

---

50 From Brandeis (1914), through the *Harvard Business Review* (Lowell, 1923) and Follett (1925/1942), to Beyer (1991), there has apparently been an ongoing need to attempt to legitimate business and business scholarship in this manner.

They attempted to define a total, coherent system of necessary knowledge within a precise territory [and] to control the intrinsic relationships of their subjects. . . . Yet, in the mind of the Mid-Victorian, professionalism meant more than all this. Professionalism was also a culture which embodied [in the ideal] a more radical idea of democracy than even the Jacksonian had dared to dream . . . a self-governing individual exercising his [*sic*] trained judgment in an open society. (Bledstein, 1976: 87–8)

At this time, according to Bledstein, one begins to find a proliferation of organizations recreating themselves in a professional mold – the mortician became the undertaker who became the funeral director. Through this web of professions, a 'culture of professionalism,' Bledstein argues that a deeply wounded society stitched itself back together. If the result did not represent everyone's idea of social equity it was at least a functioning system. Just as equality was resurrected as merely equality of *opportunity* when the ideal of material equality for all became obviously unattainable, self-employment was recast as self-discipline through occupational control structures. For the professional, occupation replaced community as the sanctioning body of individual work conduct for those of 'middling interest,' and provided a middle path between the terrors of unrestrained big business, big government and big labor.

Personal development now came to mean one or another form of service within an organizational context. For *l'employé*, service to the organization was the espoused norm. The alternative was professional service to an occupation. As society professionalized, occupation and organization became the competing sources of social authority. Within the culture of professionalism, Christian perfectionism took yet another form. The service ideal of the profession was not service to God, or to society *per se*, but to *scientific objectivity*. In a world of vested interests, the professional's claim to fame was *dis*interest. This would eventually result in the displacement of the discourse of character with a discourse of objectivity as the language within which work and knowledge of work were expressed.

The discourse of objectivity: science and the university

Professionalism managed to link service and expertise in a manner that avoided 'unamerican' connotations of service to an elite individual, class or political entity and presented at least a reasonable possibility that expertise would be applied according to criteria other than naked self-interest. Critical to this project are professionalism's relationships with the language of science and the certification of the university. Science served as a common language for the institutionalization of professional knowledge. Its cardinal value of disinterested objectivity offered a basis for claiming the 'right' or 'fair' way to proceed in a society fearful of the power of large, self-interested institutions. The imprimatur[51] of university education warranted to society

---

51 That is, the ultimate seal of approval.

that the professional was controlled by certain 'objective' standards while creating a single, controllable point of entry protecting the profession's members. An indication of the power of this new discourse and of the degree to which it differed from the prior discourse of professionalism is the fact that American medicine – the archetypal professional occupation – underwent radical 'professionalization' along scientific lines in the nineteenth century.[52] One might object that science and the university also offered instrumental knowledge. Perhaps, but we must not be too quick to assume that this was the sole reason for the university's entry into the business world. Given the many possible forms for organizing work and knowledge, why did these specific forms appear at this specific time in this particular culture? The following chapter will address this question in more detail.

Manager, employee, professional: a tripartite box

Imagine a box with three partial partitions. It is possible to move from one area to another and even to stand at the juncture of two or all three partitions. One cannot, however, leave the box. In order to become a working subject in the industrial order that emerged from Federalist reality, one has to take a place in such a box. The partitions partially segregate the areas of *l'employé*, *il maneggio* and the employed professional. There are other subjects in industrial reality – the wealthy capitalist, the craftsperson, the union member – but they are marginal to discussions of work. In organizational writing and research, a boundary condition for speaking is that one speaks *about* employees,[53] *to* managers *as* professional experts. To leave the tripartite box is to become invisible to knowledge about work. To speak as one authorized to know something about work, one must speak from a position within the box. It is not new that society have such a box, but its configuration is specific to a time and a culture. In twelfth-century England, for example, the box may have partitioned serfs, peasants, tradespeople, barons and clergy, or some similar configuration. The number of partitions, the privileges and obligations associated with each, the degree of overlap between one and another, would all have differed so thoroughly from the tripartite box of US industrial reality that no direct comparison is possible. The peasant, for example, was not a 'medieval employee;' to think this way imposes twentieth-century common sense on an era to which it does not apply.

Between the world of Freeman Hunt and the world of Frederick Taylor, a void had opened across which meanings could not be transported intact. Some ideals, such as the omnicompetence of the average person and the ideal of material equality for all, died so thoroughly that their replacements – equality of opportunity and getting 'ahead' – are now widely imagined to

52 Flexner (1915), Haller (1981), Starr (1982).

53 This becomes circular, since managers and employed professionals may also be the employees spoken about.

be founding American values. Others, such as the discourse of character, survived as empty containers which were filled with new content. The Federalist 'man of character' survived within the culture of professionalism, but character was now competitive. The *ethos* of employed professionalism could co-exist with a corporate-capitalist elite and *required* the generic labor of *l'employé*, both to do the work of production and to constitute a subject *about whom* to have professional expertise.

But, within the large organization, manager, employee and professional are *all* employees.[54] Where Federalist reality could be thought of as a game[55] played between producers and customers, and early industrial reality was a game of labor against owner-operator capital, industrial reality has become a game played by employees *against each other*. In this game, management and/or professional status are the two markers available for avoiding categorization as generic labor.[56] One may simultaneously reach for both markers. Professionals have typically striven to be *self*-managing, and management – one can look as far back as Brandeis (1914) – has sought recognition as a profession. Managers are, by definition, employees and perhaps three-quarters[57] of US professionals are employees of large organizations. There is also a huge range of occupations whose members think of themselves as professionals and in which the work relationship is usually that of organizational employee (nursing, social work, teaching and so forth). One can be a professional-managerial-employee, however, without leaving the tripartite box.

> there are trainers who beat their horses and trainers who give carrots to their horses. There may even be trainers who eat with their horses, but I have never seen a horse ride a trainer. (Shaiken, 1977: 118)

Industrial organizational knowledge: the discourse of l'employé

It is no exaggeration to say that the employee is *the* subject of knowledge about work in industrial society. Since it is this society which has produced management as a practice and management knowledge as a body of academic teaching and research, one might say that what is available as knowledge about managing workers is knowledge of *l'employé*. But is this

54 Roomkin (1989) is one of the few to explicitly name managers as employees, but the possibility of discussing the management of managers, which is a common topic, implicitly confirms this same status.

55 A 'game' need not be frivolous. Bell (1973: 487–8) distinguishes between pre-industrial, industrial and post-industrial societies by describing them respectively as 'this game against nature . . . the game against fabricated nature . . . a game between persons.' Foucault (1984a) described the relationship between subjects in society and the discourses that shape their practices as 'games of truth.' The practice of 'war games' indicates how deadly serious 'games' can become.

56 This point is made quite directly by Etzioni (1969).

57 This estimate is based on the US census category of 'technical/professional' workers. It is probably as good a figure as any, but problems of definition are so great that one should accept no statistics about 'professionals' at face value.

status changing? One regularly reads of the erosion of professional privilege, the formation by the traditional professions of large, corporate hierarchies – there is even talk of medicine entering into 'post-professional' relationships.[58] Similarly, management's privileged status may be eroding in an environment of 'downsizing,' 'migrant managers' and employers attempting to articulate a new social contract for labor, stressing employable skills rather than employer commitment to a stable career.[59] Regarding employees, there is interest and concern *both* in a post-industrial deskilling of work and in the emergence of a privileged 'knowledge worker,' although what knowledge work may be is not yet very clear.[60] In the context of work such as Mills' *White Collar* (1956), one can see the complex and shifting dynamics of skill, power and status in managerial and professional work. If one is to ask whether these dynamics are replacing *l'employé* with new organizational subjects, one must better understand the production of knowledge about *l'employé*. The following chapter places the development of this knowledge in its historical and cultural context. It is a history of today's 'common sense' about work.

58 Siler (1990: 23). Cf., Johnson (1987), O'Connor and Lanning (1990), Spence (1989). These represent but a few of the steady trickle of such articles into the scholarly and popular press.

59 Cf., Nussbaum (1991: 94), Sweeney and Nussbaum (1989). There is also an active dialogue about this topic among managers, who are not waiting for theoretical leadership (Kietchel, 1993; Fierman, 1994; O'Reilly, 1994). As the *Wall Street Journal* lectured its readers: 'If one concept has been drummed into the noggins of Americans more than any other in recent years, it is this: The social contract between employers and employees . . . is dead, dead, dead. OK, we've got it already. So what has replaced it?' (Lancaster, 1994: B1).

60 The managerialist sources cited just above are not the only ones sensing a change in the game rules. More critical perspectives dealing with the subject recently include Blackler, Reed and Whitaker (1993a, 1993b), *Socialist Review* (1991).

6

The Disciplinary World of *L'employé*

As the twentieth century began, the image of the pioneering citizen whose contact with society was a matter of free choice no longer represented the experience of most Americans. The vast majority were born within and dependent upon organizations. They expected to live their lives as wage-earners. This employment was their primary source of income and status.[1] The Federalist 'discourse of character' centered on the citizen as the ordinary subject in society was being replaced by an industrial 'discourse of objectivity' whose subject was *l'employé*. The new industrial reality was held together by a system of relationships alien to Federalist values. A society structured by the frontier, personal community relationships and local institutions was being replaced by one structured by big business, big government, big labor, a 'culture of professionalism' and science. Assumptions about the rights and responsibilities of individuals, the kinds of relationships appropriate to controlling personal and organizational practices, the purposes of organizations themselves and the nature of social good were being reconstructed. It is important to acknowledge how deeply these changes altered what was to be known about work and organizing, how it would be known and who would know it. An appreciation of the degree to which these changes restructured what is usually accepted as solid reality can help us better appreciate the difficulty today's theorists and organization members will have apprehending the emerging post-industrial order.

This chapter will contextualize *l'employé* and the discourse of objectivity in an international context by comparing the transformation of the Federalist into an industrial society with changes that occurred in industrializing Europe a century earlier.[2] In *The Order of Things*,[3] Foucault (1973b), in the tradition of Weber, attempted to represent emerging European modernity as a discontinuity in people's mode of consciousness, a rupture in common sense.[4] As Foucault describes the relationships whose emergence

1 This is not simply a matter of changing relationships with the market, it also reflects the increasing degree to which needs were met in the market at all. In other words, the aspects of life for which wages were needed have increased.

2 Another dissertation waiting to be written is a critical comparison of the US Federalist period of about 1790–1870 and the Western European classical period of about 1650–1790 with reference to their common origins, points of difference and respective influences on the discourse of modern(ist) management.

3 This periodizing is also reflected in Foucault (1972a, 1973a, 1975, 1979). It is de-emphasized, although not retracted in his later work.

4 For discussion of the relationship between Foucault and Weber, see Dreyfus and Rabinow (1983) and Clegg (1994).

ended the classical period of Western Europe, he describes a reality not unlike (and not unrelated to) the industrial relationships marking the end of Federalist reality. This chapter will frame the themes identified in Chapters 4 and 5 in Foucault's terms. This not only offers a perspective for better understanding these changes, but also helps one connect them to broader currents of world events and to other theorists. This chapter will use Foucault's term for industrial reality: *disciplinary society*.[5] It is within a disciplinary society that the discourse of objectivity speaks of the l'employé.

Federalist common sense: a 'Chinese encyclopedia'

One of the most frequently cited passages from Foucault is a commentary on a passage from Borges referring to 'a certain Chinese encyclopedia'[6] dividing animals into:

> (a) belonging to the Emperor, (b) embalmed, (c) tame, (d) sucking pigs, (e) sirens, (f) fabulous, (g) stray dogs, (h) included in the present classification, (i) frenzied, (j) innumerable, (k) drawn with a very fine camelhair brush, (l) *et cetera*, (m) having just broken the water pitcher, (n) that from a long way off look like flies. (Foucault, 1973b: xv)

Foucault notes that each item in this list may be understood individually. What makes the list incongruous is placing these groups in a series. This incongruity offers a useful insight into the industrial common sense from within which we find it odd. First, the list shows that *homogeneity* is expected. There is no common element linking these items; this makes the list look like a parody or a mistake. Second, elements are expected to be *mutually exclusive*; if these items represent the variety of animals, something in our perception wants an animal to be *either* embalmed *or* a sucking pig. Third, the categories are not *exhaustive*. From the periodic table of the elements, to phylogenetic classification of species to the Myers-Briggs, we have learned to expect a classification scheme to apply to every member of the scheme's domain. Fourth, the scheme does not link laterally and vertically to a hierarchy of other schemes; we cannot estimate its place in a *universal science*. It does not fit into a 'meta-paradigm.'[7]

Federalist reality was something of a 'Chinese encyclopedia.' Its community-based institutions neither supported nor required a universal grid of knowledge. The frontier provided a space outside of social reality; categories need not be exhaustive as long as they reached this frontier.

---

5 It would be simplistic to claim that Foucault equated the industrial era and disciplinary society. The industrial is a narrower concept favoring a single segment of the social order. In a Weberian spirit, I would say that the *ethos* of Foucault's disciplinary society is the ethos of industrialism.

6 It should be noted that this 'orientalizing' reference (cf., Said, 1979) says something about the beliefs of Argentina in Borges' time, France in Foucault's time or the place and time you, the reader, inhabit, but it should not be construed as saying anything about ancient China.

7 Such as that of Gioia and Pitre (1990). This is a recurring theme in mainstream organizational theorizing.

Radical adherence to an ideology of equality limited hierarchical categorization of knowledge about humans. Face-to-face relationships made the
specific case more important than the category to which it belonged. The
common sense which today tells us to laugh at the 'Chinese encyclopedia' is a
product of a common sense new since the days of Freeman Hunt, the
common sense of the 'second industrial revolution.'

From 'Chinese Encyclopedia' to 'Disciplinary' Reality

The 'second industrial revolution'

By about 1920, a business order built upon *l'employé* was no longer novel.
The basic questions of 'works management' had been addressed; the large
factory of scale was a functioning entity. Labor/management tensions were
intramural (if unequal) rivalries within the system; revolution was no longer
feared. The public had come to some degree of accommodation with the
'trusts;' partially regulated oligopolies[8] were the norm instead of unbridled
monopoly. Having dealt with the basic problems of rationalizing *material*
inputs, business attention turned to the rationalization of *human* inputs.[9]
Commentators at the time were well aware that a new period of business
discourse was beginning. Moore and Hartmann (1931: 4) spoke of the 'new
industrial revolution;' Jones (1916: 123) to 'the newly-opened epoch of the
administrator.' Lescohier (1930/1967) identified this as a 'third period of
industrial development,' following the application of steam power early in
the nineteenth century and the appearance of the large factory and
'industrial combinations late in the century. Drever (1929) divided Lescho-
hier's second phase into two parts. For Drever, the first phase of late
nineteenth-century industrialization had been the 'mechanical phase' which
assumed a society of 'standard economic individuals.' This, writes Drever,
was followed by an 'organic phase,' by which he means the Social Darwinist
view of society as analogous to an evolving species.

> At the present time the discussion has entered on a third phase . . . the
> *psychological* phase. . . . Neither [the mechanical or organic 'analogies'] is
> adequate, or carries us far enough. . . . Industrial relations depend essentially on
> the interests, impulses, sentiments, and passions of human beings. (Drever,
> 1929: 26; emphasis in the original).

What these observations have in common is recognition that in the years just
before 1920 industrialization was entering a new phase characterized by a
shift of focus from physical operations to the so-called 'human factor.'
    The emerging reality is well illustrated by a book first published in 1914 by
Katherine Blackford, MD, and a colleague, Arthur Newcomb. *The Job, The*

---

8 Markets dominated by a few nominally competing producers.
9 Hollway's (1991) analysis of this period augments the story told in this book, especially
since Hollway discusses both developments in the US and those in the UK.

Man, The Boss is based on 'fifteen years' experience' (1914: vii), which means that it spans the time between the coalescence of a US industrial reality and the emergence of 'disciplinary' management. Separated from Freeman Hunt by only a few decades, Blackford and Newcomb (B&N) chronicle a world as alien to Federalist reality as life on another planet. Yet separated from the present day by nearly a century, *The Job, The Man, The Boss* fits to an extraordinary degree with present-day common sense, utilizing assumptions, concepts and artifacts used today. Indeed, after excising certain passages based on now discredited scientific findings (but *not* in themselves unscientific) and updating for eighty years of personnel legislation, one could teach a present-day HRM course from this book. The surprisingly large portion of this book which is still current should be cause to wonder whether knowledge about managing the employee is *evolving*, as is generally claimed, or *revolving* around a center defined nearly a century ago. Perhaps this is a more apropos interpretation for the frequently announced management 'revolutions'!

The new common sense reflected in B&N incorporates four themes first developed by Foucault (1979) to describe the advent of industrial modernity in Europe: (1) Enclosure; (2) Classification, (3) Quantification; and (4) Rationalization.[10]

(1) Enclosure – from pioneering to conservation

As I argued in Chapter 3, the society of yeoman farmers is not a distinctly American ideal; the fifth-century Anglo-Saxon *ceorl* was culturally connected to the nineteenth-century Oklahoma sodbuster by the dream of escape from 'enclosure' by society. Although Federalist reality was based on imagining the US to be outside the international relationships of exploration, trade and exchange,[11] this was never the case. As the nineteenth century ended, the US was simply pulled back into a world on whose periphery it had developed, but from which it had never been separated.

Before the eighteenth century, society in Europe itself was composed of islands protected from the surrounding world. Society neither included all of the land nor all of the people on the land. Even the nominally great power of kings was often limited largely to taxation and military conscription; it did not necessarily intrude very deeply into day-to-day existence of the village, a group with personal and economic ties banded together against the dangers outside. At some point between the Renaissance and industrialization, this

10 Another example of the application of Foucaultian concepts to human resource practices is Townley (1993, 1994).

11 These were also, of course, relationships of conquest, but I do not wish to reinforce a historical view that has dwelt inordinately on kings, wars and geography. This book is concerned with conquest as a particular means of engaging in the struggle for control of production and exchange. If the age of conquest and colonization has stopped, it is not because humanity has reached a higher plane of morality, but because other means of gaining wealth and power are more effective in today's world.

'outside' disappears. Society becomes more of a closed system. In Britain, Tate (1967) places the main period of enclosure of common lands at 1450–1700. In France, Foucault (1973a, 1973b) notes a change between the sixteenth and seventeenth centuries.

Note the coincidence of enclosure and colonization; as the frontier was closing in Europe, it was crossing the Atlantic, both ideologically and physically. Seventeenth-century Massachusetts as a city on a hill was, to a large extent, a recapturing of the rural British 'commons' community, carried overseas at about the time the enclosure movement was bringing it to an end in Britain (one of the ironies of the American Dream is that the future toward which it is pointed often looks surprisingly like a reclamation and perfection of a past; in it, progress is not distinct from nostalgia).[12] In a sense, Turner's (1893/1956) thesis on the closing of the frontier marked the end of a chapter of *European* history as the US entered the international order from which it had so long symbolized escape. This is especially relevant to contemporary organizational thought because the US has never updated its ideology to reflect this re-entry. Today, in an emerging post-industrial order, American management is not grounded in an industrial ideology, but in an industrially-modified *Federalist* ideology. *Before it will be possible to understand the post-industrial, it will be necessary to see what aspects of the American Dream represent denial of the enclosed society.* Given the world role of the US, this is now a worldwide issue. Even 'Europe can no longer be understood by starting out from Europe itself' (Baudrillard 1989: 98).

The central feature of enclosed society is that there is no longer any 'outside.' Where sixteenth-century France could place the insane on a boat and ship them downriver into the wilderness, seventeenth-century France, having no wilderness, turned to houses of confinement.[13] Tar-and-feathering was a viable punishment when the offender could be expelled into the undefined space between towns. But, when the border of one town marked the entrance to the next, the option of expelling the individual from society ceased to exist. Society must, one way or another, make use of all its members, whatever their capabilities. In an enclosed society, those who lose the competition do not disappear. They become the 'unemployed,' the 'underclass,' the 'homeless.' If society is both competitive and enclosed, one cannot exhort individual morality as a solution for the problems of this class. Their existence is *guaranteed by the structure of the system and they cannot go away because there is no 'away.'* One person's rise assures another's fall. *Any*one may 'get ahead' through the development of 'character,' but *every*one cannot.

---

12 As I revise this chapter in January 1995, the new Republican Speaker of the House of Representatives is presenting the 'Wesleyan' (eighteenth-century Methodist) ideal of charity among private citizens as a viable alternative to government aid to the poor, and this strikes many Americans as nothing more than good common sense.

13 Foucault (1973b).

Enclosure supported and was supported by the increasing permanence of work relationships. As workers came to depend on monetary transactions for more of their needs and as fixed capital became a more prominent characteristic of employing organizations, transient work relations or self-employment began to give way to relatively permanent employment. At precisely this point, one begins to find the worker represented as 'belonging to' the organization.[14] Rather than being framed in terms of coercive power, however, this relationship quickly became couched in terms of finding an objective congruency,[15] 'fitting the man to his job and to his environment' (B&N, 1914: 198). Thus, enclosure stimulated the development of classification.

(2) Classification – ordering the human 'resource'

In the early modern British philosophy which engendered American ideals, there is a strong assumption of the approximate equality between one person and another. Hobbes (1651/1969) reflects the spirit of the times in his assertion that 'Nature hath made men so equal in the faculties of the body, and mind [that] . . . the difference between man and man is not so considerable.' Hobbes finds this to be even greater for 'faculties of the mind' than for physical strength.'[16] If people are inherently equal, the just society should provide approximate material equality for all. This was the Federalist ideal, which had, of course, been nurtured in British humanism. In the early history of industrial work, classification reflected this assumption of basic equality. It was, to use Foucault's (1979) term, 'binary.' One is within the included or excluded; punished or not punished. One's 'character' need not mark one as the best person in the community, simply as one *of* the community. This view also dovetailed neatly with the Calvinist dichotomization of people into the damned and the elect, a central thread running through Puritan/Quaker and then Federalist values. The prominence of fines as a management tool in early manufactories is an example of binary classification:

> One work rule at Haslingden Mill about 1830 read, 'Any person found from the usual place of work, except for necessary purposes, or talking with anyone out of their own alley will be fined. . . . Other fines addressed . . . singing, whistling, swearing and yelling . . . fixity of gaze . . . other fines concerned the body's smell and appearance. . . . Finally, there were fines to discourage aggressiveness, sexuality and disorderliness. (Zuboff, 1988: 33–4)

However elaborate this system might become, it only created two generic groups of workers. Unless the worker strayed into the domain of the

---

14 E.g., Martin (1877/1971: 299).

15 Again, this is not to impose twentieth-century meanings, but to show that congruency, much as it is represented in congruency/contingency theory, was understood in a sophisticated way a half-century before its 'discovery' and to question linear histories of the development of management thought.

16 *Leviathan*. Part 1, Chapters 11 and 13; cited in Jones (1969, Vol. III: 140).

forbidden, his/her behavior was untouched by management systems. Reward and punishment was based upon presence/absence, not degrees of difference. As the organization of scale became more complex, it was 'discovered' that Hobbes had been wrong; humans not only differed from each other, but they differed in a way that mirrored the needs of the hierarchized industrial organization. 'Individuals are differently endowed with those faculties of mind and body . . . which enable them to contribute to the work of the world' (Scott and Clothier, 1923: iv; note that 'faculties of the mind' is a direct echo of Hobbes above, but with the diametrically opposite interpretation of people's equivalence). As an order based on 'natural' differences replaced the former order based on 'natural' equality, worker differences could be 'fit' to different positions in the organization. If this led to status and compensation differences, it was only a reflection of the natural order of things. It was not based on self-interest, but on science, not on the untutored common sense of the businessman, but on 'a great deal of organized, classified, and verified knowledge' (B&N, 1914: 197–8).

The new disciplinary classification was no 'Chinese encyclopedia;' it was universal, exhaustive, mutually exclusive and hierarchical. Through it, the individual worker could be treated as both standardized and individualized. Standardization retained the concept that 'all men [*sic*] are created equal,' and applied it to an industrial context where they were not simply legal/ethical equivalents, but, in effect, standardized parts. At the same time, one's particular position in this standardized hierarchy was unique. This retained the rhetoric of individualism so central to the Anglo-Saxon/American heritage[17] while helping to reduce the terrifying aggregate 'labor' into individually innocuous 'employés.' In Europe, Foucault traces the emergence of classification to military barracks, the hospital, the asylum, the school and, of course, the factory[18] from the eighteenth century; it only appears in the US near the beginning of the twentieth century. While there is something to the platitude that the large organization was modeled on the military, *both* the large organization *and* the military were re-created during this period in conformance with more fundamental social changes.[19]

Comprehensive classification was also facilitated by Scientific Management's standardization of work tasks. Taylor's reliance on the principle of selection to match the right worker to the right job reflects this consciousness. In Scientific Management, one can see the flowing together of Quaker

17 Another area for further investigation is the role of individualism in Western development. Based on his study of old records, Macfarlane (1978) concludes that as far back as the thirteenth century – well before industrialization became a strong social force – England was inhabited by people who placed a distinct emphasis on the individual. If capitalism often reinforces individualism, it may well be that individualism was at least partially responsible for producing capitalism as it is known today in the West.

18 This is most accessible in Part Three, sections 1 and 2 of Foucault (1979), but it is a central theme appearing in all his major studies prior the *History of Sexuality* (1980).

19 'Is it surprising that prisons resemble factories, schools, barracks, hospitals, which all resemble prisons?' (Foucault, 1979: 228).

perfectionism,[20] Federalist common sense and industrial rationality, but this movement is still part of the pre-history of *l'employé*, a transitional position between Federalist and industrial constructions of human nature. For Scientific Management, the worker remained largely a dependent variable. The problems of motivation, commitment and quality of effort could be answered by engineering the work flow and the piece-rate system. Taylor and his contemporaries never required access to the interior of the worker's life.[21] Classification of worker 'types,' 'traits' and 'aptitudes' was a product of the 'new industrial revolution' of the 1910s. The new language of this revolution was that of quantification.

(3) Quantification – 'a world ruled by number'

In describing computerization of the paper manufacturing process in a mill in the 1980s, Zuboff (1988) identifies two conflicting realities between which workers are caught. The computerized system replaces an older, sentient reality of touching, looking and doing with a new abstract reality of data. Workers no longer go into the plant to control it; they look at a computer screen and type at a keyboard. As the workers struggle to find meaning in the numbers produced by the computer, they are replaying a shift from Federalist to industrial reality. The disciplinary shift regarding quantification was that numbers replaced sensory experience as the *primary reality* of work. For the Federalist, numbers were tallied simply to mark one's profit/loss position. For the industrialist, numbers – budgets, output statistics, trends, variances and expert data – *were* the organization. In 1880 Marston Whiting spoke to his foremen to learn the status of the organization. In 1984 Harold Geneen spoke to his financial analysts.

It is easy today to forget what a radical event the quantification of business discourse was in the nineteenth century. Even in economics, long known as the dismal *science*, 'it was not until the last third of the nineteenth century that mathematics took hold within it, and much later, somewhere in the 1930s or 1940s, that economic theorists began to study the calculus as a matter of course' (Schabas, 1990: 3). Schabas notes that this is odd, since the knowledge and techniques for creating 'a world ruled by number' had been available at least since the eighteenth century. The popular management account of this lag might relate to the assumption that 'pre-industrial societies were largely biased against the concept of managing organizations effectively and efficiently' (Bowditch and Buono, 1994: 7), but this fails to account for the attention to capitalizing time and space characteristic of the Protestant business tradition. More explanatory is the observation that

20 Taylor, like so many figures in the history of management, came from a Quaker background.

21 Taylor was more sensitive to process than he is generally credited with being. Such interpersonal skills as were required by Taylor's interventions did not require more knowledge of the worker's interior life than Freeman Hunt would need in order to deal with his Federalist colleagues.

mathematization emerges at the same time as the 'general office,' which creates the possibility of *general management*.

Today's business student will be taught to begin formulating business policy by asking, 'what is our business?' S/he will learn that managerial stewardship means maximizing the value of 'the organization' by maximizing 'shareholder value' (market value of stock). The entities they manage to accomplish this work are 'cash flows'.[22] The centrality of these concepts reflects the dominance of what Chandler called the 'general office,' a level at which the primary activity is to 'allocate resources for a number of quasi-autonomous, fairly self-contained divisions' (1962: 9). The general office exists primarily as an asset manager, as able to buy a titanium foundry as a frozen yogurt chain, depending on which business offers the highest return on investment and speculative growth potential. This general office was *not* produced by the coming of the organization of scale. Entire organizations of scale are mere *divisions* within the general office organization. Scale technologies facilitated the centralization of industries producing the early general office organizations, but the critical factor in their emergence was the financial combination, then consolidation, of the trust movement of roughly 1890–1910.

The rise of the trust represented the decline of owner-entrepreneurs whose source of wealth was the sale of goods and services. Replacing them were 'public investors with a speculative trend of mind' (Dewing, 1920: 23). The so-called 'robber barons' of this era may appear to contradict this change, but they are transitional figures. John D. Rockefeller came to dominate the kerosene market when he *stopped* selling kerosene and started buying kerosene *companies*. Significantly, Rockefeller was, by training, an accountant, not an 'oil man.' Andrew Carnegie was both an 'oil man' and later a 'steel man,' but his legendary wealth was made from an office in New York where he bought and sold steel companies. It was more important in this enterprise to be close to investors than to 'the works.' 'Financiering,' was no longer the path to perdition in business; it had become 'the organization' itself. In a half-century, the US had passed through its 'Mercantile Revolution' (more commonly called the American Revolution), into an Industrial Revolution and on to a Financial Revolution. Only with this last revolution, generally ignored by business historians, did the possibility of general management appear. With the appearance of general management does a 'world ruled by number' begin to form. Mathematization was a new language that fit with this new source of authority.

Morris's comment in 1910 that 'statistics are the clinical thermometer of industry' (1920: 221) would have made no sense to Freeman Hunt fifty years

---

22 E.g., Thompson and Strickland (1987: 5); Collins and Devanna (1990: 172). This may sound simplistic, but it was reflected in a recent Email bulletin board exchange about stakeholder theory in which several Organizational Behavior professors argued that management is self-evidently bound to privilege the interests of stockholders because they are the only legally recognized stakeholder and that is that.

before, but it was repeated almost verbatim by Harold Geneen seventy-four years later.[23] Quantification of the employee was an adaptation of a process that had begun a generation earlier to quantify physical resources of the organization. Statistical reality was the ultimate uniform and universal framework, within which large businesses and small, bakeries and coal mines, became perfectly comparable. Numbers could travel readily and reliably in an era when hands-on control was giving way to management at a distance. Not suprisingly, this method of control appeared first with railroads.

> By a gradual process of concentration, the workings of the road are reported with detail constantly reduced, to officers increasing in rank until the president is reached, while certain statistical detail may keep right on until it reaches the executive committee of the board of directors. (Morris, 1920: 230)

Morris notes the competitive advantage of such a mode of perception as a *productivity* tool in a time of increased business size, competition and shrinking margins. Statistical reality was a radical break with the past. It replaced the governance of tradition with that of science. Jones (1916), presenting one of the first explications of 'the scientific method'[24] in a text on administration, explicitly contrasts 'the efficiency of science and the inefficiency of tradition. . . . Industry is the greatest exponent of action in modern life: science is the chief exponent of modern thought: much is to be hoped from the union of the two' (Jones, 1916: 4). Only as this new reality sediments does it become possible to be a 'bottom line' manager; one can 'get to the bottom line' only through a financial statement.

There is a second site from which mathematization developed. From within the works the increasing complexity and mechanical operation of work produced an ever-widening web of experts whose mode of expression was scientific 'data.' Looking backward, Carnegie (1920: 174) found it 'incredible' that in 1870 chemistry was 'almost an unknown agent' in iron production. It did not take long, however, before the large-scale production of steel using the Bessemer process led to scientific analysis of ore qualities and quantitative data replaced the puddling-foreman's experience as a guideline for proceeding. Taylor argues that while the question of what feed and what cutting speed to use in setting a lathe may 'sound so simple that they would appear to call for merely the trained judgment of any good

---

23 'Numbers serve as a sort of thermometer' (Geneen, 1984: 190).

24 This is not simply an addition to such texts; it is part and parcel of a more general transformation. Nineteenth-century books on the operation of businesses were typically written by business people for an audience in a particular industry or sector. At some point, authors become trained experts rather than business people; administration of people becomes a specialized topic (it was nearly absent in the older books); the primary audience is a student – or an organizational 'scientist' – not a 'young merchant;' and the domain of discussion is general management, not managing in a specific industry (cf., Jenks, 1960). As part of these changes, it eventually became the norm to explain 'the scientific method' because the author was an expert appealing to science, rather than business experience, for authority. In this genre, Jones (1916) is probably not the first example, but he is among the earliest.

mechanic,' the 'fact' is that 'the answer in every case involves the solution of an intricate mathematical problem' (1911: 106–7). Because such complex mathematics is beyond the skill of most machinists, movement from 'trial and error' to mathematization is not simply a new language for describing the same practices; like any language, it plays a role in *shaping* the practices. Quantification in this case implied a shift of knowledge (and thus authority) from the worker to the expert. It resulted in exteriorization of knowledge; it no longer resided in the worker, but in tables and slide rules which could be controlled differently. The complexity of adjustment implied that repetitious work was desirable and strengthened the argument to specialize lathe operation using a set-up expert trained in the mathematics and less-skilled operators who were merely machine-tenders.

Coming from these two directions, finance and science, quantification was changing the language and the practices of work. Enclosed, classified and quantified, work in the US was beginning to look recognizably like it does today. As these practices of mathematization encountered the idea of progress – endless growth – it left the world of absolute magnitudes for the abstract stratosphere of *ratios*.

(4) Ratio-nalization – progress mathematized

According to Marx, what is distinctive about capitalism as a mode of production and distribution is that it exists, not to turn goods into more goods, but to turn money into more money. This is captured succinctly in his famous expression *M-C-M'*.[25] Marxian economics is often represented as the intellectual antithesis of management thought, but on this point one finds an almost identical statement behind the basic managerialist tenet that 'ROI [Return on Investment] is the most frequently used criterion for divisional performance measurement' (Dominiak and Louderback, 1985).[26] This idea was still radical as a managerial strategy as late as the time of the 'second industrial revolution.' In 1919 Alfred Sloan had to argue to the Executive Committee of General Motors that 'it is not, therefore, a matter of the amount of profit but of the relation of that profit to the real worth of invested capital.' In his memoir, Sloan describes this idea as 'an accepted part of management doctrine today,' but 'not so well known then' (Sloan, 1964: 49).

At the heart of ratio-nality is the concept of *ratio*, the proportional equivalence of two things. Three ways this ratio-nality represented a specific consciousness in business were investment, conservation and – once again – the legacy of Protestant perfectionism.

Investment Both codes – *M-C-M'* and *ROI* – signify a radical shift in the

---

25 Marx (1867/1967: 150).

26 This source was chosen arbitrarily; any mainstream text on the subject would be likely to express the point similarly.

meaning of 'the organization.' The Federalist owner-operated business existed primarily to produce wealth for the owner through fulfillment of customer needs. Some Federalists did become wealthy and customer 'needs' did grow as the means for fulfilling them elaborated, but the measure of business success remained *wealth*. With the coming of a disciplinary common sense, the criterion of measurement increasingly became the *rate of increase* of wealth. This is analogous to a shift from measuring the speed of a car to measuring its acceleration. Within ratio-nal perception, *no absolute size is ever adequately large*. This is illustrated by two articles about IBM. In January 1988, CEO John Akers told the *New York Times* 'We haven't liked hanging around $50 billion all that much.' This article was downbeat despite the fact that a business generating a billion dollars a week in revenues is employing thousands of people, presumably satisfying millions of consumers and contributing a great deal to the economy. All that was important in this article was IBM's *increase* in size. In June 1991, *Business Week* refers to Akers' 'six disappointing years' as CEO – and to company sales of $69 billion in 1990. In two years the company had grown enough – $19 billion – that *the difference alone* was larger than the annual sales of three of *Business Week*'s ten most valuable companies in the US – but the *rate* of growth was 'disappointing.'[27] This is rational reasoning – *ratio-nal*. To be rational is not synonymous with being sensible. Ratio-nality is a specific form of sense-making and, like any sense-making, can be done well or poorly. One can be sensible without being ratio-nal and vice versa.[28] One can be reliant upon a valid means of sense-making without being specifically rational or irrational.

Ask yourself what interests are served by thinking about business in proportional terms. The owner-operator is primarily concerned with absolute levels of profit; the employee (managerial employees included) with absolute levels of labor and compensation; the consumer with the absolute price and quality of the output; the suppliers with absolute prices for goods sold to the organization; and the community with the organization's absolute effect on the quality of community life. One party stands apart from this interest in absolute measures – the 'investor.' Only when one sees the business as competing with every other business through the purchase and sale of stocks, bonds and banking instruments does proportional return become the most important form of information. That general management has come to be shaped by the language of ratios is significant. The purchase and sale of goods and services is only loosely related to the purchase and sale of capital. Even a defender of finance capitalism must recognize this distinction if s/he is to be capable of separating the logic of producing goods and services from the logic of

27 Byrne et al. (1991). *Business Week* (1990: 28). Sanger (1988).

28 Kafka is peerless in his ability to illustrate how one can be ratio-nal but not what would generally be considered sensible. 'The Burrow' and 'In the Penal Colony' are especially vivid examples. Gilligan (1982) offers an excellent contrast between two forms of sense-making which show what is ordinarily represented as 'rational' to be only one form of valid sense-making.

financial management. The ratio is not simply a 'fact;' its very existence expresses values about what counts and what does not in the world of production and exchange.

Conservation   As this ratio-nal attitude of business was emerging around the turn of the century, it was supported by a growing interest in *conservation*, which, in turn, appears to have been inspired by the closing of the frontier. A prominent advocate of Scientific Management, Harlow Person, noted that 'the paradox of pioneering is that, for the industrial pioneer waste is economical' (1926: 194). Because there is an excess of resources, inefficient methods – such as slash-and-burn agriculture or strip mining – are often the most profitable. Person credits the disappearance of this frontier of excess resources with the coalescence of 'the management movement,' as he called it. There was an affinity between the general spirit of the times and the emergence of management. Taylor's introduction to *The Principles of Scientific Management* does not begin with the needs of industry; it recaps the then President Roosevelt's campaign to conserve the country's natural resources (this was the period when the most famous national parks were founded). Less appreciated, notes Taylor, but equally important for 'national efficiency' is 'our larger wastes of human effort' (1911: 5). The transition from command[29] to management, from the 'officer' to *il maneggio*, was accompanied by a new image of responsibility. The business pioneer might have been seen as meeting nature 'red in tooth and claw,' but the emerging industrial conservationist cultivated the image of the good steward. Quick's (1913) image of humanity as the crew *On Board the Good Ship Earth* may have a post-Sputnik flavor to present-day readers, but it is an excellent reflection of perception at the turn of the last, as well as the next, century.[30]

Perfectionism   The image of the steward resurrects yet again a model of social responsibility hugely indebted to the Puritan/Quaker worldview of seventeenth-century Britain. The disciplinary reality of this steward operating as a 'machinery for adding up and capitalizing time' (Foucault, 1979: 157) was easily adaptable to an ideal of conservation. Succeeding the industrial warrior would be the industrial custodian. For contrast in this

---

29 This is yet another area for study. Today, one is likely to hear post-industrial organizing spoken of as representing a shift from the command-and-control organizational form, but there are also important ways in which the formation of the hierarchical industrial bureaucracy, which was largely complete by about 1920 (cf., Dupont and General Motors chronicled by Chandler, 1962), represented a transition from command-and-control decades ago.

30 Placed in this perspective, one might look anew at present thinking about the 'greening' of management and business policy (a.k.a. the relationship between business and the natural environment) in a different light. Many qualities of the discussions *c.* 1995 mirror others *c.* 1915. To what extent is new ground being broken and to what extent is a timely problem being coopted into a discourse that saps its transformative potential and poses as a 'solution' business conservation themes of 1920?

respect, one might consider Andrew Carnegie and Alfred Sloan. Carnegie is described by admirers and detractors alike as fiercely competitive and accustomed to being obeyed. He described himself as an admirer of Spencer's Social Darwinist theories, within which those who rise to the top through ruthless competition strengthen society by those very actions. Sloan, roughly two generations younger, was one of the key architects of the tremendous success General Motors enjoyed for the half-century beginning about 1920. Sloan was no less an empire builder than Carnegie. He was certainly acting from self-interest, earning several hundred million dollars for his efforts. But Sloan was the quintessential man in the grey flannel suit, a consensus builder, an architect of committees.[31] The Carnegie mills advocated *laissez-faire* competition and sought to control the market. General Motors operated within interlocking domains of 'countervailing power'[32] and sought a constant *proportion* of a publicly scrutinized and partially regulated market. The General Motors' strategy was also shared by US Steel, the consolidation which swallowed the Carnegie mills in 1900.[33] Like Sloan, Elbert Gary, who was chosen to head US Steel, was not idealized as a pseudo-warrior, but as one who 'is never intolerant. He seeks the opinions of associates, listens to everybody . . . and he gives up when there is a majority against him' (Tarbell, 1925: 349). The image of stewardship reflected the interests of industrialists of this period, who were beginning to worry more about 'wasteful competition' than about the dangers of public or government interference;[34] they accepted 'that cooperation is bound to take the place of competition' (Tarbell, 1925: 232).

What one finds at this time is that ratio-nalization does not appear from any one place in the emerging order, nor is it the property of one interest group. At the highest level of finance, it represents a shift from the era of owner-operator robber barons to a new generation of financially trained and investment-oriented decision makers. In the plant, interpersonal relations are changing to reflect, in the prescient words of Taylor, the ideal that '[i]n the past the man has been first; in the future the system must be first' (1911: 7). With the closing of the frontier, government and the public at large are learning a new term: 'conservation.' Through all of this floats the Federalist incarnation of the Puritan/Quaker man of character, reborn as the custodial steward of the work group, the industrial order and the planet. From this emerging consciousness comes a new measure of value, reflecting the perfectionist concern with order and efficiency, expressed as a ratio representing maximization of output with minimal input. For the first time, a business person can speak of *productivity.*

31 Cf., Carnegie (1920), Chandler (1962), Sloan (1964).
32 Cf., Galbraith (1967).
33 This is detailed in Tarbell (1925).
34 This phrase is from Hoyt (1966: 177), but it is reflected in Chernow (1990) and Tarbell (1925). That this produced an industrial order focused on issues other than profit maximization can be found in a stream of thought from Berle and Means (1932) to Galbraith (1967), Thompson (1967) and others.

Enclosed, classified, quantified and ratio-nalized

It makes little sense to ask what was the prime mover of these changes. Each is simultaneously produced by and producing the others. But determining the cause is not a necessary condition for learning from this analysis. At some point, we can see the accumulation of changes in degree leading to a change in kind. We can see that the centrality of productivity as a measure of business success is not a timeless yardstick. It makes sense only within a certain web of relationships. Although one can produce productivity *data* in any culture, this data takes on *meaning* only to one properly conditioned to understand experience through a disciplinary consciousness. Such data was not merely unknown to prior business cultures; it was *irrelevant*. The very idea of being productive relies on conditions of enclosure, classification, quantification and ratio-nality. Given that the idea of productivity rests on such industrially specific relationships, one should be wary of assessing post-industrial forms of managing in terms of whether they are productive. This point will arise again in Chapter 8.

Not a hegemonic conspiracy

The social control of work practices changed radically between Federalist and industrial discourses. To ignore this is to ignore the conditions from which the institutions of management emerged. But this is not to say that industrial reality was produced by a hegemonic conspiracy.[35] Even the 'captains of industry' were often surprised at what their efforts created. Thomas Edison, who perhaps contributed more than any one individual to 'modern' entertainments (movies, phonographs, electric lights) condemned the resultant society for seeking too many things 'for the stimulation of the nerves' (Wachhorst, 1981: 140). John D. Rockefeller, the founder of Exxon and eighteen other Standard Oil companies, wrapped his Bar Harbor summer home with carriage trails because he never did overcome his dislike of the motor car.[36] Few could claim as large or purposeful a role in creating the oligopolistic, highly regulated business environment as J.P. Morgan, yet, once created, this new environment had no place for men such as Morgan.[37] While we do not weep for these powerful and privileged men, we

35 This does not *per se* invalidate critical perspectives utilizing Marxist/socialist assumptions of hegemonic class dominance. Reconciling these critical perspectives with the discursive view represented by this book is not without conflict, but it may be possible (cf., Alvesson and Wilmott, 1992a, 1992b). Very roughly, one might think of *both* critical and managerialist perspectives as *industrial* versions of tension between the more and less privileged members of society. Pre-industrial tensions were enacted between other groups and grounded in other ideologies. It may also be that *post*-industrial tensions will take a form that is *both* post-Marxist *and* post-managerialist.

36 This is the story the National Park Service tells of the Rockefeller carriage trails, which are now part of Acadia National Park.

37 Cf., Chernow (1990) regarding the generation of Morgans following Pierpont.

should also not go to the extreme of assuming they understood what their self-interested behavior was creating.

One of the most profound statements made about social groups (albeit in a clinical context) is Bion's observation that, 'people come together as a group for purposes of preserving the group' (1959: 63). In the self-interested clashing of capitalists, managers, the middle-class, welfare workers, educators, social scientists and others, allegiances and tradeoffs were complex. Corporations supported welfare workers who condemned capitalism. Unions accepted the organization of scale and employers accepted unions; nobody was enthusiastic about these compromises. Workers at every step of entry into the disciplinary society faced double-edged tradeoffs. For accepting Taylorism (in the form advocated by Taylor) they might increase their salary.[38] In exchange for permitting regimentation of work hours, they might receive health and sanitation reforms (not to die from cholera transmitted at work may be a negative benefit, but it is a big one). In exchange for becoming 'human capital' within a personnel system geared to permanent, full-time employment, they might experience the novelty of regular raises and occasional promotion. As Kanter (1977) noted, the least empowered in an organization often support the very rules they might be expected to resist because, lacking other forms of power, they can use rules to limit what others can do to them.[39]

An excellent illustration of these conflicted relationships is Struck's description of the 1906 founding of the National Society for the Promotion of Industrial Education. While such industrialists as the Presidents of Norton Co. & General Electric were among the charter members, the initial meeting also contained an address by Jane Addams of Hull House, a highly regarded social reformer. Addams[40] praised the goals of the organization because those who leave school early are 'much harder to control and more difficult to teach.' Such students leave 'without adequate preparation,

---

38 Taylor (1911) explicitly recommends that bonuses in his system be structured to yield a 60–100 per cent increase in worker compensation. Whether this was 'generous' is highly dependent on one's baseline assumption. For workers of the 1880s, it was less important than retaining control of the work process, but for workers of the early 1900s, who had lost this control and were less and less optimistic of regaining it, a 60 per cent increase in wages was not inconsiderable.

39 This observation could be usefully extended theoretically using De Certeau's (1984) framework of 'strategic' versus 'tactical' discourses; e.g., Jacques (1992a: Chapter 9).

40 The settlement house movement, of which Addams is the best-known participant (Addams, 1910/1981), is an excellent early example of what was to elaborate into Bledstein's culture of professionalism. If the settlement house movement was considered 'anarchistic' by the powers that be, it was liberal and middle-class from the perspective of the poor. Rudolph (1962: 366) appropriately describes it as 'a characteristic collegiate expression of Progressivism.' Like current liberal reform efforts, the settlement house movement helped to prepare the poor for participation in society; it did not otherwise attempt to change the social structure. As a college-driven, middle-class movement, it participated in the same flow of energy that had transformed Christian perfectionism into Federalist 'character' and which was transforming character into professionalism.

either for the responsibilities of citizenship or vocational life' (Struck, 1930: 168–73).

For Hunt (1857) or Terry (1869), Addams' words would be incomprehensible as those of a 'citizen.' What, they might ask, is 'vocational' about wage work? How is that a 'calling?'[41] Since when must one attend school to learn citizenship? To understand how Addams, activist author and keeper of a settlement house the police considered 'a nest of anarchists' (Smith, 1984: 412), could become a spokesperson for industry requires setting aside traditional managerialist or radical perspectives. What had happened in the time between Hunt and Addams was a shift in the *terms* of debate. For Addams to speak at all, she had to speak with reference to certain social relationships represented by the tripartite box of *l'employé*. A new reality had emerged. This new world of disciplinary power relations was not simply a system of oppression, but neither was it benign. For better or worse, it became the primary form of social control shaping industrial society. It is not a form of privilege *per se* because nobody controls it or stands outside of it. It is, rather, the framework *within which* issues of control, reward and influence are contested.

Normalization, Observation, Examination: a Dynamics of Disciplinary Organizing

Within an order of work structured by these 'disciplinary' relationships, new possibilities emerged for structuring work. In their general form, the possibilities that were enacted bear a strong family resemblance to what Foucault (1979: 104) called 'the gentle way in punishment' emerging in eighteenth-century European barracks, asylums, schools and factories. Foucault describes these relationships in the following three terms: 'hierarchical observation, normalizing judgement [*sic*] and their combination in . . . the examination' (Foucault, 1979: 170). These three form a useful framework for looking at the emerging relationships for managing *l'employé*. Once again, one must fight the ingrained habits of thought which tell us these relationships are – well – 'normal.' They are characteristics of qualitatively different ways of understanding work, the worker and the world.

---

41 Originally, in Christian usage, a vocation was the receipt of a calling from God to devote one's life to His work. The Puritan/Quaker vocation was secularized without relinquishing the religious connotation; one pursued the work of God by doing good work in the world. The Federalist was a product of this tradition, but did not apotheosize work. Significantly, the old connotation of vocation, calling up several centuries' association with service to God, was resurrected as a term for knowledge related to blue-collar wage work (e.g., 'vocational' training) – and not by the workers themselves.

The 'normal' worker: from Paul Bunyan to Taylor's Schmidt

Paul Bunyan, the folk hero, could do the work of several men. He was an ideal because he was larger than life. Frederick Taylor's 'Schmidt' is also legendary in the history of work. He was ideal because he was more or less like everyone else. Foucault (1979) identifies a similar transformation in the European ideal of the soldier. In the early seventeenth century, he was recognizable by signs of his courage, pride and bearing. By the end of the following century, he is 'a formless clay' (Foucault, 1979: 135) to be constructed as a part in a mechanical system. It is a sign of correct training that he does *not* stand out as different. There are traces of Paul Bunyan in Carnegie's ideal of the early industrial puddling foreman who was both 'able to knock down a man now and then as a lesson' while possessing 'some almost supernatural power of divination' for diagnosing the state of the furnace (Carnegie, 1920: 174). There are traces of Taylor's Schmidt in everything written about 'the employee.'

Douglas McGregor (1960) identifies the mid-nineteenth century as the place of emergence of a new form of authority not rooted in authoritarian punishment. Punishment had suited the binary classification of manufactories preceding the industrial factory. Rules punished offenders, but non-offenders formed a homogeneous group. Regular job evaluation, pay scales, routes of advancement from one job to another and other marks of differentiation between workers were radical developments appearing much later. These developments were both an example and a product of the new 'normalizing' way of seeing the worker.

A symbol for this type of power is the 'normal' curve of statistics, representing a measure of central tendency (mean, median, mode) and 'deviation.' The characteristics of this familiar tool embody the ways the employee differed from his/her Federalist antecedents. First, the ideal is not the strong*est*, the *most* skilled or even the *most* compliant worker, but the 'normally' qualified worker able to hold a standardized job. Second, all degrees of difference from the norm are measurable and subject to 'correction.' Where binary classification had only punished violations, normalizing relationships reached into all aspects of behavior. Within the non-offending group, internal differences of rank and grade can be developed to mark each worker's relationship to a norm toward which they are 'developed.' Third, punishment is no longer used as a deterrent (for example, fines), but as a form of *training*. Offense no longer operates as a means of dichotomizing the offending and the non-offending. Offense becomes a matter of degree and 'discipline,' in the form of corrective exercise, and replaces punishment. Workers up to this date had possessed or not possessed *skills*. Now, they possessed *aptitudes*. Aptitudes could be developed into skills, but only with knowledge built into systems controlled by the employer. Personal development gradually, but steadily leaves a domain of self-control shaped by a discourse of character and enters a domain of organizational control shaped by a discourse of science; it becomes *personnel* development. The goal of personal development is no longer the perfect, but the normal. This emerged as the new mode of understanding in at least three interconnected ways. Normalization became the new mode of interpersonal control; the normal came to be synonymous with the real and the normal subject replaced the 'great man' as an ideal.

Normalizing interpersonal relationships

Through the interaction of normalizing relationships and disciplinary classification, a work environment can be conceived which is 'individualized' in a standardized manner. Every worker has a unique place within a system of grades, steps, training and reward schedules, but every position is a routine combination of elements *within one universal system*. As control increasingly shifted from the foreman to 'personnel' experts within an office bureaucracy, normalizing classification came to replace the person of the master as the source of authority. As the nation experienced a loss of an 'outside' with the closing of the frontier, a parallel change occurred in human relationships. A steadily decreasing portion of one's individual experience as a subject in society was outside of the relationships which shaped and influenced that experience. Not only was the exemplary being replaced by the normative as an ideal, the aspects of experience being 'normalized' were increasing. Authority was not limited to worker behaviors; it had discovered 'constructive and destructive mental states.' Since employers are purchasing 'mental and psychical forces rather than muscle power,' the goal of employment management is not simply to make the person perform work, but to 'conserve' (see above reference to enclosure, p. 99) 'the highest and best constructive thoughts and feelings of those employed.' As Weber recognized, this form of authority pervades the experience of the worker very deeply: '[t]he individual bureaucrat cannot squirm out of the apparatus in which he is harnessed . . . [he] is chained to his activity by his entire material and ideal existence' (Gerth and Mills, 1946: 228).

The normal as the ideal

Histories of leadership research note a shift away from 'great man' theories early in this century without relating this observation to historical context.[42] There is little to support the idea that such theorizing, or any theorizing for that matter,[43] was the victim of failure to produce empirical evidence. In fact, it survives in good health on the popular management book shelf.[44] The

42 Cf., Yukl (1989) or any introductory text covering leadership research.
43 Kuhn (1962/1970) and Webster and Starbuck (1988) note that theories are seldom, if ever, rejected because they are empirically unsupported and offer several reasons.
44 For instance, in the constant stream of hagiographic biographies. It is less significant that these are written than that they are purchased in quantity.

demise of 'great man' theorizing does, however, coincide with a general cultural shift from idealization of the exemplary to idealization of the norm. Mintzberg (1971), which is widely cited as having 'discovered' that managers do not do what Fayol (1916) claimed, does not emphasize the historical context which may account for the discrepancy between Fayolian and Mintzbergian 'norms' of management. Unlike the Federalist owner-operator, Mintzberg's CEOs are represented as existing *within* the disciplinary apparatus of their organizations. Authority is not a personal perquisite, even at this privileged level. One must instead 'exploit situations that appear as obligations' (Mintzberg, 1971: B102). Somewhere in between Freeman Hunt and Henry Mintzberg, as a transitional character in the history of work in the US, it is entirely likely that a generation of administrators found their reality best described by Fayol.[45]

The greater the stature of Carnegie's 'Paul Bunyan' foreman, the higher the output of the work crew. But as work became increasingly mechanized, divided and interdependent, heroes became liabilities. In management, as in production, what was needed for smooth operation at high levels was a worker possessing 'standard requirements in aptitudes, training, experience, and consequent efficiency for that job' (B&N, 1914: 16–17). 'In the future,' Taylor accurately predicted, 'it will be appreciated . . . that no great man can (with the old system of personal management) hope to compete with a number of ordinary men who have been properly organized so as to efficiently cooperate' (Taylor, 1911: 6–7).

The normal as the real

Implicit in most usage of the term 'normal' regarding subjectivity in Anglo-US society, is the presumption that normality and non-normality are qualities which change only at the slow pace of evolution. Historical perspective shows the normal to have a more volatile history.[46] Elton Mayo, famous for his connection with the Hawthorne experiments, was indirectly noting that this normalization of the worker was still a work in progress when he reminded readers of the new journal *Personnel Research* 'that sanity is an achievement rather than a merely natural condition of mind' (Mayo, 1922: 419). One characteristic of normalizing relationships is that they are not primarily constituted between the worker and the owner, foreman or even manager. Normalization is maintained through the apparently neutral

---

45 Little is made of the fact that Fayol was not just describing another time, but another place. France was the first industrialized country in the world. By the turn of the twentieth century it had been eclipsed by Britain and Germany and would soon be passed by the US, but its experience with the large work organization, the *administration*, the *bureau*, was based on a long and culturally distinct industrial history. To read Fayol apart from this context is to distort him into the shape of another, inappropriate context.

46 An excellent starting point for thinking about the normal as a social construction is the section of Berger and Luckmann (1967) in which they describe the processes of reification, sedimentation and institutionalization.

objectivity of externalized rules and practices which have authority, not because they are supported by the power of this or that individual, but because they have been empirically derived by experts and certified by 'the scientific method.' They are not presented as forms of power or as values and preferences, but as forms of truth. Normalizing practices produce the ubiquitous, disembodied 'they,' as in 'they won't let us do it any other way.'

The normal as Other: 'Schmidt plus or minus 1.96 standard deviations'

Whether normalizing relationships restricted or extended employee freedom is impossible to say. It is more important that it was a new *mode* of authority relationships *within which* employee freedom and managerial control were contested. The employee's authority relationships exist, not as a contest of strength with an embodied authority figure, but as a contest of knowledge with a web of experts and with 'the files.' S/he was no longer an embodied collection of skills, but an aptitude, a 'bundle of possibilities.'[47] S/he was no longer one of the subjects within the discourse about work, but an object of experts who spoke for her/him. Maximization as a goal of personal attainment was replaced by achievement of the norm. Behavior that was above was as subject to correction as behavior below. To be normal, one must be 'Schmidt plus or minus 1.96 standard deviations.'

As the present decade searches for 'excellence,' it might help to consider how excellence constitutes deviant behavior within today's systems of evaluation, promotion and reward. Neither will it be sufficient to become 'anti-normalization.' Do you want systems in place to assure pay equity with your fellow workers? Do you want regular performance reviews in which you are evaluated on the same criteria as co-workers? Do you favor affirmative hiring legislation or want rules in place to limit patronage and nepotism? Do you vote with your consumer dollar to create or maintain highly normalizing jobs such as those in the burgeoning fast-food industries? Normalizing relationships are embedded in aspects of life we would defend as much as in those we would prefer to change.

Observation: decoding the worker

'Other things being equal,' write Blackford and Newcomb 'we select for employment supervisors those who have the keenest and most accurate powers of observation' (B&N, 1914:220). Why 'observation' one might wonder? In 1880, the closest thing Marston Whiting had to an 'employment supervisor' was the foreman. In selecting a foreman, work-related skills might be criteria; the ability to influence others, especially through physical

---

47 Facing the title page of Blackford and Newcomb (1914) is a photograph of about 20 men captioned 'Applicants at the door of an Employment Department. Every man a bundle of possibilities.'

intimidation, might have been important, but observing was not part of that picture. The importance of observation reflects the degree to which the worker had changed from being a *subject with* whom one shared knowledge to an *object about* whom one had knowledge. This is a critical characteristic of expert discourse; it is carried on about, not with, a person. In fact, the subject's very disagreement with expert judgment will have an expert interpretation. For example, a physician pronounces a patient to be an alcoholic. The patient refutes this diagnosis. This supports the diagnosis because denial is a symptom of alcoholism. Whether the subject is a non-alcoholic or an alcoholic-in-denial is entirely subject to expert judgment.

Without exception, early twentieth-century commentaries cited in this book, when dealing with the rise of the large organization, mention the loss of the direct owner/worker relationship as a source of the problems of industrial society. After the Terror of the period of capital/labor struggle for control of the workplace, the discourse of the employee had reproduced a person-to-person relationship within the large organization. But the manager/employee relationship was not comparable to that of the owner/worker. The employee was not primarily an individual, but a 'case' (the Weberian 'file'). This case was 'read' by an 'expert' specially trained to read a language inaccessible to the lay person. Observation of the external signs indicating the employee's hidden meanings becomes the critical skill of the personnel expert.

Textualizing the worker: the Weberian 'case'

The term 'observation' is a bit misleading because it conjures up the already anachronistic image of the overseer. More characteristic of disciplinary relationships – and far more pervasive – was the *textualizing* observation which began at this time.[48] Both the work itself and the worker were increasingly represented in standardized and systematically analyzed tables, files, and manuals. Thus, certain aspects of the employee's experience were encoded into a text perpetually visible to those authorized to read it. Gradually, the employee-as-file became the primary reality to which organizational relationships connect. The employee-as-body was a matter of decreasing importance.

For instance, suppose one's distinctive competency is something valuable, but 'soft,' such as the ability to connect between different people in an organization to solve problems and get projects completed. After a century

48 This is why Foucault's (1979) description of panopticism and the 'gaze,' which has been so strongly emphasized in organizational writing influenced by Foucault, appeals little to me. The panopticon suggests the image of a literal gaze, one more applicable to a spy network. What has been developing for some time is an *auto*-panoptic society in which all are observed by all, but there is no central observation point and all are both observers and observed. '[L]et us not look for the headquarters that presides over its rationality' (Foucault, 1980: 95). It is important to remember that the panopticon describes emerging industrial modernity, not the present day.

of personnel research, this cannot be represented directly to potential employers. What can be represented is college degrees, intelligence and personality test scores, a record of positions held, the industries within which one has worked, the amount of time one has used specific technologies and so forth. The critical skill – connecting and problem solving – can only be represented indirectly through standardized responses to standard categories which can be accumulated into a textualized representation of the employee. What does not fit into the text is not 'real.'

One finds a similar silencing occurring through practices of textualizing gender, race, and so forth, where salient elements of experience are not represented or representable in 'the file.'[49] For instance, Pelavin (1995) has concluded from her interviews with working mothers that the experience of 'managing' domestic issues[50] and balancing competing work/family demands provides a great deal of 'management training' relevant to performing in an organizational role. Yet, the organization does not reward, nurture or formally recognize the value of such experience. The bias that one does not look to the domestic sphere as the source of work-related skills is part of the problem. Additionally, the absence of objective measures – domestic performance review – prevents domestic work from being codified as part of the 'real' performance of the worker. Here is a classically ambivalent disciplinary situation; to increase recognition of domestic work by making it more present in the textual record is simultaneously to make domestic activity more vulnerable to greater disciplinary control. One cannot choose to step outside of these relationships, however. Radical, liberal or conservative strategies for dealing with this situation must start from an understanding of the disciplinary logic of these relationships in order to be effective. The question is not whether to textualize the worker, but how to influence the process.

The decoding expert: the employment manager

The expert produced to decode the encrypted meaning of the employee was the 'employment manager.' The 'employment managers' movement' was not initially connected to the academy. As employers increasingly created offices to deal with the personnel issues that had formerly rested with the foremen, the employment managers in these offices eventually became numerous enough to form trade associations and begin sharing information about what would now be called 'best practices.' Employment managers claimed some turf formerly the foreman's, some from other managers and some from employers.

---

49 Cf., Mills and Tancred (1992).

50 One of the ways it has been made clear to her that these mothers are the domestic 'managers' is their gratitude when their husbands 'help' around the house. Pelavin interprets this to mean that the husbands are not acting as full partners.

The first duty of the employment department . . . is to relieve foremen, heads of departments, and other line officers of the responsibility and trouble of interviewing applicants, selecting employees, making transfers and adjustments, discharging employees, and all similar duties and obligations. (B&N, 1914: 32)

B&N refer to their system as 'character analysis by the observational method' (B&N, 1914: vii). Note both the survival and the transformation of Federalist character. The name survives, but character is no longer the inviolate property of each citizen. In industrial society one subject's character is analyzed and 'developed' by another. This raises a critical question. If the environments constructed by society can determine, to a significant degree, who the individual becomes, 'who is to construct the controlling environment and to what end?' (Skinner, 1971: 17). Skinner may seem an odd source to cite in this regard, but he is one of the few prominent theorists of recent years to attempt to make this question central to debates in behavioral science. Skinner argued that the 'literatures of freedom and dignity' and the myth of the 'autonomous man' served to buffer discourse from the conflict between a rhetoric of participation, empowerment and development, and practices which systematically attempt to effect the control of the behavior of one group by another. Skinner did not, of course, condemn the shaping of behavior; he condemned shaping behavior within a rhetoric of egalitarianism that prevents frank discussion of practices and their consequences. His point is, if anything, reinforced by the perdition *Beyond Freedom and Dignity* has encountered in the behavioral sciences. Far more popular, at least in the US, is a 'win-win'[51] rhetoric which posits the organization as an institution in which every participant can find self-fulfillment and which acknowledges no potential conflict regarding who will have authority over others.

Examination: certifying 'development' in the human 'resource'

Within disciplinary relations, correction is not intended to function as punishment, but as education. A half-century before McGregor's 'discovery' of what has come to be called Theory Y,[52] theorists were asserting that 'an intelligent, efficient employee strives to excel' and 'possesses a natural, healthy love of work'[53] (B&N, 1914: 56–7). What was needed to unleash this potential was for supervisors to learn to 'discipline' through training rather than punishment; 'every factory, every store, every office is

51 'Habit' number four of Covey's (1990b) best-selling *The 7 Habits of Highly Effective People*.

52 The current popular version of Theories X and Y is such a travesty of *The Human Side of Enterprise* – an essay urging organization studies to rethink its basic assumptions – that I prefer not to blame McGregor for what has come to be called Theory Y.

53 Taylor (1911: 13) was heading in this direction as well when he noted that the average worker would give his all at sporting events on Sunday, yet 'soldier' through work producing as little as possible on Monday. The implication is that employers simply need to remove industrial barriers to this natural desire to excel.

in the best and truest sense of the word a school' (B&N, 1914: 23). The conventional wisdom of the earlier period of industrialization had been to leave a worker in one job at one rate of pay until that worker complained, quit or was fired.[54] With the production of universalizing classifications and normalizing practices came the realization that, '[a] periodic appraisal held every six months enables management to know the lines along which each employee is developing or failing to develop' (Scott and Clothier, 1923: 116–17). This ritual of examination might be periodic, but the constant visibility of one's 'case' communicates to the worker 'that his record is under inspection constantly and that he is being graded fairly for both failures and successes' (Murphy, 1917a: 19). Consequently, it 'impels the employee to exercise conscious effort in improving himself in those specific qualities deemed important by the management' (Scott and Clothier, 1923: 117). This form of development permitted the worker to excel while remaining normal. One could advance progressively through a series of increasingly complex jobs, each with its own norm of performance. In addition, the periodic examination made the process of continual (textualizing) observation a spur to employee performance.

Normalizing compensation and 'quality of work life'

To review, the appearance of an *enclosed* society, as opposed to one surrounded by frontier, had been associated with a new way of viewing relationships between people in society. This way of seeing was distinguished by increasingly universal schemes of *classification*; *quantified* information was increasingly preferred over other forms of knowledge and a distinct form of *rationality* which was both a continuation and a radical transformation of the discourse of character. This new way of seeing was associated with new relationships of social control governed by idealization of the norm-al rather than the exemplary. *Normalizing* discipline was corrective rather than punishing; it required an expert to *observe* and decode the meanings of the working subject; 'getting ahead' was measured through a process of regular, but periodic *examination*.

The development of these relationships leaves a distinct trail in the form of new types of compensation appearing at this time. One central theme in the emergence of these new relationships was stabilization of the work force, which had only become a goal since the 'second industrial revolution.' Between 1912 and 1913, Ford reduced 'five-day men' (those who quit after receiving one paycheck) from 3,594 to 322.[55] Ford was a pioneer in this effort, which indicates that the idea of stabilization was still new. Stabilizing relationships developed, at Ford and elsewhere, through the creation of many disciplinary ties between the worker and the organization.

54 E.g., Porter (1917b), Murphy (1917a).
55 Porter (1917b: 171).

Welfare work   The interests of social reformers and employers intersected in a number of early 'quality of work life' programs then called 'welfare work.' These might include inexpensive meals, music at meal times, dances, fashion shows and group discounts on mass purchases of consumer items.[56] While these programs did not specifically entail commitment of the worker to longer terms of employment, they reflect the emergence of a new goal: ensuring worker *loyalty*. A generation earlier, employers were less likely to seek cooperation than to demand compliance. This idea of loyalty as an objective suggests that having a mere 'hand' in the works was already being seen as inadequate. In some ways, the worker's judgment and/or knowledge were already recognized as valuable.

Employee health   At the turn of the century, a workplace free of diphtheria, cholera or the like was no small benefit.[57] Workplace health went a step beyond the lunchtime concert in creating a disciplinary relationship with the worker. In order to obtain assurance that one's co-workers were disease free, one had to submit one's personal health, hygiene and habits to a company expert who applied the disciplinary rules of nursing, public health and medicine. To receive freedom from contagious disease, the worker had to surrender a degree of organizational access to his/her body and personal life.

Profit sharing   Deferred rewards rely less on worker sentiment by creating economic ties contingent upon long-term compliance with organizational practices. Fisher (1917: 158) acknowledged that 'most profit-sharing plans, in fact, look more to stabilizing the force than to increasing profits through the incentive of larger volumes of production.' What is being introduced as progressive in 1917 is in some sense a partial return to the co-entrepreneurial, job-lot based system of compensation pushed out of the workplace by the organization of scale. Maximizing production is no longer the only, or necessarily the primary criterion of the good worker. More important is the worker who can be 'developed' in a normalizing fashion over a long period of time to be committed to goals established by others calling themselves 'the organization.'

Savings, pensions, loans   Other disciplinary relationships extended even beyond the fiscal year. As workers became increasingly dependent upon wage income, business fluctuations became more damaging. The formation of company credit unions[58] offered some insurance against these cycles at the price of commitment to a multi-year employment relationship. Where this was combined with loans, especially mortgages, the relationship was even tighter; 'where men buy homes,' wrote Thomas approvingly, 'there is

56 Ommer (1917), Niven (1967).
57 Cf., Thomas (1917)
58 E.g., Stanley (1917).

opportunity for holding down ill-considered resignations' (1917: 100). The ultimate long-term reward was the pension. Some early plans could actually make a discretionary determination of the pension amount at retirement.[59] The worker was not rewarded incrementally for incremental contributions. The price of old-age security was a lifetime of compliance.

Families, community status, morality Capitalists of the Gilded Age had aided the 'improvement' of the masses through the funding of parks, libraries and other public amenities. As such, they were transitional figures. They retained the Federalist value of *self*-improvement, (for example, making libraries available), but they accepted a very un-Federalist *noblesse oblige*. Some citizens now provided the means of improvement while others did the improving. Disciplinary management of the early 1900s carried this a step further and took charge of both the means and the process itself. Ford investigators examined employees' personal conduct, installment purchases and housing arrangements, intervening when these were deemed to be out of hand. Compliance with these investigations was tied to the famous five-dollar day.

These developments show both the continuing atrophy of the family as a multidimensional social unit and the 'work transfer'[60] through which organizations could increasingly demand that the family unit conform itself to providing what amounted to free services as providers of workers properly clothed, fed and socialized. At Ford, c. 1920, women were not eligible for profit sharing because they were not viewed as heads of families;[61] at one point marriage was even a requirement of eligibility for men. When it suited the organization, such transfers could follow another pattern; skills of the homemaker could be brought into the world of paid labor. For instance, Table 1.2 in Chapter 1 of this book represents the 1914 'discovery' that women's socialization made them well-suited for jobs as employment managers. Whichever way this transfer went, what remained constant was that the relationship was increasingly likely to be determined by the needs of large employers rather than those of workers or families.

'Home Incorporated'[62] The family's increasingly specialized role as a unit of consumption only was, itself, a strong influence in stabilizing work relationships. For the Federalist factory worker like 'Nailer Tom' Hazard (see Chapter 5), employment merely supplemented a more or less traditional peasant existence sustained by a wide variety of productive

---

59 E.g., Disston (1917).
60 This term is taken from the more detailed analysis on this subject done by Glazer (1993).
61 This benefit could have been made available based on whether one was a head-of-family. Instead, men were presumed to be supporting a household, whether they were or not, and women were assumed to be secondary wage earners regardless of their actual family status. One was not rewarded for heading a household, but for being male. If an exception was made, it was to exclude single men, not to include female heads of households.
62 This term was coined by Burns (1975).

activities centered on home-based work.[63] For the employee of 1920, the domestic sphere was being deskilled through the introduction of 'labor saving devices' a shift from passive marketing to the active creation of consumer needs.[64] The production of ready-to-wear clothing was replacing domestic sewing. Prepared foods lessened the skill required for cooking and restaurants eliminated that need entirely. Birth, illness and death went increasingly to the physician, hospital or mortician. Work and social skill needs were increasingly claimed by schools, colleges and universities. Recreation became more and more a matter of paying to be a tourist, a spectator, a user of recreational facilities[65] or purchaser of sporting goods. Production for the market, of course, had largely left the home in earlier stages of industrialization. All in all, then, the worker's needs were increasingly of a form that could only be met through earning money and a regular employment relationship was the best assurance of a regular supply of money. As regular grade/step wage systems with periodic review began to be instituted, the strategy of going from job to job seeking the highest wage became less viable than seeking tenure in one job.

L'employé, *the disciplinary subject*

For the first time in this period, wage work became a primary identity around which family and community practices were arranged. Note that this is not simply a shift in the meanings of work; *it is a change in the place of work itself within social life*. No longer is one primarily known by one's community identity. The employment relationship assumes more and more responsibility from both the 'public' domain of community and from the 'private' domain of family life. At least two fundamental shifts in belief about human nature changed radically at this time. First, it became accepted that it is the normal state of society for some to have the power to develop others. Society did not simply sanction development of character with inclusion in and exclusion from community; some people were authorized to shape the character of others. Second, the industrial subject was 'discovered' to have a need for *achievement*. Federalist society had been a closer reflection of the pre-industrial Europe described by Weber in which 'a man does not by

63 Cf., Braudel (1982) on the traditional economic resources of peasants and the slow conversion of this group into an industrial proletariat – 'The peasant survived, managed to pull through, and this was true everywhere. But it was usually thanks to plying a hundred extra trades' (1982: 255). The Federalist citizen lacked a lord extracting rents, and this was no doubt a source of relative prosperity, but it did not qualitatively change the worker's mode of relating to the large employer.

64 The half-century (1888–1938) anniversary issue of *Printers' Ink*, the US advertising trade journal, boasts that 'marketers' have ceased to simply advertise products. They have 'provided new uses for leisure . . . increased the standards of cleanliness and sanitation . . . wrought a new understanding of and desire for healthful living . . . kept alive the desire for personal betterment . . . played a leading role in the upbuilding of the highest standard of living in the world' (*Printers' Ink*, 1938: 6). Note that these activities do not satisfy needs; they *create* them.

65 This is also about the time the National Park system was created.

"nature" want to earn more and more money, but simply to live as he is accustomed to live and to earn as much as is necessary for that purpose' (Weber, 1904/1958: 60).

It is ironic that when *employers* were concerned with maximizing daily output, the employee was 'known' to have a short-term orientation,[66] but that when the self-interest of employers shifted, the employee was 'discovered' to have different motivations, consistent with the new goals. If human 'nature' was so thoroughly transformed within two generations, this argues strongly for the social constitution of the worker's 'nature.' As issues such as 'pay for performance' arise at the turn of the twenty-first century, today's student of 'post-industrial' pay schemes would do well to study how, for a century, there has been a dynamic relationship between social context and what is supposedly 'inherent' in worker motivation. There has also been a pronounced tendency to blame the worker rather than to look at what can be done to change the context (see Bardwick, 1991 and Zaleznik, 1989: Chapter 2).

As complex as the relationships tabulated thus far had become, they constitute only the early history of the disciplinary subject. Most of these programs began during the period of Systematic or Scientific Management, when the meaning of 'the employee' was not considered so complex as to require specialized knowledge. Blackford and Newcomb reflect a turning point reached with the emergence of the 'employment managers' movement.' This movement could not have occurred had the new disciplinary common sense not become the dominant reality of society. One of the main effects of this shift in common sense was an 'industrial revolution' of education. Through this transformation, education became (and remains) a powerful force for socializing an industrial way of seeing into the values, beliefs and expectations of every industrial subject.

The 'Industrial Revolution' of Education

Business organized predominantly in the form of market capitalism dates back several centuries. Education organized according to something recognizable today as a university dates back to the thirteenth century.[67] A relationship between the two, however, is much more recent. In the US, it barely predates the beginning of the present century. This is extremely important to realize as one contemplates the future of management education, research and consulting in the twenty-first century; if business

66 Taylor's (1911) discussion of the proper time frame for incentives reflects the spirit of the times when he states as fact that piece rates are superior to profit sharing because of the short-term orientation of the worker.

67 Campbell et al. (1987: 151) date the university of Paris from 1215; Salamanca from 1218; Padua from 1222; Oxford from 1249; and Cambridge from 1284. I take this as one of the first signs of the growth of a secular-capitalist society as the power of knowledge leaves the monastery and enters the secular institution.

has not always needed academia, it may not always need it in the future. For managers, this means asking what academia can offer to 'post-industrial' organizations. For students, it means assessing the value-added of a degree program. For business academics, the issue is whether we have a future. All of these questions are better understood if one appreciates the degree to which today's educational practices have been transformed by the industrialization of society.

Between about 1880 and 1920, the knowledge demands of organizations, the supplies of knowledge and the social context of organizing had changed in several profound ways. There was great demand for an ever-increasing array of technical specialities which were not traditionally supplied by anyone, since they were needed only in the organization of scale. The industrial chemist, for instance, has no antecedent in the Federalist order of work. The industrial order, which had produced the need, had also to produce the worker. As for supply, the apprentice system virtually disappeared when crafts lost control of their work.[68] Throughout the late 1800s, immigration of skilled labor from Europe eased the shortage of domestic knowledge production, but a 75 per cent decline in immigration of skilled 'mechanics' from Europe between 1905 and 1925 reduced this source to a trickle when demands were rapidly increasing.[69] For the labor force as a whole, this resulted in an environment of labor scarcity. Baer (1917) cites spending $125 [roughly $1400 in 1990 dollars] on newspaper advertising and drawing only six applicants for a firm installing sixty new machines. The organization of scale appeared during a time of abundant immigrant labor, but that had been a generation before. The 'second industrial revolution' was founded on the recognition that 'the greatest problem before us today is not so much the further improvement of machinery, but the development of an increased efficiency in men' (Murphy 1917a: 23).[70]

In the early twentieth century there was an explosion of new institutions for learning. 'Americanization' became a formal subject of study for the foreign-born; the US was no longer an open frontier to be settled as one wished, but a complex society with relatively explicit rules for becoming a 'real' American.[71] Employers established vestibule schools to teach new employees a combination of work-related and cultural skills (for example,

68 Explicit recognition of this event by employers is common in this period; cf., Steinmetz, (1918), Scott and Clothier (1923).

69 Struck (1930: 68).

70 Citing the Chairman of the United States Envelope Company.

71 For instance, in the early 1920s Harper and Brothers produced an eleven-volume series of books on 'Americanization Studies' funded, significantly, by the Carnegie Corporation. While couched in a language of respect for the immigrant, this series reflects the spirit of the times in the assumption that (a) the culture brought from Europe is inadequate and (b) the way of adapting to the new country is through formal education. The cartoon facing the title page of Davis (1921) succinctly captures the new attitude. Captioned 'What way of teaching immigrants habits of health is more effective in America?', it shows three pictures subtitled 'By force,' 'By letting them blindly grope' and 'By education.' Punishment and personal freedom, both characteristic of the Federal order, were being replaced by corrective training.

English language, 'Americanization'). Companies established reading rooms and libraries, funded lectures and supported company newspapers. The now ubiquitous company bulletin board is a product of this period.[72] Training outside the workplace was facilitated through the growth of night schools and correspondence courses. Throughout this new web of relationships, one can discern both the survival of a very perfectionist theme of self-improvement interacting with a distinctly new theme of selves being studied and developed by others.

Three periods in US education

It is important to look at the changes of this period in terms of the broader history of US education. Present-day accounts of problems with the educational system often appear to imagine current problems against some past golden age when education was done 'right.' A closer look at history shows education in the US to have a dynamic and contested history.[73] Like the Jews, but unlike most other cultures until their time, both the Puritans and Quakers were people of the book. Protestant belief combined the faith that the individual could know God without the mediation of priestly experts with emphasis on the Bible and books written by believers as a means for attaining divine knowledge; this presumed literacy. The Massachusetts Bay Colony was only six years old when it founded a university (Harvard, 1636). At that time there were probably more university graduates per capita in New than in Old England.[74]

As colonial life became more secular, the quality of education fell. It experienced a revival in the Federalist period; the spirit of radical democracy dictated that the average citizen be able to read and compute sufficiently to conduct the public business of the state. This revival did not reverse the stagnation of college education, since the Federalist could learn what a citizen needed to know in the primary grades. Through most of the nineteenth century, colleges were a poorly funded patchwork of institutions, largely affiliated with religious bodies and desperate for students. It was common to pay students for attendance, not as a competitive scholarship, but routinely, as a cost of proselytizing borne by the church supporting the school.[75] As late as the second half of the nineteenth century, the Harvard BA, even the MA, was primarily an attendance prize – one simply attended for the required amount of time and paid a graduation fee.[76] At about this time, a professor of surgery at Harvard argued that written examinations for

---

72 Cf., Yates (1989). What I call the emergence of disciplinary reality, she calls the rise of 'system.' Through Yates' eyes, innumerable mundane details such as the bulletin board become part of the story of this elaborating network of new relationships.

73 Valuable for insight into this history are Bruce (1987), Hofstadter (1963), Rudolph (1962), Travers (1983) – especially Rudolph.

74 Rowse (1959: 155).

75 Rudolph (1962).

76 Bledstein (1976).

the degree of MD would wreck the medical school because, among those graduating from the program, 'more than half of them can barely write. Of course they can't pass written examinations' (Bledstein, 1976: 275–6).

The shaping of education in the US[77] has had little to do with the pursuit of Truth in the groves of academe and everything to do with the knowledge needs (or lack thereof) of the dominant institutions of society. This is not necessarily bad, but it is contrary to the popular image of education as beholden only to the needs of Knowledge.[78] By 1890, education had come and gone as a weapon against Satan. It had come and gone as a tool of self-governance for the Federalist citizen. The periods of decline following each of these eras showed that education was not a necessary institution of society, but one that would thrive only where it provided a service valued by important social constituencies. In the late 1800s, US education was on the verge of yet another rebirth. It would produce an educational system that today is often taken as a natural evolution and progression from eight centuries of Western history, but which is stamped in every detail with the cultural context of an industrializing US.

The vocational movement

With the apprentice system gone, employers required new suppliers of knowledge[79] and workers sought new paths to the higher wages of skilled employment. The 'vocational movement' at the turn of the century continued the ambiguous alliance of those interested in bettering the condition of the worker and those attempting to increase the worker's value as human capital to the organization.[80] In 1905, Massachusetts appointed the Douglas Commission to evaluate educational institutions and recommend changes to bring education in line with industrial needs. The following year saw the formation of the National Society for the Promotion of Industrial Education (Struck, 1930). By 1917, congress passed the National Vocational Education Act. Once again, perfectionism legitimates industrial social change. As the training for skilled blue-collar work from control of

---

77 This is generally so, but my focus is the US.

78 An image that education itself actively encourages. The motto of Harvard University is simply Truth (*Veritas*). Written in Latin (the Puritans spoke in English and were a force for the translation of even the Scriptures from Latin), the motto borrows its ancient aura from a dead culture instead of the one out of which Harvard has grown.

79 Another potentially valuable study yet to be undertaken is to research the conditions under which organizations will 'produce' knowledge in-house and those under which they will 'subcontract' it to others. Of the potential suppliers of knowledge – public education, professional and technical training, consulting and training organizations – what changing social conditions are associated with changes in their relationships to business and society? The history of industrialization suggests that these relationships are extremely dynamic. If, today, an informed dialogue is to be conducted regarding the knowledge needs of society and the role of business in creating and filling those needs (particularly as corporations increasingly become involved with public education), this history must become better understood.

80 Cf., Niven (1967).

occupations to control of employers and experts, the term 'vocation' – literally, divine 'calling' – replaces traditional names.

This movement illustrates the diffuseness and complexity of the developing web of disciplinary relationships between the worker, the organization, public education, government and middle-class society. Did the vocational movement exist to promote worker welfare? To increase organizational capital? To stabilize the working class? Was it an early 'workfare' program? Was it fostered by the self-interest of educators? Does it show government and public education to be at the service of industry? All of these forces were at work simultaneously. The vocational movement was a reflection in public education of the new 'common sense' transforming society. Just as the work force was being divided into 'officers' and 'men,' the educational system was forming two corresponding spheres. Public education no longer prepared the independent citizen for participation in running society. It prepared workers to be 'controlled' and 'taught' (Jane Addams' words), so that they could be led by the officers of industry. Of course, education was also involved in training officers.

Training 'officers'

Frederick Taylor (1911) sanguinely notes that his early efforts were made possible because, being a 'college man' and not 'of working parents,' the owners felt he 'had the interest of the works more at heart than the other workmen.'[81] Colleges offered an institutional framework within which development of an 'officer corps' could combine acquisition of instrumental knowledge with class socialization. One of the early 'experiments' was cooperation between several railroads and the University of Chicago which, between 1904 and 1906, created the 'Chicago courses in railway organization and operation' (Dewsnup, 1906). In a 1906 address to the Railway Club of St Louis regarding this program, Earnest Dewsnup candidly touted it as having 'a direct bearing upon the labor problem' by training young men 'to see far above and beyond the petty aims and strifes of unregulated unionism' (1906: 413–14).

This experiment represents two significant changes. Most evident is industry's entry into the area of training traditionally reserved for the clergy and, more recently, law and medicine. Dewsnup is aware of this as well, noting that the railways are seeking 'those bright minds that find their way into a frequently thankless professional occupation' (Dewsnup, 1906: vii). This was creating a new partnership between business and education, and not just at Chicago: 'the educational movements at Montreal [McGill], Chicago, and elsewhere are significant' (Dewsnup, 1906: vi). Less evident is the radicality of railroads cooperating to create a shared resource. Prior to this time, it was common sense that one did not share competitive knowledge. This is a sign of the growing dominance of the spirit of

81 Taylor (1911: 50–1, 55–6). ·

rationalizing resources replacing the earlier spirit of *laissez-faire* competition.

It is at this point that the paramilitary railway 'officer' begins the transformation into *il maneggio*. Even 'the head of a great system,' wrote Haines, will come to see that 'managing' is 'not the originating of ideas or the institution of reforms so much as the coordination of the efforts of others [using] the reasoning faculties, developed by education and by experience' (Haines, 1919: 485). What one sees under construction at this point is the disciplinary manager 'discovered' by Mintzberg (1968) half a century later. Fayol's (1916) administrator corresponds to the railway 'officer,' who had been the source of authority during the period 1870–1920. Accounts from this period show an acute awareness of the need to replace paramilitary administration with disciplinary management. If the nature of managerial work was surprising in the 1960s, it was not so in the 1920s. As early as Dewsnup in 1906, one can trace the replacement of 'great man' leadership with the 'managerial mystique' cursed by Zaleznik in 1989. Such a mystique may be a problem today, but one must understand it as a form of practice produced through the dominant industrial-social relationships of seven decades. *Il maneggio* has always been a coordinator within, not a producer of, disciplinary relationships. 'He' is neither the robber baron nor the railroad officer. If we wish to change him, we must understand the world that has produced and that maintains him.

The new 'industrial' university

Dewsnup recognized that this new partnership would transform the university and defended the change as an extension of its traditional mission in society:

> One of the features of the educational history of the past half-century has been the specialization of education. . . . So far as the universities are concerned, this utilitarian aim is, after all, in accord with their earliest policy [to train lawyers, theologians and physicians]. . . . Even if this had not been the case, there would have been every reason to suppose that the modern trend of higher education is in accord with the spirit of the times and with the logic of events. . . . [The proliferation of professional departments is] greater and greater indication of the influence of the spirit of specialization, which, after all, is but a response to the demand that education shall adapt itself to the necessities of life. (1906: 402–3)

What may sound like cross self-interest in Dewsnup actually reflects awareness of broad trends that had been transforming education in the decades since the 1870s. For two centuries the university had been a minor actor in society, largely church supported and modeled after the medieval Oxford and Cambridge from which many Puritan leaders had come in the years around 1600.[82] By 1920 the university was a more central player in

---

82 The inner life of these universities was a better reflection of the thirteenth than the seventeenth century at this time.

Table 6.1 *'Radical' nineteenth-century innovations in education*

Course of study
Numeric grading
Competitive entrance
Regalia
Medieval architecture
Professional schools/science/secularization of humanities
PhD for university professors
College for public teachers
Standardized tests
Job connections: licensing, hiring preference
Graduate school
Tenure/academic freedom
Research
Scientifization

---

society, dominated by secular interests and modeled after the technology-oriented German polytechnic institute. University status was secured in this new relationship as the final arbiter of the discourse of objectivity, whose ideal was represented by laboratory science. For the emerging 'culture of professionalism' the university both guarded entry through its awarding of degrees and certified the knowledge taught to be above self-interest (in the ideal) because it was based on scientific investigation and 'most Americans learned to associate the scientific way with openness and fairness' (Bledstein, 1976: 124).

For all intents and purposes, the US college and university system was created from scratch between 1870 and 1920. Table 6.1 lists some of the central icons of present-day education which were radical innovations in the late 1800s. Through these changes, the university became a *producer* (often a mass producer) of knowledge as well as a user. Like industry, it geared up for production using the latest technology, which happened to be German science. Various reasons are given for the preeminence and adoption of German education at this point. French education in the nineteenth century was a casualty of the Napoleonic wars. British university knowledge was dominated by a royally appointed theocracy; the British contributions to this period most often came from 'amateurs,' gentleman of leisure such as Galton and Darwin. Nonetheless, it is interesting that at this particular point in time, the US breaks away from a British heritage whose extreme individualism was consistent with (and a parent to) Federalist reality in order to remodel knowledge around the more statist German system within which the individual occupies a much more subordinate place.[83]

83 Consider as an example Hegel's influential *Phenomenology of Spirit*, in which none of the higher levels of consciousness can be attained by an individual. The levels of Spirit, Religion and Absolute Knowledge can only be experienced through social experience. Contrast this to Hegel's utilitarian contemporary in England, Jeremy Bentham. Following in a tradition of Hobbes, Locke and Hume, Bentham's universe subordinated the social to the individual (Norman, 1976; Jones, 1975).

Like the factory, the university became a standardized producer of knowledge. Implementation of research programs created a hierarchy of professorial status strengthened by the creation of graduate programs. The graduate student, as today, was privileged relative to undergraduates, but researched and taught at a level subordinate to the lowest status professor. The PhD, first awarded by Yale in 1861, became increasingly commonplace for university professors. The American Association of University Professors was founded in 1915 'dedicated in particular to the development and protection of standards of freedom and tenure' (Rudolph, 1962: 415). Both, along with the development of a national job market, facilitated the development of a 'normalized' professorate. Standardized testing, curriculum committees, licensing and grading of students produced an increasingly standardized industrial 'product.' Whatever the successes and failures of the US university in the twentieth century, they have been *industrial* successes and failures, produced by a factory configured as an organization of scale.

The 'evolution' of evolutionary thought

In 1859, a son-in-law of the pottery magnate, Josiah Wedgwood, and a cousin of Francis Galton, the founder of eugenics, published a fateful book. It was *The Origin of Species* by Charles Darwin. Like many epochal books, *The Origin of Species* is not so much a cause of evolutionary thinking as it is a crystallization of the spirit of an era.[84] Evolutionary thinking is not necessarily Darwinian any more than socialist thinking is necessarily Marxian or psychological thinking necessarily Freudian. In fact, most social applications would more appropriately be labeled 'Social Lamarckianism' than Social Darwinism because Lamarck, but not Darwin, believed that individuals pass on adaptations gained in their lifetimes.[85]

Emphasis on the conflict between evolution and religion obscures some powerful similarities between the two. Perhaps it is not coincidental that Galton came from a Quaker family. *Nineteenth-century biology 'discovered' in the animal kingdom a form of progressive development. Sixteenth-century perfectionism had 'discovered' the possibility of an individual's progressive development toward Grace. Eighteenth-and nineteenth-century capitalist economics 'discovered' the progressive growth of economies. At the individual, social and biological levels, each of these potentially conflicting systems of thought diverges from Renaissance reality in a similar way: it replaces a reality centered on the* status quo *with one centered on growth.* What matters, for the individual, for society and for life itself is not where it is, but where it is going. This is appropriately symbolized by Darwin's connections to

84 What Darwin may really have written or thought is irrelevant to my arguments. My concern is with the uses of evolutionary theory and the effects these uses have had on knowledge. This is not, then, a critique of Darwin.

85 Natural selection as defined by Darwin is based on mutation. Favorable mutations are 'selected' by the environment if those possessing them are more likely to reproduce. Whether the individual organism can change itself is not relevant.

Wedgwood and Galton. As a wealthy Briton who was not a member of the landed aristocracy, Darwin was a product of the tremendous optimism and economic growth of the British eighteenth century. It takes nothing away from his accomplishments to say that the theory of evolution *could* be thought in this time period because it fit into broader changes in ways of understanding the world. It was a short jump from the 'evolution' of Wedgwood's Etruria works to the evolution of species – and yet another short jump to Galton's societal evolution.[86]

Evolutionary thinking transformed the physical sciences, serving as a new central organizing concept. Today, from the Big Bang theory in physics to biological categorization of species to chemical explanations of physiological and organic processes, science is told as a story of unfolding and ongoing development. The past has 'evolved' into the present which is 'progressing' into the future. At the social level, society was explained as a response to environmental forces. Anglo-US society was no longer justified simply in patriotic terms as superior to others; it was explained as the 'natural' result of response to a harsh climate. This provided a new 'objective' framework for racism and xenophobia since a 'progressive' response within this framework was to help 'savage' cultures more quickly 'evolve' into 'civilized' forms.[87] At home, eugenic thinking about the development of 'the race' provided a weapon against certain groups outside the Anglo-Saxon mainstream. In the 1924 scientific treatise *The Fruit of the Family Tree*, Albert Wiggam uses the discourse of objectivity to assert that '[i]nvestigation proves that an enormous proportion of [America's] undesirable citizens are descended from undesirable blood overseas. America's immigration problem is mainly a problem of blood' (Wiggam, 1924: 6–7).

Such assertions are easily dismissed today as simply 'bad' science. This helps to distance Anglo-US society from complicity in the Holocaust,[88] but it creates a huge blind spot for understanding our own history. Eugenic thinking was ubiquitous during the half-century which formed the US scientific establishment of today. *To dismiss this as deviant thinking on the part of a few is to ignore the container within which management and management theory were formed.*[89] *Eugenics formed the necessary link*

---

86 Langton (1984) brings this line of thought full circle, arguing that Wedgwood pottery be understood in Darwinian terms as an example of organizational selection.

87 Takaki (1993, 1979), Shipman (1994).

88 Perhaps inappropriately so. US internment of Japanese Americans and the tragicomedy that was McCarthyism have convinced me that the difference between the Germany of 1933 and the US of today is primarily one of circumstance and opportunity, not one of social morality.

89 Veblen (1899/1983) and Borsodi (1929) build on such thinking, as do Carnegie (1920) and Blackford and Newcomb (1914). Marx himself could not have espoused his theory of social evolution toward scientific socialism without a social context in which science and evolution were central concepts. But only when one begins to search through old books does it become apparent what a popular tide of thinking has been erased from our histories. Used bookstores abound in blatant eugenic/evolutionist tracts; some that I have found include Dopp (1902), Keller (1915/1973), Millikan (1924), Wiggam (1922, 1924). More pervasive is a sympathy with these attitudes that is ubiquitous in scientific and social thought from the turn of the century until the Second World War.

between biological change and the question of which employees would have
the authority to 'develop' others and which would be the objects of
development. 'All men are born unequal' declared Wiggam (1924: 330), who
re-interpreted the Declaration of Independence as simply a notice to King
George of the social equality of colonists – in the aggregate – with citizens of
England. This was not a view reserved for the conservative. Borsodi (1929),
who is critical of the factory system, estimates that those who can rise above
'the herd' are only about three in a thousand. Between 'Mr. Potentially
Superior' and 'Mr. Potentially Inferior,' the relationship is: '[i]nferior can
never rise above the herd. . . . But superior can . . . *if he is free to make the*
necessary effort (Borsodi, 1929: 389; emphasis in the original).

Today, Social Darwinism is routinely dismissed as an erroneous view
briefly held in the dawning years of organizational thought, primarily as
legitimation for the robber baron generation. This dismissal-in-caricature
diverts attention from the central influence still exerted in organizational
thought by the assumptions so concisely expressed by Borsodi: (1) People
are naturally unequal in their abilities; (2) People are not simply diverse, but
differ systematically in their social value; (3) These values can be placed on a
continuum or in a hierarchy; (4) A free society does not make all people
equal, but allows them to rise as far in this hierarchy as their abilities permit;
and (5) Removing barriers to each person rising to his/her highest and best
place in the social order is the job of those whose knowledge is most
'evolved,' that is, those at the top of the social order. This schema makes a
place for a version of the Federalist discourse of character because each
person must 'make the necessary effort' to rise to his/her place. But equality
now operates within a hierarchy presented 'objectively' as the natural order
of things. Inequality is not the result of oppression or privilege. It is the act of
placing everyone where they can be of best service to society. By
assumption, this aggregate benefit to 'society' creates the greatest overall
benefit to individuals. What has been reduced over the years is the degree to
which women and non-Anglo-Saxons have been found scientifically 'inferior' by confusing social disadvantage with biological inferiority.[90] Metaphors of evolution in social thought – such as Weick (1969) or Hannan and
Freeman (1977) – have become more technically Darwinian. Perhaps it
should be said that knowledge has emerged from the Social *Lamarckianism*
of the Gilded Age in order to be shaped by a more properly Social Darwinist
perspective.

Conditioning theory

In addition to Germanization of the university and the spread of evolutionary thinking, Travers (1983) suggests that a third major influence on

---

90 Even this change may have more to do with the events of the Second World War making
talk of racial types and racial differences unthinkable than with any 'evolution' of science. For
the past half-century it has been a tenet of faith in Western countries that *inherently*, large
groups of people are basically alike (cf., Takaki, 1993; especially Chapter 14).

the 'industrial revolution' in education was Russian behaviorism. At first blush it is odd that such an extreme mechanistic view of human activity could take root in a society founded on the freedom and self-determination of the individual, especially when one considers that humanist loyalties resulted in these beliefs finding less acceptance in supposedly class-stratified Europe. On reflection, however, behaviorism fits quite well with one strain of American ideology. From the Puritans onward, being 'American' has meant learning from immediate experience. Theory, intellect and reflection have been suspect qualities.[91] A science of behavior presumed to emerge from data, unencumbered by grand theorizing, philosophy of knowledge or history, reproduced within academic discourse the common sense 'omni-competence' of the average competent observer that, while disappearing as a social practice, lived – and lives – on as an ideal.

As Skinner (1971) scathingly argued, the study of human interaction has continued to mingle a science of behavior with what scientifically amounts to a superstitious belief in internal attributes. Behavioral scientists have shown a preference for a discourse focused on these internal states and traits – motivation, satisfaction, personal hardiness and so forth – and for a rhetoric of humanism. Behaviorism is strangely marginal in management texts despite the discrepancy between behaviorism's relatively strong empirical support (especially compared to the work of Herzberg or Maslow) and the frequent claim that organizational science is an empirical discipline. Where the legacy of behaviorism has become pervasive is in the now dominant belief system which values 'data' over ideas, which values 'descriptive' research and imagines it can be distinguished from 'normative' research, and which places faith in the quasi-religious tenet that once enough measurements and computations are made, they will produce a science of social interaction.

The disciplinary revolution of everything

To speak of an 'industrial revolution' as the producer of modern society is simplistic. Granted, science and education experienced a transformation that might be called an industrial revolution, but one could understand this period equally well speaking of the *scientific revolution* of industry and education or the *educational* revolution of industry and science. To speak of a *managerial revolution* in government, labor, industry – even religion – comes closer, but management was produced by the changes in industry, education and science. Slotkin (1992) has argued that modernization was a militarization, and this analogy will take one far, but the militarization of industry produced an industrialization of the military.[92] Just as one cannot

---

91 The Quakers' belief in direct communication with the Divine (Reay, 1985); lionizing men of practical wisdom such as Franklin and Edison (Goodman, 1945; Wachhorst, 1981); the Jeffersonian citizen farmer (Boorstein, 1960); and contemporary America (Hofstadter, 1963; Baudrillard, 1989) all show this theme to have remained strong through changing times.

92 Cf., McGregor's (1960) introduction to *The Human Side of Enterprise* regarding the change between early and mid-twentieth-century military authority.

find a social group or class which orchestrated the construction of disciplinary society, one cannot find a social institution that was the prime mover. 'Is it surprising,' asked Foucault, 'that prisons resemble factories, schools, barracks, hospitals, which all resemble prisons?' (1979: 228). It may be conventional to refer to this period as 'industrial,' but industry was as transformed as the rest of society by disciplinary changes.[93]

How does one comprehend changes which produce new social groups and new institutions while altering the meanings of the good society and the good citizen as well as producing new criteria for what counts as knowledge and new modes of producing, articulating and applying it? This is an unprecedented challenge produced, at least in part, by the accumulation of recorded knowledge and by the accelerating pace of social change. It has led an increasing number to attempt to describe 'modernity' as a distinct cultural system corresponding, very roughly, to European/American industrial society. The growing suspicion that we are now at the tail end of this modern period has stimulated bodies of theory about the possibility of the 'postmodern.' Present debates often center on what postmodernity *really* is and whether theory self-labeled as postmodern is important. These debates may be premature. As Foucault once commented:

> I wonder whether we may not envisage modernity rather as an attitude than as a period of history. And by 'attitude,' I mean a mode of relating to contemporary reality. . . . And, consequently, rather than seeking to distinguish the 'modern era' from the 'premodern' or 'postmodern,' I think it would be more useful to try to find out how the attitude of modernity, ever since its formation, has found itself struggling with attitudes of 'countermodernity'. (1984b: 39)

After the fall of Rome, the structures of the classical world lingered in developing medieval society for about five centuries. Between the last execution of empiricists as heretics and the modern world lie at least two centuries. Perhaps it is unrealistic to expect that in our lifetimes we will understand the meanings of today's social shifts. A useful start can be made, however, by inquiring how the present 'attitude of modernity' reflects a specific constellation of historical and cultural values. This book has been describing the preconditions for, the emergence of, and the coalescence of such an 'attitude of modernity.' As such, it has been a prologue to a history of management. Only with the sedimentation of this society into something that appeared solid – and with the growth of a populace who did not remember the old order – could management as we know it finally emerge. By 1910–20, social reality had been thoroughly reshaped along 'modern' disciplinary lines. Capital and labor increasingly contested wages and hours

---

93 The traditional way of speaking of a transition from an agrarian to an industrial society is misleading. With industrialization, farming did not disappear. Both farm and factory were reconstructed within a new common sense which is as well illustrated by the industrialization of farming as by the development of the factory. Similarly, the advent of the post-industrial does not herald the disappearance of industry, but yet another reconstruction of society on the basis of a new logic not yet clearly seen.

rather than social relationships and work technologies. The average worker expected to be employed by others. Corporate ownership and endless industrial growth were accepted as desirable, or at least inevitable, by most. Legislative systems, education, social institutions and the workplace had been interwoven with disciplinary relationships, legitimated through a discourse of objectivity and mediated by 'professional' experts. This new way of understanding the work, the worker and the world was organized around new problems, was structured by new kinds of institutions and, consequently, produced new objects of knowledge, new concepts for understanding and new knowers to articulate what would be known. It is this conjunction of events that produced the possibility for what we now know as organization science.

Scientific Management had created the *possibility* of a science of the worker by bringing 'the labor question' into the domain of engineering. Scientific Management, however, did not pose the worker as a problem of understanding for scientific inquiry.[94] Today, the discursive descendants of Scientific Management are industrial engineering, production operations management and management science, disciplines related only indirectly to organizational behavior, organizational theory, human resources management or business policy. The mind of the worker first emerges as an object of scientific inquiry only about the time of the First World War, when discursive relationships had developed sufficiently for *l'employé* and *il maneggio* to support 'the new profession of handling men.'

The Management Movement

Management as a high-profile 'movement' was, Person noted in 1926, a result of these historical events. This movement represented the convergence of three internally complex forces. The first was *Scientific Management*, which had established the relationships between science, the university, professionalism, business interests and the worker. To this was added the force of the *'employment managers' movement'* and, later, the theoretical weight of *industrial psychology*. This coalescing of 'disciplines' created another compatible axis of disciplinary power by applying the language of scientifically managing *material* resources to the Scientific Management of *human* resources. It is from this point that a discourse recognizably connected to today's organizational knowledge begins to appear.

94 One can find in Taylor's thought the seeds of what subsequently became known as Organizational Development. Taylor was not insensitive to the importance of worker attitudes (for this observation, I am indebted to the unpublished doctoral research of CSPP student Mark Dunaway). Scientific Management, however, remained largely reliant on two tools (wage bonuses and decreasing fatigue) which did not require knowledge of the worker's psychological traits or 'sentiments' (cf., Hollway, 1991).

This is the point of emergence of *il maneggio*, the 'handler.' At about this time, a literature emerges in which appear titles such as 'The Building of Men' (Murphy, 1917b), 'Shaping Men to the Work' (Slocum, 1917), 'Human Being Management' (*Industrial Management*, 1916), 'The New Profession of Handling Men' (Bloomfield, 1916). This idea of 'managing,' especially as a form of 'handling' and 'shaping,' would have made no sense to readers a generation earlier. 'Human resource management'[95] would have been both alien and counterproductive in a pre-disciplinary world of seasonal production, short-term employment relationships and occupationally controlled skill maintainance. As this world changed, large organizations began a process of 'backward integration' into the development of the labor force as a resource. The employment managers' movement emerges as employers begin to assume greater authority for developing the worker as a 'disciplinary' subject.

The employment managers' movement

Beginning just before the turn of the century, welfare work, the interests of employers and the vocational movement began to coalesce in the new 'profession' of employment management. One arm of the vocational movement had entered public schools to reform the training of workers. Another entered the large organization, promising to bring order and increase productivity by classifying workers and work and matching the one to the other. Much of what would today be recognized as the basis for the academic discipline of human resource management developed in these factories, not the university. In *The Job, The Man, The Boss* (1914), Blackford and Newcomb utilize interview and evaluation forms, rate-step payroll schemes and most of the other contemporary objects and concepts of the HRM department. Their point of reference for the group developing this knowledge is a loose professional association of employment managers. Promoting 'a plan of employment based on scientific principles' (B&N, 1914: xvii) is their main claim for assuming authority once held by the employer or foreman. This group has already allied with science, but they have not yet allied with the university.

It has become traditional for organizational texts to describe a progressive 'evolution' from mechanistic Taylorism to 'softer' human resources/human relations perspectives. This was colorfully described by Perrow (1973: 8) as a conflict between 'the forces of light and the forces of darkness,' and is propagated by virtually every current organizational textbook. Of course, the story usually told skips from Taylor to the Hawthorne studies. Leaving out the employment managers' movement severs a critical link between mechanical and human engineering. Far from being an opposing force to Scientific Management, the employment managers' movement sought to position itself as an *extension* of Taylorist principles. The movement

---

95 Both the idea of humans as 'resources' and the idea of 'management.'

appealed quite explicitly to the Taylorist principle of matching workers to jobs and to the theme of 'conserving human values' (B&N, 1914: xvi).[96] The new movement did attempt to distinguish itself from 'a tactless Taylorism' (Moore and Hartmann, 1931: 507),[97] but claimed that

> [a]dmiration for these results [of Scientific Management] has generated a demand that, in another department of industry there should be introduced something which might, by analogy, be called 'human engineering'. . . . As the engineers, or technical executives, learned to control physical resources by science, it now remains . . . to control the human factors in industry in accordance with the fundamental principles of human nature. (Jones, 1916: 125–7)

Employment management went beyond Taylor in recognizing that correct placement of the worker in a properly engineered task was only the first step in a comprehensive process of analysis, counseling, training and placement which would change the subject from a fixed capacity to be merely optimized into a constantly increasing aptitude to be *progressively* increased. Implementing this process required an expert capable of systematically categorizing the worker based on 'natural' traits only indirectly observable.

> When a man writes his name, address, and other items, *he tells far more about himself than he thinks.* Like voice, handwriting is an expression of *character.* . . . The rapidity with which he fills in the blank will indicate, to some degree, his quickness of thought. . . . Germans and Englishmen do not harmonize readily, nor do Irishmen and negroes. . . . For the same reason, it is often desirable to know the religion of the applicant. . . . Happily married men, other things being equal, do the best work. They are the most permanent. Bachelors come next. The man with serious domestic trouble is least efficient and least satisfactory of all. . . . This is not difficult to ascertain by *indirect methods* if the interviewer is tactful and *sympathetic.* . . . [The list of the applicant's qualities] is not submitted to applicants for the purpose of obtaining direct information from them. . . . In many ways applicants *reveal* in some measure their characters, their aptitudes, and their habits as they react to this list. (B&N, 1914: 184–8; emphasis added)

This, finally, is the language of *il maneggio*. The threat of punishment has given way to sympathetic tact. The worker's embodied traits, once legible to the average person, have been recast as a hidden language decipherable only by the trained expert who understands the internal meanings of superficial signs. Through the disciplinary apparatus developed by this profession, the unknown interior of the worker becomes visible as 'variables' arrayed within precise grids of 'organized, classified and verified knowledge' (B&N, 1914: 198). The employment managers' movement worked in tandem with Scientific Management. The latter produced standardized *jobs*; the former standardized job *holders*. Although Blackford and Newcomb (1914) advocate certain topics that no longer fit the discourse of the employee, it is surprising to a present-day reader how much of *The Job, The Man, The Boss*

96 Also Gilbreth and Cook (1947).
97 Which was very mild criticism, since Taylor himself is candid about his occasional lack of tact (1911: 88).

could still be used in an HRM class. Today's HRM text is less a product of 'evolution,' than of revision. One finds in Blackford and Newcomb, a fully developed theoretical and practical framework for the selection, classification and development of workers as a human 'resource.' On this framework, one can hang virtually any topic represented in human resource textbooks of the 1980s.[98]

Industrial psychology

The employment manager spoke the discourse of science, but in an applied fashion. The model for this profession was the (itself newly professionalized) practical discipline of mechanical engineering. In the second decade of the twentieth century, employment management intersected with another expert discourse, one rooted in German university practice. Just as employment management presented itself as an extension of Scientific Management, industrial psychology presented itself as the theoretical foundation of employment management. 'Psychologists and management engineers,' wrote Bingham in 1925, 'are drawing together. They are becoming more aware of each other's problems and points of view' (1925: 29). The psychologist was presented as an advisor who 'can be of great value to the [employment] experts,' who would be the ones 'required to work out the details' (Link, 1924: 230). Industrial psychology granted the employment manager the claim to greater specific knowledge of his/her industrial domain, but psychology claimed 'knowledge of the workings of the mind,' and familiarity 'with the requirements of an exact technique [experimental methodology] such as will be essential if these phases of employment are to be placed upon a sound and scientific basis' (Link, 1924: 230). The psychologist would 'test tests rather than applicants' (Link, 1924: 20). It would also be a producer of new knowledge, which would no longer come solely from practice.

> The employment psychology which will prevail, and which will increasingly contribute to the unravelling of employment problems, is the psychology which rests on continuous research and experimentation in the field of employment itself. And this research must in turn be conducted by psychologists trained in the best practices of the university laboratory. (Link, 1924: 390–1)

As reflected in Link's comment, the entry of industrial psychology into the discourse of the employee was a point from which the extensive interpenetration of the university and the organization began to produce a

98 It might be appropriate to include the 1990s, but it is possible that strategic human resource management, Total Quality Management/Business Process Re-engineering concepts and management of knowledge-intensive workers and work environments will produce some fundamentally new thinking before the end of the 1990s.

distinct product. Industrial psychology was the first institution of management[99] to be enunciated primarily by academics. This is reflected in a flurry of new academic journals appearing at this time, including *Personnel Journal* (1914), which became the *Journal of Applied Psychology*; the *Journal of Personnel Research* (1922); the *Journal of Industrial Psychology* (1922).

The First World War was 'a red-letter date for applied psychology' (Moore and Hartmann, 1931: 5). During the war 'scores upon scores of thousands of skilled men went to France – to their death' (Scott and Clothier, 1923: 10). The carnage *per se* is not lamented. The problem was that those dying were the skilled. The scientific classification of recruits allowed those sent to their deaths to be more consistently those with less value to industry. After the war, the experience of the army 'had a tremendous educational and inspirational effect' (Scott and Clothier, 1923: 11) on employers in influencing them to apply industrial psychology to the workplace.

The 'phenomenological shift'

The convergence of Scientific Management with the vocational, employment managers' and industrial psychology movements indicated and accelerated a profound shift in the reality of work. Because of the strong influence of German idealism in this transformation, I will refer to it as the 'phenomenological shift.'[100] It was manifested in a decentering of the material and economic aspects of work in favor of an emphasis on work as what would today be called a social construction. Bell (1973) noted this shift as a characteristic of what he termed 'post-industrial' society; post-industrial reality, wrote Bell, is no longer located in either physical nature or machines, but in '*the social world*. . . . Society itself becomes a web of consciousness, a form of imagination to be realized as a social construction' (Bell, 1973: 488; emphasis in the original). But Blackford and Newcomb anticipate Bell by six decades as they announce a dawning awareness of 'the purely psychological nature of business . . . the other tangible factors in our commerce and industry are but the visible counters in a game played solely by the invisible forces of mind and soul' (B&N, 1914: 4).

Calás (1987: 159) is one of the few who has noted this 'Hegelian connection' between German idealism and organization theory, citing it as an influence on Chester Barnard. A similar foundation of dialectical

---

99 The first institution of *management*, not of the 'utilitarian aim' noted by *business*. The university first entered business as a partner in financial administration (see, Dewsnup on p. 129). If one examines early issues of the *Harvard Business Review* (from 1922), one of the earliest regular business school publications, one finds nothing in the early years directed at the human problems of organizing. The focus is strictly on material and financial systems – topics which would be of interest to the new 'general office' level of the organization.

100 An ungainly term, but one which emphasizes that even among mainstream, 'bottom line' types, the meanings of work were already leaving the hard reality of physical objects and moving into a socially constructed realm where 'reality' would increasingly refer to the phenomena of social experience.

idealism can be detected in the early industrial psychology writings. The following, from the first edition of Scott and Clothier's *Personnel Management,* went through six printings and was widely used into the 1960s (with this section abridged in the sixth edition).

> Personnel work consists of man-analysis, job-analysis and the bringing of man and job together. . . . The job is never the same job when filled by different persons. . . . And M is never quite the same man in two different jobs. . . . This leads us to the concept of the worker-in-his-work as an entity all by itself. . . . [Hiring] is the creation of a worker-in-his-work unit. . . . [Firing] is the destruction of that particular worker-in-his-work unit. The hiring of a new worker for the job will not reproduce the same worker-in-his-work unit; a new worker-in-his-work unit has been brought about. (Scott and Clothier, 1923: 13–14)

The 'worker-in-his-work' indicates a quiet shift in the basis of reality that industrial psychology brought to the discourse of the employee. This shift is compatible with the emerging discourse of objectivity because it is located firmly within the scientific project, but it radically recasts the objects of knowledge. Machines, output and money are now peripheral phenomena, markers of what is happening in the 'real' world of values, perceptions and symbols.

This may sound like academic hocus-pocus until one considers the degree to which such phenomenological slip has entered the discourse of work. How often does some expert claim that the solution to overcoming worker resistance to management agendas is to make them 'feel empowered' or 'feel that they are being heard'? It is not inappropriate *per se* to focus on employee attitudes, but what can easily happen is a loss of the connection between employee perceptions and employment conditions. *Feeling* empowered is not the same as *being* empowered. A science of perception facilitates disconnecting the '*sentiment*'[101] of empowerment from actual sharing of authority, reward or decision making. This is not to say that behavioral science is designed as a tool of oppression. Rather, it indicates a power-laden relationship between work practices and organizational authority. If managers and experts speaking about the worker diverge from the workers' opinions about themselves, it is the workers' opinions which are not supported. Within a discourse of objectivity, their opinions are reduced to *data*; beneath what they *think* they experience, the expert measures what they *really* experience.[102]

As theorists look toward the problems of post-industrial management, this problem becomes critical. In so-called 'knowledge-intensive firms,' it is critical that workers use their discretion to perform beyond the formal requirements of evaluation and reward systems. If the worker's 'perception' of empowerment or inclusion is more effected by basic organizational

---

101 Hollway (1991).

102 Again, this is not simply theoretical. In previous consulting work I have been struck by the degree to which, even in relatively open organizations, the tabulated results of the consulting survey constitute a far more 'real' object in terms of managerial influence than the often perceptive written comments of employees.

practices rather than 'motivational' add-ons, managers will have to make difficult choices between the expediency of continuing a dialogue between experts about the worker and the longer-term self-interest of nurturing organizational performance. Recently, this and other concerns have crystallized around the concept of the 'knowledge worker.'

L'employé: *always a knowledge worker?*

One critical problem with the concept of the post-industrial knowledge worker as emergent is this: *the constitution of the worker as a 'knowledge worker' is the central event marking the emergence of* l'employé c. *1920 and creating the possibility of the current discourse of management.* The discourse of the employee was not an immediate response to problems of works management – it took almost half a century. The 300,000 cars Ford made in 1914[103] suggest that it had gone a long way toward dealing with works management. Its employment policy at that time, however, was described by a Ford executive himself as, 'hiring men at the back door for as little as we could get them, putting them in the shop and making them work as long as they would stick, and not giving them an advance until we had to' (Porter, 1917b: 168). Mechanistic production systems requiring little worker knowledge could function with unskilled labor as long as violent resistance could be avoided. Even today, assembly work, data entry and the like are often taken to cultures where a worker's primary qualification is a lack of other work opportunities.

Particularly because the Ford assembly line has given its name to work deskilling ('fordism'),[104] it is interesting that Porter reflects recognition, before 1920, that the system of disposable workers is outdated and that production requires a loyal and enthusiastic work force. Ford was already looked to by industry as an exemplar of efficiently deskilling tasks and, at that particular time, a buyer's market for labor (reinforced by a pro-business legal and legislative context) precluded problems of worker resistance. Nonetheless, at this time when one might expect workers to become *more* disposable, Ford entered the 'new industrial revolution' of that decade to seek further gains from 'human being management' (*Industrial Management*, 1916). In less mechanized environments, the discourse of the employee had even more appeal. Even before 1920, mechanistic production facilities in which the workers were – as Taylor imagined – mere 'hands' was already limited to specific areas of business. Fisher (1917) noted that the cooperation and judgment of the worker was necessary in process technologies; Bloomfield (1916: 444) makes similar observations about 'organizations which sell service.'[105]

103 Georgano (1982: 252).

104 Braverman's (1974) description does not actually use the term, but has been central to subsequent discussion.

105 This 'contingency' of fit between technologies and business environments was 'discovered' again by Woodward (1965).

The constitutive problem of the employee has, from the beginning, been that of knowledge. During the clashes between capital and labor in the late 1800s, employers had fought to obtain a work environment in which knowledge was built into technical systems. The ideal employee was unskilled and interchangeable. But the 'second industrial revolution' around 1920 was founded on the recognition that even in the most regimented environment only limited success could be achieved without workers possessing several forms of special knowledge. The least skilled worker was more valuable when retained over a long period and educated in the practices of a good employee.

Before 1920, Thomas Edison, founder of General Electric, saw it as 'an important part of my duties, as a business executive,' to 'make capital' from worker knowledge (A.W. Shaw Co., 1917: 81). Hays (1917) tells a story more commonly associated today with 'high'-tech companies of the 1980s, of a company bankrupted when an employee quit, selling proprietary technical knowledge to competitors. The shift to 'handling' workers, in order to win their loyalty or to secure them with deferred benefits, reflects a shift in the locus of knowledge. Rights to capital in machines could be established in court or, if need be, by Pinkerton guns. Rights to human capital could not be so coerced. Thus, a discourse emerges emphasizing kinder, gentler industrial relations designed to induce workers to voluntarily 'give us the very finest products of their heads and hearts, and, therefore, of their hands' (B&N, 1914: 9).

Knowledge worker or 'learning worker'?

Perhaps, instead of imagining the knowledge worker to be newly emergent as a *post*-industrial worker, we should imagine him/her as a worker who has been there all along and who is now in the spotlight due to the confluence of certain socio-economic accidents – new technologies, redefined market boundaries, global redistribution of classes of work, and so forth, which placed this worker at the confluence of critical relations of power. After all, Weber clearly identifies bureaucracy as an organizational form built on the rational distribution of technical expertise, employing disciplinary knowledge (of the 'files') as a form of power. Perhaps what is changing today is not the *importance* of worker knowledge, but the *kind* of knowledge that is important. For three generations, systems have been refined to produce worker knowledge leading to *compliance* with decisions made by a specialized subgroup of employees ('management'). Increasingly, post-industrial organizations are seeking systems producing worker knowledge leading to *initiative*. This is not simply a different goal; it is one that conflicts with every element of disciplinary work practices.

Another possibility is that what is called 'knowledge work' is badly labeled. Perhaps the employee *c.* 1870–1990 should be called the knowledge worker. What may be emerging today is the *learning worker*. Edison knew how to capitalize knowledge in 1917. Foucault called eighteenth-century disciplinary society a machine for capitalizing knowledge. Knowledge is a static, if intangible, entity. Hofstadter captures this well in referring to the knowledge component of work as a 'store of frozen ideas' (1963:26). Increasingly, the problem of organizing has to do, not with the content of worker knowledge, but with the ability to revise this content as required. This ability is not effectively nurtured or controlled by the reward and evaluation systems of disciplinary organizing – indeed, it is suppressed; one's 'human capital' is one's frozen knowledge. *The difficulty of capitalizing the time and action of the worker is again the central challenge to organizing.* Who will gain the authority to accumulate, develop and apply this knowledge will be the central power issue of post-industrial organizing. If researchers today merely study knowledge and knowledge work, they are studying problems emergent in 1920, not the twenty-first century.

Is craft work knowledge work?

One might appropriately ask if Federalist craft knowledge was not also 'knowledge work.' Certainly there is knowledge, often sophisticated knowledge, demanded of craft work, but once again the difference between Federalist and industrial realities provides a point of rupture across which meanings cannot be transported. Craft work relationships defined the shape of work in Federalist society. The spectre of class warfare at the end of the nineteenth century stemmed from the incompatibility of craft and industrial assumptions about the organization of work. Craft, in the form of the 'trade unions,' was the site of organized *opposition to* the creation of the disciplinary organization. Had craft relations survived, they would have made industrial organization impossible. Similarly, in a society of industrial work relationships, craft work survives only in marginal spaces not claimed by industrial organizations.

To date, the three enabling processes for bringing craft-controlled work within large organizations have been mechanization, formalization and professionalization. Each of these transforms the work by removing control of power-knowledge from the body of the craftsperson. Mechanization physically builds knowledge into organizationally controlled assets, which are then run by interchangeable 'hands.' Formalization is disciplinary mechanization; although it resides in procedures rather than machines, it is directly analogous. Similarly, professionalization routinizes knowledge in the program-and-pigeonhole processes of an occupation whose assumptions are compatible with those of industrial discourse.[106] The passage of clients through a profession is quite comparable to the passage of inputs through a factory.

If one thinks of these three elements of disciplinary relationships as forming a web, craft work exists largely outside and in opposition to this web; knowledge work exists between the strands, potentially enabling or

---

106　Robbins (1990), Mintzberg (1979), Perrow (1986).

resisting the functioning of the relationships. What I am calling knowledge work is both *produced within* and claimed by the organization, but is *embodied in* – and also claimed by – the worker. There is a contest for ownership of knowledge, but it is a conflict bounded by the terms of industrial discourse. The employee cannot fundamentally oppose the system because one can work only as *l'employé* and *l'employé* can exist only *within* the system. Conversely, one can 'manage' more or less successfully to maintain organizational ownership of knowledge, but one cannot be *il maneggio* without employees.

The ghost of Freeman Hunt

The central point of this chapter has been that what are today known as 'management' and 'the employee' are products of the 'second industrial revolution' of about 1920. I have described the features of this emergent reality as 'disciplinary society' in order to contextualize them in relation to the emergence of industrial modernity in Europe. I have traced the coalescence of an entire social order around this new logic, focusing on the disciplinary revolution of education and the new relations this spawned between the school and the work organization. As these institutions come together, one can begin to speak of the emergence of management. As Scientific Management, the employment managers' movement and industrial psychology converge, this story reaches the Pacific coast against which it has been 'westering.'[107]

The following chapter will explore some contemporary implications of this story. Prominent among these will be the degree to which the industrial US of the twentieth century has maintained elements of a Federalist ideology of self-sufficiency, equality and individualism incongruously within a society structured through practices of interdependence, stratification and social construction of the individual. One result of this anachronism is a curious redundancy to the themes of 'managing for the twenty-first century.' What does it say about the status of knowledge if the 'emerging' themes of the post-industrial are the same as the themes of concern at the emergence of the *industrial*? Compounding this problem is a sort of collective amnesia; the relations documented in this book have been largely forgotten. As a result, their social specificity is unsuspected. They are exported to the world simply as 'management,' not as 'US industrial management.' In this way, the ghost of Freeman Hunt is not simply a spectre haunting US post-industrial discourse. Through the international exportation of knowledge 'he doth bestride the narrow world like a colossus.'[108].

107 Cf., Steinbeck, cited in Chapter 3.
108 W. Shakespeare, *Julius Caesar*, Act 1 Scene II: 'Why, man, he doth bestride the narrow world/Like a colossus; and we petty men/Walk under his huge legs, and peep about/To find ourselves dishonorable graves.'

7

The Struggle of Memory Against Forgetting: Managerialist Thought as a Conceptual Prison

'The struggle of humanity against power,' says a character in a Milan Kundera novel, 'is the struggle of memory against forgetting.'[1] History has not been treated as a major reference discipline for understanding present-day management problems. Where historical perspective is not ignored completely, it is most often used to explain the supposedly steady 'evolution' of a nearly perfected body of thought. If not, it is likely to be used to show the constancy through time of currently accepted belief or the repetitive cyclicality of the order of things.[2] This chapter will reflect a different perspective. It begins from the premise that knowledge and relationships specific to the US and to industrial society have slipped into 'common sense,' where they can no longer be questioned and where they prevent looking with fresh eyes on the emerging problems of post-industrial organizing. The remainder of this chapter will examine ways that historical analysis of this common sense can offer new possibilities for practice in a post-industrial world, both as organization members and as organization scholars.

Historical perspective as a management tool? 'Y' not?

There is a lesson to be learned from the interplay of memory and forgetting in the fate of McGregor's 'Theory Y.' In *The Human Side of Enterprise* (1960), McGregor characterized traditional managerialist thinking as 'Theory X' and outlined an alternative set of assumptions he called 'Theory Y.' McGregor stated that in the history of civilization there had been only two great transformations of authority in work organizations. The first was the shift from direct coercion to financial inducement, which produced the modern organization and the assumptions he labeled Theory X. The second

---

1 Kundera (1981: 3). What is translated 'man' I have reinterpreted as 'humanity'.

2 The evolutionary perspective forms the central theme of virtually every organization studies textbook history of the field. Starbuck et al. (1994) represent the eternal-theme view; this is summarized in McKinley's (1994) comment on the Starbuck *et al.* symposium: 'Could it be that there is a core of strategic and structural problems that are common to all organized enterprises in all historical contexts, and that all managers have to attend to?' McKinley argues that there is. The cyclicality perspective is present to a degree in Perrow (1973) and is more formalized in Barley and Kunda (1993).

great transformation, McGregor argued, was then underway and its future path was not yet clear. 'If anyone had been able to predict in 1900 what life in the United States would be like in 1960,' McGregor wrote, 'he would have been regarded as a complete fool.' Similarly, looking at the year 2000 from the vantage point of 1960, the future was unclear. McGregor was, however, convinced that although 'the modern industrial enterprise is an invention of great historical importance', '[u]nfortunately, it is already obsolete. In its present form it is simply not an adequate means for meeting the future economic requirements of society' (1960: 244–5). Rather than give his new theory a concrete name, then, McGregor used the scientific variable 'Y' to indicate that he was only outlining the barest bones of a new way of looking at work relationships. Theory Y was presented explicitly to mark an emerging and unknown area.

> It is not important that management accept the assumptions of Theory Y. These are one man's interpretations . . . and they will be modified – possibly supplanted – by new knowledge within a short time. . . . The purpose of this volume is not to entice management to choose sides over Theory X or Theory Y. It is, rather, to encourage the realization that theory is important, to urge management to examine its assumptions and make them explicit. (McGregor, 1960: 245–6)

Thirty-odd years later, what has become of Theory Y? It has been frozen in time. The central principles McGregor tentatively proposed for further elaboration are presented as dogma in introductory organizational texts for students to accept or reject as is. The meaning of Theory Y as a starting point in a dialogue has been lost. In addition, it has been forgotten that McGregor ever aspired to do anything other than to pronounce a piece of universal and timeless truth. McGregor propounded what, since Kuhn, might be called a new 'paradigm' of knowledge in the sense that *The Human Side of Enterprise* called for establishment of a new basis for dialogue about the nature of work, workers and the structure of society. Instead, McGregor has been 'normalized' into organizational science. Through a form of discursive taxidermy, Theory Y – abstracted from its socio-historical context, stuffed and mounted – is presented as a claim to be empirically proven or disproven. This has neither led to deeper understanding of the person at work, nor has it created the dialogue called for by McGregor.

Some key points so far

This book has been written as a tool for examining the discursive process through which 'Theory Y' has been desiccated. It explicitly associates the dream of a science of managing with the American Dream and its construction. Thus, values brought to America by the original Puritan and Quaker colonists are stressed. Prominent among these are perfectionism, a discourse centered on 'character,' an anti-intellectual belief in pragmatic action and the omnicompetent knowledge of the average citizen, a belief in social progress and an orientation toward capitalizing time and activity. All of these values would change dramatically as the colonial social order gave way to the Federalist and the Federalist to the industrial, but they would continue to be present at the heart of American 'common sense.'

Early signals of the emergence of the modern order were the closing of the frontier and the decline of community as the locus of social institutions. Society survived the appearance of the large organization of scope, but the coming of the organization of scale precipitated 'the Terror,' within which Federalist institutions and social relations collapsed. Prominent at this time, the three central questions of organizing were the 'labor question,' the 'works management question,' and, slightly later, the 'trust question.' Out of the 'financial revolution' of the trust-question times came a business order controlled at the investor, as opposed to the works, levels. This created the possibility – but still not the actuality – of general management.

Through this time, the business order saw a steady remapping of authority from occupations to organizations, from foremen and owners to 'management,' from foreman and management to a general office organization operating through 'the files,' from the operational to the financial level, from direct to encoded knowledge of the worker. It was associated with and influenced by an 'industrial revolution' of education and science as well as a 'scientific revolution' of education and industry. The final sedimentation of a new order was the point at which welfare work, the vocational movement, Scientific Management, the employment managers' movement and industrial psychology coalesced into the 'management movement' of about 1920.

Within this new order, Federalist 'common sense' no longer made sense. Radically new concepts became 'knowledge' (that is, belief that has forgotten it is belief, assuming the status of self-evident truth). Conservation of natural, and later human, resources succeeded 'pioneering' and re-centered knowledge around the new, ratio-nal concepts of efficiency and productivity. Wage work for life, the permanent 'job' and a new division of labor producing 'task work' were perquisites to building the organization of scale. As the trusts 'rationalized' business, cooperation was touted as the ideal replacing 'destructive competition.' The Puritan ideal of progress toward perfection was recast as endless progress, social 'evolution.' In the new 'culture of professionalism,' this new discourse based on objectivity succeeded the Federalist discourse based on character. This new 'disciplinary' reality embodied a 'phenomenological shift' away from the materiality of work practices; the material world was replaced by a web of perceptions as the domain necessary to understand if one wished to speak about managing. This new reality was a numeric, not a sensory, domain.

This new reality produced new subjects. Workers were now visible as subjects of knowledge only to the extent that they entered the tripartite box and assumed one or more of the three subjectivities it offered: there was *il maneggio*, the horse handler, now redirected to be a handler of 'men;' there was the professional, no longer appealing to social caste, but to technical knowledge for authority and status; there was *l'employé*, the good, the permanent, the organizationally owned, the subordinate, the task-working, the wage-earning, the typologized, the divided, the childlike and ignorant worker. Outside of work, everyone was 'the consumer.' Increasingly, it was 'discovered' that this social subject had a 'human nature' quite at odds with the nature of the Federalist self. S/he sought good wages, not occupational autonomy; idealized the normal, not the heroic; was composed of 'aptitudes' instead of skills; and wanted to steadily 'develop, but required the aid of an increasingly complex web of experts to learn how to do this. Ironically, despite this engineering of knowledge out of the individual and into various systems, the central problem of the worker shifted from worker effort to worker knowledge. A new American Dream had been constructed, containing all the by now traditional signifiers – freedom, individuality, self-knowledge, achievable Utopia – but with a radically different content. On examination, destruction and reconstruction of the American Dream has been a distinctive theme for three centuries, an invisible thread of the dream itself.

The Instability of the American Dream

Scanning the successive reconstructions of the American Dream offers several lessons for organizational scholarship. First, one finds a striking similarity between the crystallization of cultural values in American Utopian thinking and the relationships scientifically 'discovered' to exist in the modern organization. Second, the plasticity of the Dream over time undermines the naive idea that today's American shares a set of core values with the founding 'fathers.' Third, the durability of certain terms and themes despite profound changes in the practices they connote is an indication of relatively well-defined banks through which the river of social life in America has flowed.[3] Studying how each construction of the dream has contained within itself the seeds of its own destruction, might offer hints for understanding how similar forces may be operating today.

If one treats the American Dream as a product of colonization, that is, as being unconnected to the beliefs of the indigenous peoples, the first American Dream was of the Augustinian City of God. The irony of the Puritan ideal was that a work ethic coupled to austere social practices led to accumulation.[4] In noting this dilemma, Johnson (1976) cites Cotton Mather's awareness of the problem as it was occurring: '*Religion* brought forth *prosperity*, and the *daughter* destroyed the *mother*' (1976: 423). In addition, the growth of international capitalism which had made it possible for these neomedieval visionaries to receive funds also led quickly to the

---

3 In Saussurian terms, the superficial appearance of constancy in the central signs connoting the myth (or dream) of America has masked a profound shift in practices *signified* while the *signifiers* used to represent them have changed little. The complex power relations signified by and producing this constancy-within-change constitute a relatively unexplored area for research.

4 Johnson (1976), Bradford (1856/1981).

demise of the ideal of the City of God. Within a generation, settlers moved outward to their 'great lots' leaving the original colony 'very thin and in a short time almost desolate' (Bradford, 1856/1981: 281–2). Within a few generations, the attempt to build a City of God resulted in a society of capitalist farmers and merchants whose spirit for commerce was unencumbered by pre-industrial social structures and, paradoxically, fed by redirecting the Puritan/Quaker ethos into secular channels.

The secular colonial order was not a radical democracy, but a somewhat 'flat' social order with an elite whose source of authority was the claim to have succeeded within the commercial order.[5] Service to the state was, for this class, a form of *noblesse oblige* – duty incumbent on the gentleman of character. After conducting the American Revolution, this class also undercut its dream by successfully pursuing it. A revolution produced by an elite resulted in the erosion of rule by an elite.

The language of the revolution had been that of a radical democracy that far exceeded the equality of actual social relations. The destruction of a large portion of the well-to-do who had sided with the Tories led to the reorganization of state governments 'in a radical democratic spirit . . . which, for the most part . . . was insubordinate, factious, and extremely independent' (Croly, 1909: 31). This existed contradictorily with the belief that the institutions constructed by this group were nearly perfect and the dangers of further improvement outweighed the dangers of stagnation.[6] This has 'kept them peculiarly liable to intellectual ineptitude and conformity, [a] mixture of optimism, conservatism, and superficiality' (Croly, 1909: 50). Thus a generation willing to experiment with the most radical social change produced its antithesis. Not only did this result in the ossification of what was designed to be a dynamic system (think of McGregor and Theory Y), it has also made Americans 'blind to the true lessons of their own national experience' (Croly, 1909: 50).

The Jacksonian period also sowed the seeds for the industrial destruction of the Federalist order. No one could have foreseen this effect; again, the successful pursuit of the dream killed the dream. For two centuries and more, the American farmer could (erroneously) imagine his/her world to be beyond the margins of international trade, but by 1870 the pioneer farmer had largely been replaced by members of an industrial order who borrowed money and used an increasing amount of capital equipment. Eventually, and unintentionally, these farmers produced an order dominated by industry and by the expert, an order within which the farmer was a marginal player. 'This was a result that had never entered into the calculations of the pioneer democrat. He had disliked specialization, because, as he thought, it narrowed and impoverished the individual' (Croly, 1909: 102).

Paradoxically, this shift was greatly facilitated by the most radical spirit of

5 Commercial, in this sense, may be applied to either farming for the market or trade. Manufacture was not yet significant.

6 See Croly (1909), in Chapter 5.

democracy ever seen in the US. The early nineteenth-century Jacksonians permitted the translation of individual privilege into corporate privilege; the corporation was seen less as the agent of protected monopoly – which it had traditionally been – and more as an agent of free competition. 'The Jacksonian Democrats took a giant step, perhaps the decisive one, in translating Jefferson's agrarian individualism into the industrial *laissez-faire* of the latter part of the century' (Davis, 1905/1961: ix–x).[7] This would have appeared to have made great sense at the time notes Davis. 'Distrust in the state as organized caused the accumulation of political powers in the hands of minor states, corporations' (1905/1961: II–267). These 'excited no apprehension because they were democratically organized and did not seriously conflict in their activity with established industrial relations' (1905/1961: II–267). The conflict would not become pronounced for another three or four decades.

> Moreover, were they not based substantially on individual contract and was not 'freedom of association' one element of liberty? If the entire state had been formed and organized like the corporation, would not philosophers and political theorists have had to confess that it was an ideal state? (Davis, 1905/1961: II–267)

Thus in protecting the community from the dangers of big government, the Jacksonians left it wide open to the dangers of big business. But one need not stop here. The age of the robber barons was also both the fulfillment and the death of an American Dream. The great 'trusts' created by Elbert Gary and J.P. Morgan were based on a form of baronial agreement between business leaders. This was not unprecedented – Adam Smith comments on the spirit of collusion among merchants – but it led to the creation of public scrutiny and government regulation which would make such methods of operating illegal.

The strict Protestant ethos and the Darwinian interpretation of *noblesse oblige* driving the founders of the Vanderbilt, Carnegie and Rockefeller fortunes led them to participate in constructing a finance-capitalist order ruled by 'financiering' speculation[8] alien to their own values. J. Pierpont Morgan is an especially ironic figure. Perhaps more responsible than any other single person for creating the corporate-capitalist order of the turn of the century, Morgan was able to do so because he was *not* part of that order, but part of a hereditary, trinational banking aristocracy. Further, the world he created was one into which (after the securities laws of the 1930s) his kind

---

7 In this shift, the US was once again entering late into a relationship that had been proceeding apace in Europe since the Enlightenment. 'A great change that is still not without its effect on the law of corporations took place, or more properly, culminated in the sixteenth century. The standpoint from which all institutions were viewed was shifted from society as a whole to the individual. Social forces were conceived as moving from below and not from above. The destruction of tradition and the elevation of reason was one phase of the change. . . . Corporations were viewed not so much as *divisions of society* as *associations of individuals*' (Davis, 1905/1961: II–246).

8 Daniel Drew and Jim Fiske are perhaps the archetypes of this orientation. Cf., Gordon (1988) for one account of their careers.

did not fit. Barely two generations separate Vanderbilt, the first of the notorious robber barons, and Alfred Sloan, the harbinger of a new, managerial mode of control. Wachhorst (1981) notes the rapidity with which General Electric marginalized then eliminated its founder, the anti-scientific Edison, replacing him with team players working within the discourse of science, such as Jacob Steinmetz. The disapproval of Edison and John D. Rockefeller of the world they helped create has already been mentioned (Chapter 5).

From 1620 until 1890 it is relatively easy to see how the achievement of a Utopian vision created a society within which that vision became untenable.[9] Within the last century, this process is harder to see; there is too little space to provide historical perspective. If society is changing dramatically, however, it is likely that such processes are underway. Where are they operating and what is their effect likely to be? It would be prudent to avoid simple answers to this question, but one might consider it whenever one encounters – as one frequently does – statements about how America has 'always been ___' (fill in the blank).

The basic vocabulary of dream signifiers remains in circulation: opportunity, equality, self-determination, rationality, hard work, progress, salvation, merit. However, this constancy of terms masks profound shifts that have occurred in their meanings. Further, as Croly noted almost a century ago, America's ability to analyze America is limited by the belief that the founding institutions and documents of the country are basically perfect. Americans may well wonder, then, what will emerge from this latest crisis of American values. Others might wonder what they purchase from a US exporting this knowledge as value-free scientific findings.

Progress and Addiction: a Culture of Denial

Humankind has not always been preoccupied with filling needs. Weber (1904/1958) noted that it was more common to seek a given level of material well-being with the minimum of effort rather than to seek the greatest wealth with the greatest effort. A central obstacle to the builders of colonial empires was that colonized populations often felt no need for the benefits of wage labor until their indigenous social relationships had been undermined and their ability to support themselves outside the market economy was eliminated. In contrast, consider the conditions one finds in the US today, amid the greatest profusion of material goods owned by any society in

9 Baudrillard's (1989) characterization of America as an 'achieved Utopia' fails to capture this dynamic dimension, which shows achievement and destruction to go hand in hand. America has yet to produce a *sustainable* dream. Every incarnation has been predicated on escaping, rather than nurturing the relationships on which society depends. This has implications for the applicability of American thought to the issue of sustainable economic development.

history. The overwhelming sense is one of *need*, the need for more time, the need for support services, the need to get 'ahead,' and the need for the economy to grow. Economic and business thought is founded on the principle of scarcity. One rarely even sees measures of aggregate wealth or poverty. It is not even the need to grow. The basis for social debate is the (ratio-nal) *rate* of growth. However, if growth could solve the problem of need, one would expect it to become less, rather than more, prominent as society grows.

Galbraith long ago made this point in *The Affluent Society* (1958) . Later, in *The New Industrial State* (1967), he more explicitly addressed a source of this paradox – the same industrial processes which have resulted in the mass production of goods and services have been applied to the mass production of needs themselves. A special half-century (1938) anniversary issue of *Printers' Ink* (the trade periodical of the US advertising industry) implicitly supports Galbraith by tracing the slow development of national markets for advertising, technologies of reproduction and new relationships between media outlets, producers and advertisers. That modern advertising creates needs is not a revelation,[10] but the circularity of this system bears mention.

Walter Dill Scott was one of the industrial psychologists whose career ticket was involvement in the army's use of psychological selection in the First World War. He went on to found one of the first consulting companies (1920) and to publish one of the most durable texts on personnel management.[11] Scott also wrote *The Theory and Practice of Advertising*[12] (1903). In other words, *the same knowledge used to produce the producers of products became the knowledge used to produce the needs of the consumer.* This is the point at which the system becomes independent of any requirement that it contribute to social welfare. It is self-sufficient, producing goods, services, the producers of goods and services and the needs for goods and services. All it needs from external constituencies is constant growth. This is the short circuit which results in the simultaneous existence in the US of an unprecedented level of material wealth *and* an unprecedented level of need.

In a world of increasingly limited resources, this is untenable. Yet it is fundamental to the discourse of management to direct conservation of resources toward perpetual growth. As long as the primary responsibility of 'management' is thought to be stewardship to stockholders seeking to maximize investment growth, absolute levels of business production and social wealth are irrelevant; the absolute amount of growth must increase. Schaef and Fassel[13] have perceptively identified this as an addictive

---

10 Also worth browsing are Packard (1958) and Ewen (1976).

11 Scott and Clothier (1923); new editions 1931, 1941, 1949, 1954, 1961.

12 It appears this was a popular book. The preface notes that most of its chapters were originally serialized in *Mahin's Magazine*. The copy I have found was printed in 1916, indicating a fairly long in-print life.

13 Schaef (1987) and Schaef and Fassel (1988).

perspective. Their insightful books analyze organizational practices using the framework of 12-step recovery groups. Unfortunately, perhaps because they write for a popular audience, Schaef and Fassel have had no impact on organization theory. Within the context of history, one could go beyond Schaef and Fassel to say that not only do dysfunctional organizations produce addictive behaviors, *the very structure of industrial, corporate-capitalist organizing is based on an addictive understanding of experience in the world*. At one time, this could be dismissed as a problem only for social critics. Today it is also a problem for those with no goal other than long-term productivity. The short-term 'quarterly report' mentality of American management is soundly and regularly criticized, but seldom does the critic reflect an understanding that this dysfunctionality is the logical production of the relationships put in place between 1870 and 1920. Today, even the business conservative, if s/he is interested in building viable organizations, must question the Ponzi logic of 'general management.' But this is difficult to do when organizational knowledge is taught as an evolving science.

(R)evolving Science or Procrustean Bed?

In Greek mythology, Procrustes was a somewhat less than customer-centered host who either stretched or amputated his guests to fit the length of the bed in which they were to sleep. If one is seeking a metaphor for understanding organizational knowledge, the myth of Procrustes may be more timely than the myth of evolution.[14] As Table 7.1 illustrates, the view that organizational knowledge is steadily evolving can only be held if one systematically refuses to look at a great deal of the historical material that is available.[15] By 1920, the poles of difference today characterized as hard *versus* soft, X *versus* Y or 'macro' *versus* 'micro' were both clearly articulated and interrelated. If this relationship has never been entirely trouble-free, then neither is it clear that present-day integrative perspectives have a great deal to add to what was known by the employment managers' movement and Scientific Management. However, in the last several decades one can trace several 'procrustean revolutions,'[16] which continue to this day.[17] Where the pattern of 'evolution' is constant change based on

14 The term 'myth' in this context is not used to connote erroneous or merely superstitious belief. My perspective is closer to that of Barthes (1972). Even scientific cultures, as Midgeley (1985) notes, must contextualize scientific data within larger structures of meaning which are themselves not subject to falsification. Newell and Simon (1976: 115) call these 'laws of qualitative structure;' I prefer the more anthropological term 'myth.'

15 This is not to say that the landmark studies cited made no contribution to theory. However, to see them as formulating what had previously been observed into a hypothetico-deductive discursive language is very different from believing these were the first ones to have the insights at the heart of those formulations.

16 My neologism.

17 This is also discussed in White and Jacques (1995).

processes of adaptation to a changing environment, a procrustean revolution fosters the appearance of change by incorporating the new, but only after stretching and/or truncating it so that what is incorporated retains the shape of the old. This procrustean transformation is literally a 'revolution' in the facetious sense used above; it continues to revolve around the same issues and continues to present the same limited range of potential solutions. Perhaps it is in this spirit that we should understand the new 'revolutionaries' of Chapter 1.

A century's perspective: Procrustes in action

The evisceration of McGregor is one example of this process, but there are many others, including Frederick Taylor. Today, Taylor is widely associated with McGregor's Theory X vision of management, but if one compares *The Principles of Scientific Management* to *The Human Side of Enterprise*, both authors paint quite a similar picture of the prevailing managerial norms they are criticizing. Taylor can be constructed as McGregor's opposite only by neglecting Taylor's advocacy of higher wages and lower overall effort for workers, as well as his sensitivity to the process of implementing work process change. Similarly, maintaining this dichotomy requires that McGregor must be constructed as a simple-minded advocate of impression management with no regard for work process design.

Then there is Hawthorne, the Gettysburg of management history. Within the mainstream story of management history, the Hawthorne studies are credited with discovering the informal organization and the importance of social relations. This alleged discovery is generally cited as the foundation of the human relations movement. What was and was not discovered at Hawthorne is being debated to this day,[18] but this event can only stand out as radically changing the dimensions of management knowledge if one selectively forgets a great deal of background information (most of Chapters 5 and 6). *Management and the Worker* 'discovered' much that was already believed by Elton Mayo in his article 'The Irrational Factor in Society (1922).' It was a central theme of industrial psychology and the employment managers' movement. It was well recognized by Taylor who argued that implementation of Scientific Management in 'even a simple establishment' would take 'from two to three years' because of the need to effect a 'change in the mental attitude of the workman,' starting with one worker and building to 'a complete revolution in the public opinion of the whole establishment' (Taylor, 1911: 131–2).

This procrustean interplay of memory and forgetting can result in the amputation of entire streams of thought. Consider the irony of behaviorism. Narrative and textual research or theory based on critical social thought is routinely dismissed from mainstream organizational research circles with the claim that organizational science is an empirical discipline. At the same

18 See discussion in Hollway (1991), Gillespie (1991).

Table 7.1   *Is organizational knowledge 'evolving'?*

The conventional wisdom . . .	. . . fails to account for
Expectancy theory was first articulated by Vroom in 1964.	Taylor (1911:131–2). Change should be introduced by first convincing one worker of the gains s/he will experience, then 'tactfully' changing others over, one by one as others become 'desirous to share in the benefits.'*
Mintzberg discovered in 1968 that managers do not do what Fayol (1916) had claimed.	Fayol wrote of the French 'bureau' just prior to the emergence of 'the new profession of handling men' (Bloomfield, 1916). The change articulated in 1968 by Mintzberg is noted by Bloomfield, A.W. Shaw Co. (1917) and others during the 'new industrial revolution'.
Contingency theory grew out of a Systems Theory perspective. Early formulations were Woodward (1965), Lawrence and Lorsch (1967).	Fisher (1917) noted the cooperation of workers was necessary in process technology environments; Bloomfield (1916) notes the special needs of service organizations. This documents three (industrial, process, service) contingent structures before 1920.
'Congruency' between internal systems and external environments was developed in Salter (1973) and subsequently (cf., Fry and Smith, 1987).	Perkins (1885) and Dewsnup (1906) discuss 'congruency' between departmental/divisional and line/staff functions in terms of varying external environments. Blackford and Newcomb (1914:198) reflect the spirit of the employment managers' movement when they speak of 'fitting the man to his job and to his environment.'
According to Yukl (1989), 'Great Man' theories were discredited early in this century as leadership theory evolved.	Consistent with Carnegie (1920), but what is missed is that 'Great Man' theories may have been not erroneous, but characteristic of a set of social relations then passing into history as 'the manager' emerged.
The distinction of mechanistic/organic organizational forms dates from Burns and Stalker (1961). It is widely believed post-industrial organizations will be more organic.	Drever (1929) identifies organizations having moved through a 'mechanistic' phase into an 'organic' phase and claims that the needs of organizations are entering a third phase which must go beyond both.
The 1994 formation by the Academy of Management of an interest group dedicated to Business and the Natural Environment represents the emergence of a new 'green' business consciousness.	The very *idea* of management and the manager was based on a pervasive shift from 'pioneering' conquest to managerial stewardship of increasingly scarce and exhaustible natural and human resources (Taylor, 1911; Person, 1926; Blackford and Newcomb, 1914; Quick, 1913).
Job enrichment/enlargement expanded the narrow time/motion perspective of Taylorism to advocate worker control of a 'natural' unit of work (e.g., Hackman, Oldham, Janson and Purdy, 1975).	This was quite consistent with industrial psychology's advocacy of the 'worker-in-his-work unit' articulated at least as early as 1923 by Scott and Clothier.

Table 7.1   *continued*

The conventional wisdom . . .	. . . fails to account for
McGregor (1960: 47) found that 'The expenditure of physical and mental effort in work is as natural as play or rest.'	'Industry, like health, is normal,' wrote Blackford and Newcomb (1914: 12), articulating an already fully developed perspective of employment management and industrial psychology shared by McGregor two generations later.
'The Term Quality of Work Life (QWL) was initially introduced during the 1960s to emphasize the prevailing poor quality of life in the work place' (Bowditch and Buono, 1994).	QWL reproduces the concerns of welfare work, the vocational movement and the employment managers' movement between the late 1800s and about 1920.
Management thought is steadily evolving.	Compare a contemporary HRM text with Blackford & Newcomb (1914) to see how fully the boundaries of this area were staked out before the First World War.

* I thank Mark Dunaway, doctoral student at CSPP, for this observation.

time, Behaviorist research has been marginalized *despite* its relatively strong empirical support, a relatively clear methodology for rejection of false hypotheses and a concise language of variables and causal relations upon which to build cumulative results. On center stage in this 'empirical' discipline, one finds theorists such as Maslow and Herzberg, despite the questionable empirical support generated for their positions.

In the last quarter-century, every new theme in organization studies has been subject to this procrustean trimming. As of about 1970, the human problems of management could be adequately described as clustering around a few core problems of the worker: motivation, satisfaction, productivity and leadership. Since that time, new topics have not so much represented additional topic areas or refinements of categories, but new *lenses through which* to view all of the knowledge of the field. Gender, race, culture, the 'paradigm' debates, international management, diversity,[19] and post-industrialism have each created a tension between those who see in the emerging topic a new way of looking at organizing and those who see only a new variable to be added to the conventional wisdom. White and Jacques (1995) discuss this point with reference to the rise and fall of organizational culture:

> In the late 1970s, it seemed possible that the concept of organizational culture as a
> new metaphor for understanding social systems would challenge theorists to more

19 This is not redundant. Race entered US organizational discourse about 1968; gender about 1973. The main theme of these research streams has been the underlying similarity of all people once one 'controls for' differences of socialization. Diversity emerged as a topic about 1988 emphasizing fundamental differences between identity groups. It is not directly contradictory to earlier thinking about race and gender, but fusing the two periods of thought is a delicate matter not free of contradiction (cf., Scott, 1990; Vogel, 1990; Jacobson and Jacques, 1990).

cautiously contextualize the benefits and limits of research modeled on the physical sciences by comparing such models of inquiry with the more interpretive models of anthropology and sociology. Very quickly, however, culture began to be absorbed into mainstream theorizing. As a result, its critical potential was seriously diluted or entirely lost. As early as 1980, Morgan and Smircich warned of this trend. Smircich (1983) attempted to distinguish between approaches treating culture as a 'variable' and those treating culture as a 'root metaphor.' For the former, culture was an attribute of organizations, something an organization *had*. For the latter, culture was something an organization *was*.

This literature has been assimilated into organizational discourse in the last decade – but not uniformly. In the process, the critical potential of this literature has been marginalized while more functionalist theory demonstrating manipulation of the culture 'variable' has taken center stage (cf., Deal and Kennedy, 1982; Schein, 1985, Hampden-Turner 1990). By the late 1980s, concern was being expressed that the critical potential of the culture movement had been lost (Calás and Smircich, 1987; Frost, 1988; White and Jacques, 1995: 47).

After enough cycles, the pattern becomes clear. Organizational knowledge is not evolving, except in a peripheral way, adopting new terms and sites of application as times change. However, from 1920 to date the central concepts, problems and methods of evaluating what will count as significant new knowledge have remained rock solid. As they enter organizational discourse, new topics lose whatever is challenging to this core.[20] Revolving around this central axis, organizational knowledge remains dominated by the labor question, the works management question and the trust question.

Re-framing Old Questions

How does one develop a critically reflective perspective on this core knowledge, one that will scrutinize it in light of its cultural and historical context rather than religiously assuming it as a prerequisite for expertise? It is fashionable in the quick-draw culture of the US – as argued in earlier chapters – to prescribe answers, assuming that questions are clear to all. This book will advocate the more modest goal of asking what *questions* are the most critical to ask. The following pages will discuss several current organizational topics, applying the perspectives of earlier chapters to suggest new ways of framing the questions usually asked by managers and academics. Note how each topic exhibits the following qualities: (1) It is currently framed in a way that reflects embedded US cultural values; thus, they may not reflect the experiences of other societies; (2) These values are predominantly values of an *industrial* period; thus, they are increasingly outdated for *any* society; (3) Discussion around these issues is shaped by the survival into the industrial order of US *Federalist* values which were not even current to the period which is *passing*. This book will not presume to say what action is appropriate relative to these issues. The purpose of these

---

20 For instance, the issue of paradigmatic incommensurability is regularly pronounced a false problem after having been trivialized into the very different question of whether 'qualitative methods' are acceptable in mainstream inquiry.

pages is to contribute to re-framing these issues in terms central to today's problems and conflicts rather than those of another era.

Motivation research

At the center of the present management knowledge universe are the interrelated topics of motivation and leadership (scan management texts and the management shelves of the local book superstore). Although they will be discussed separately here, each is the complement of the other. Motivation makes sense only where a group is divided into those who wish to direct the actions of others and others who, for whatever reason, are resistant to being directed. Leadership theory offers both instrumental knowledge for overcoming the resistance of followers and criteria for who will be recognized as having legitimate power to lead. It may seem that these problems are so fundamental that any grouping of people through time must have encountered them. Indeed, Robbins (1990: 36) finds Moses having these problems. Rindova (1994) finds Theories X, Y and Z[21] applicable to analysis of ancient Chinese organizing. No doubt these authors identify documentable similarities, but they must also be aware of the operation of what might be termed the *semantic eclipse*.

In a lunar eclipse, observers on Earth see a small body blocking the view of a much larger one. In a semantic eclipse, a relatively small subset of meanings comes to block sight of a broader set of potential meanings. For instance, when a mode of rationality normative to Western culture, masculine behavior and the modern era is simply called rationality, the only category remaining for the reasoning of other cultures, women and other historical periods is *ir*rationality or *non*-rationality. Only a small area of the domain of rational behavior is visible; the rest is eclipsed by it. In this manner, the seemingly extensive body of motivation research draws attention to a specific subset of motivation problems and solutions while blinding the observer to a broader range of problems and possibilities.

What distinguishes the industrial problem of worker motivation from organizing problems of other times? Prior to the appearance of bureaucratized organizations, two 'motivators' were widely effective. The first was connection to output. Control of the worker was not important where survival dictated the production of a marketable product. This was true both of the free tradesperson and farmer and of the peasant. One could not neglect the master's share of the harvest without starving oneself. Where self-interest did not ensure worker participation, coercion was widely effective (bureaucratization itself does not preclude physical and non-physical forms of coercion from being applied to rule breakers). The limitation of bureaucracy is that, while it permits an ever-finer punitive mechanism to operate, it does not provide a means for positively eliciting worker cooperation. *Only where self-interest, coercion and rules are*

---

21 Theory Z (Ouchi, 1981) was the response to 'Japanese management' a decade ago.

insufficient does 'motivation' as it is currently understood appear as a topic for organizing. The worker is separated from output through division of labor. Coercion is socially proscribed or simply ineffective for the kind of effort required. Rules fail to secure worker discretion, as the phenomena of 'learned ignorance,' 'malicious compliance' and 'work to rule' indicate.

In this sense, motivation is an industrial concept. One can also find in it traces of the American Dream. Consider Hackett, Buycio and Guion's article (1989) on absenteeism. Positioning themselves within a broader stream of research, the authors frame the problem of being absent from work as an individual choice made by the 'absenteeist.'[22] They then explain their results in terms of differences in 'work ethic.' Under a veneer of scientific objectivity is the cultural artifact of perfectionist work-as-salvation. One should be cautious in accepting this interpretation. It easily becomes circular reasoning, since 'work ethic' is both a cause of absenteeism and a variable indicated *by* absenteeism. Were the term not a cultural artifact buffered by common sense, the authors' conclusions might be seen simply as a tautology. At minimum, their interpretation posits Protestant perfectionism as a basic human quality. This focus on the individual as the source of problems (in this case absence) can also blind one to important structural factors. Miller and Norton (1986), who were more attuned to the worker's context than her ethos, found the most important reason for absence was responsibility for sick children. It is very unlikely that such a finding could have emerged from a study that framed absence as a personal choice and was predisposed to understand absence as a function of personal work ethic.

The 'common sense' that the worker is a self-determining individual for whom work is part of an 'ethic' of improving oneself while doing the work of God and society (who are one) reflects the worldview of Freeman Hunt. Even in Hunt's time, the quasi-religious status of work reflected the past time of the Puritan/Quaker theocracies. This embeddedness of outdated Federalist values in an industrial situation is an obstacle to understanding the industrial subject – who would not even be a subject of motivation research were s/he not part of a complex, interdependent society. Although the motivation theorist explicitly seeks to facilitate managerial control of the worker, this goal cannot be named because of these archaically surviving cultural values. Control must be exercised within a rhetoric of self-determination and free individual choice which, if valid, would invalidate the very basis of motivation research itself![23]

22 This is not Hackett, Buycio and Guion's term. It is used to underscore the curious construction of work absence as an ideology, an *ism*. Through this construction, objective science serves a powerful ideological function *itself*, by institutionalizing work attendance – a novelty of modern industrial settings – as a normal aspect of human personality and by pathologizing absence as an ideology of which the worker is to be cured by proper motivation.

23 The possibility of gathering empirically valid data presumes that people will respond deterministically (within a range of probability) to situational stimuli; only to the extent that this is *not* so can subjects be said to be exercising free choice.

After studying nurses as examples of post-industrial knowledge workers[24] I would make a more extreme observation. What confirmatory motivation studies will never show is the possibility that the very concept of motivation, as it has been operationalized, actually exacerbates many contemporary problems of organizing. Theories of motivation have developed since the 'phenomenological shift' of organizational discourse and require separability of work practices from worker perceptions. One need not create meaning in work if one can create 'experienced meaningfulness'[25] in the worker. 'Motivation' has increasingly been removed from the worker and placed in the hands of managers and experts. Meaningful involvement with work practices has been separated from the design of work practices. To merely call for a proactive problem-solver in such a context amounts to no more than wishful thinking.

For massaging the perceptions of the alienated worker, motivation theory is ideally suited to assembly-line environments like Ford's River Rouge plant (and even they are changing). Of even greater importance are the vast groups of workers who do not need motivation in *any* traditional sense. Products of disciplinary education and disciplinary society in general, they have internalized a desire to do the job as a means of getting 'ahead'[26] and require of management that it *remove barriers* rather than *induce effort*. This would generally be the case of workers who think of themselves as professionals as well as those so-called 'knowledge workers' who are increasingly being touted as the critical post-industrial worker. Consider the example of nurses, the largest occupational group in the US. Colonized by business theories, nursing management has often applied traditional theories of motivation, and often wondered why they had so little effect. Increasingly, voices within the literature are recognizing that, for many nurses, work systems which facilitate discretionary nursing activity directed toward developing a relationship with the patient are the most effective motivators.[27] That is, nurses do not have to be *motivated* to do the work; they are motivated when they are *supported* in doing the work *effectively*. For these workers, what has been the central topic of micro organizational theorizing is, for all intents and purposes, irrelevant[28] as formulated. Worse, motivation theory is functioning as a barrier to understanding this form of work. Management researchers studying nursing have confirmed or failed to confirm hypotheses generated elsewhere, but they have not discovered the potential irrelevance of their hypotheses to the situations studied, nor have they discovered new forms of working.[29]

24 Jacques (1992a, 1993).

25 The term is a variable in the Hackman and Oldham job characteristics model (Hackman et al., 1975).

26 Ahead of what? Nobody knows.

27 Benner and Wrubel (1989), Chandler (1992), Gordon (1991b).

28 Nursing satisfaction surveys routinely reflect a desire to be given the authority and support to perform the work effectively Jacques (1992a).

29 Jacques (1992a).

Leadership

The other side of motivation is leadership. If workers need to be motivated, they need to be motivated *by* someone or some group. One could say that leadership is the study of how to effectively and legitimately motivate members of an organization. But who or what is a leader? To what extent is 'leadership', as it has come to be constructed as an organizational research topic (and business publishing and consulting 'industry'[30]), based on Federalist cultural values rather than the universal needs of organizing, as the literature presumes? Writing for *Newsweek*, Michael Elliott recently commented that '"Leadership" is a peculiarly American word.' Elliott noted the absence of an equivalent term in Germany (*'Führerschaft'*?), France or even Britain. 'Non-Americans typically think history moves because great social motors of demography, culture, technology and economics hum away.' But even 'very sophisticated Americans,' he writes, 'tend to think epochs are shaped by "leaders."' (Elliott, 1994: 67) – one week later, *Fortune* magazine ran a cover feature crediting Lee Iacocca with the development of Chrysler's minivan.[31] Within the leadership literature, the 'universal' leader tends to look very much like the following *Business Week* description of the typical US CEO based on demographics of the 'Business Week Corporate Elite.'[32]

> Is there a typical big-company chief executive? As it happens, there is. . . . Henry Schacht of Cummins Engine . . . happens to fit comfortably in many of the categories of *Business Week*'s Corporate Elite. . . . Schacht's age is right: 55 (the average is 56). He was born in a Middle Atlantic state (Pennsylvania). He graduated from Yale with a Bachelor of Science degree, among CEOs the most popular degree at the most popular undergraduate college, and took an MBA from Harvard, which leads the list of graduate schools. He came up on the finance/accounting side, the most common career track. (Mims and Lewis, 1989: 23)

The article also notes that the average 'elite'[33] CEO has been a 'boss' for sixteen years, owns 55,000 shares of stock and has been with the organization for twenty-three years. Perhaps too obvious for comment, Schacht is also the normative sex (male) and race (white). This analysis is very revealing of the 'universal' subject of organizational studies: a male, a mid-American, a carrier of mainstream class values, an Anglo-Saxon[34] or someone easily mistaken for one.

30 This characterization is not mine but *Fortune* magazine's (Huey, 1994b: 54).

31 Taylor (1994).

32 Some will argue whether a manager and a leader are the same. Without addressing this question, if those with the formal responsibility for leading the 1000 largest companies in the country are not the subjects of leadership theorizing, it is difficult to imagine who might be.

33 These are the CEOs of the 1000 most valuable US companies based on stock value.

34 This has been a dynamic, yet very real boundary through American history. Benjamin Franklin might have thought Schacht one of the 'Palatine boors,' but German-Americans were 'white' compared with the 'brunette types' from Eastern Europe who composed much of the late nineteenth-century wave of immigrants – and they have become 'white' while African-American, Latino, native American and Asian American citizens have not.

In the early industrial organization, there was a close relationship between the power to lead and bureaucratic authority. The 'leader' was the owner-operator who built and owned the organization. As ownership moved to investors uninvolved with operations, and control moved to the general office (a level above the individual business enterprise), 'leaders' such as Elbert Gary and Alfred Sloan[35] emerged who were neither adventurers nor Darwinian predators, but builders of committees, proselytizers of 'cooperation' and skilled players of the game of consensus building. It has been seventy or more years since leader*ship* was embodied in a single leader.

> [I]f the president of a telephone company for good reasons orders two poles carrying a cable removed from the north side of First Street between A and B Streets to the opposite side of First Street, it can, I think, be approximately demonstrated that carrying out that order involves perhaps 10,000 decisions of 100 men located at 15 points, requiring successive analyses of several environments, including social, moral, legal, economic, and physical facts of the environment, and requiring 9000 redefinitions and refinements of purpose, and 1000 changes of purpose. . . . [W]ithin organizations, especially of complex types, there is a technique of decision, an organizational process of thinking, which may not be analogous to that of the individual. (Barnard, 1938: 198–9)

In the bureaucratic, market-capitalist world of large organizations that has become the present-day US, the influence of highly placed individuals acting on their own initiative represents a very small portion of the overall direction and control that shapes the organization. It represents a legitimate topic of study, certainly, but a narrow one. Through what semantic eclipse has *the leader* blossomed into an entire industry to the exclusion of the other areas of leader*ship*? Why, more than half a century after Barnard, do we have so much knowledge about the 'great man' and so much less about the 'functions of the executive'?[36] Once again, a profitable first step toward usefully theorizing leadership in the post-industrial would be to exorcise the ghost of Freeman Hunt from today's discourse of leadership.

Pioneering, conquest and manifest destiny continue to sell well as expertise on leadership. Learn *The Leadership Secrets of Attila the Hun* (Roberts, 1986), study Machiavelli or Sun Tsu and plunder the vanquished. Kanter literally names this view 'cowboy management,' criticizing companies where 'the cowboy is viewed as the ultimate entrepreneur and the frontier metaphor is invoked frequently' (1989a: 70). The turn-of-the-century 'Morganization' of industry was based on the principle of cooperation between producers. In 1911, Taylor announced that system was already preeminent over the individual in the workplace. By 1926, Person would characterize the 'management movement' as emerging from the triumph of stewardship and conservation over pioneering wastefulness.

---

35 Of US Steel and General Motors respectively (Chandler, 1962; Sloan, 1964; Tarbell, 1925).

36 One might note that 'the executive' is not necessarily even an individual. The executive *function* may well be predominantly interpersonal rather than personal.

Within an American cultural context, the image of the trailblazer may flatter the person who imagines him/herself to be a leader, but what does it have to do with the world of large-organization functioning?

A more recent, and seemingly divergent stream of thinking about leadership shares surprisingly similar cultural roots. A plethora of contemporary titles emphasize leadership as a form of cooperation, communication and, above all, service:[37] *Principle Centered Leadership, The Visionary Leader, Lost Profit [sic]: The Art of Caring Leadership, The Leader Within: An Empowering Path of Self-Discovery, The Soul of Business: Managing for Profit and the Common Good, How to Make a Buck and Still be a Decent Human Being.*[38] The themes of these books follow a strong path from Cotton Mather, through Benjamin Franklin to Freeman Hunt. Unfortunately, they reflect a world that disappeared in Hunt's century, – the world of self-employed and self-governing individuals working in a system where individual interest, community interest and the teachings of God converge.[39] Remembering this Federalist community helps to explain the oxymoron 'servant leadership.'[40] Consider Max DePree, the celebrity CEO of Hermann Miller. DePree (1989) makes much of business as a custodial responsibility. This, in itself, is laudable. What easily misses one's attention is that the primary custodial responsibility is not to the workers, but to God – the same Protestant God one serves through success in business, which is equated with serving society and advancing the welfare of the community. Robert Greenleaf's *Servant Leadership* is published by the Paulist religious order who have also published the more straightforwardly titled *Servant Leaders of the People of God* (Schwartz, 1989). The servant leader is not a servant to those 'below' but to the One 'above.' Servant leadership is not post-hierarchical, but pre-hierarchical, reverting to a seigneurial sense of obligation and responsibility, a premodern Great Chain of Being.

Through these beliefs, a specific religious/cultural ethos has been held up as universally representative of the values, perceptions and behaviours of people in organizations. Because the roots of these ideals are not evident, they cannot be understood. Because they are not understood, nostalgia for a lost Federalist community passes as progressive thinking about the future of large organizations. This is not a critique of religious belief or of the benevolence of business people like Max DePree. It is an attempt to point to the disjunction between these ideals and present social practices. The Puritan/Quaker, the Jeffersonian and the Federalist circulate freely through this discourse, but industrial – to say nothing of post-industrial – social practices have yet to penetrate this common sense. This is evident in a recent *Fortune* cover story on 'post-heroic leadership' (Huey, 1994b). Intending to

37 Stephen Covey, discussed in Chapter 3, is also an example of this growing body of writing.
38 Autry (1991), Champlin (1993), Chappell (1993), Covey (1990b), Haas (1992), Rose and Garrett (1992).
39 This is admittedly a simplistic characterization; see Chapters 3–5.
40 Greenleaf (1977), Schwartz (1989), Stevens and Schoberg (1990).

announce the emergence of post-industrial leader-follower relations, the article continually notes changing conditions whose demise signalled the *arrival*, not the *passing* of industrial reality. Leadership, supposedly, used to be 'in the cut of your jib;' forget training, 'you had it or you didn't' (Huey, 1994b: 42). The author cites Warren Bennis as saying 'whips and chains are no longer an alternative' (Huey, 1994b: 44). Nonetheless, the post-heroic situation 'still requires many of the attributes that have always distinguished the best leaders' and 'the *pioneers* who forge ahead are most likely to claim the future' (Huey, 1994b: 50; emphasis added). What passes for progressive analysis in 1994 would have been accepted as a good description of the 'new industrial revolution' by *its* 'pioneers' in the 1920s. Until these ideas are studied as the product of a discourse specific to a particular culture and era, this recycling of folk belief, presented as serious critique of emerging trends, will continue.

Management and the manager: one and the same?

Just as leadership can be envisioned as something more than the self-determining actions of a special elite defined as leaders, so also might the industrial image of the manager create a semantic eclipse blinding observers to the broader issues of managing. 'Management' is the collection of activities which constitute organizing; it is not necessarily embodied in an organizational group of that name.

In my prior research, observing primary-care nurses, two points impressed me. One was that the nurse manager, who worked twelve-hour days, was seldom present on the nursing unit. She explained her job as managing the environment so the staff could manage the unit. The other point had to do with the Fayolian 'management' responsibilities handled by the direct care providers themselves. The complex coordination of tasks and interrelationship of specialists and specialized departments necessary for the daily operation of a tertiary-care medical unit operated with an 'autokinetic ease' reminiscent of the pre-managerial Whitin Machine Works.[41] One could extrapolate from the nurses to ask how many engineers, software developers, and other more normative post-industrial knowledge workers 'manage' in this sense. This raises a serious challenge to the habit of assuming management to be the work done by a specialized group of employees called managers. The manager appeared with two key roles. One was to maintain order and to see that the interests of employers were carried

---

41 Cf., Navin (1950: Chapter 4). While I have not had the opportunity to do so, one might profitably apply the 'co-entrepreneurial' model of Whitin Machine's early years to this situation. Thinking of these nurses as 'foremen' [*sic*] might be illuminating as a model for creating the appropriate authority, responsibility and reward structure for these 'knowledge workers.' Ironically, this model might fit better than the management models that have 'evolved' over the last century.

out.[42] The other was to function as a bearer of expertise.[43] It is unclear whether there is the need for a specialized group of employees to perform either function in many of today's work environments.

The current platitude (that in post-industrial organizations increasing worker self-management will be the norm) appears to address this issue more directly than it does. Do 'self-managing' workers give themselves promotions? Do they set production goals or make production technology decisions? What are the limits of self-management? The completely self-managing worker or work group would become an independent contractor. This is not without precedent. The 'job' lot worker and the steel puddling group were 'self-managing' in today's terms. Were this to become the norm, academic organizational knowledge would be without a constituency, since it exists to train that specialized group called 'managers', speaks most frequently from that group's perspective,[44] and is structured institutionally to speak *to* managers *about* employees. Within present management discourse, managers represent 'the' organization; workers are merely a contingent resource need.[45] What does this imply for the distribution of authority, and reward, in organizations? How can change agents hired under the sole authority of managers have any degree of effectiveness in creating a post-managerial work climate? *To whom* does one address knowledge about self-managing employees, managers? Management knowledge would have to be institutionally transformed for it to be able to speak to representatives of 'the organization' and workers contracting with them in a way that reflected the two parties' interests equally. The manager, like the leader, has sedimented into American management ideology by filling the hole left by the disappearance of the Federalist 'man of reason.' Management today might be most usefully understood as the power to influence the flow of information and the authority relationships through which work is organized. While this flow is embodied at various points by specific individuals, it does not emanate from a distinct body of 'managers' who own it. While it results in differences of authority and reward, these must increasingly be legitimated through criteria other than mere position in a management hierarchy. The emerging world will be held together through different patterns of relationships from the world with which we are familiar.

42 Marglin (1974) claims this was the only reason for management. Whether one agrees with him or not, his article raises a number of provocative points.

43 Taylor's system (1911) required the creation of seven types of factory floor 'bosses'.

44 A request for funding proposals distributed at the 1994 Academy of Management meeting by the Foundation for Excellence in Consulting and Management exemplifies this reincorporation of the new into the familiar. The proposals solicited are on the subject of work, meaning and motivation as 'the business world is redefining itself.' The proposal explicitly requires that such thinking address issues *from a management perspective* (emphasis in the original). This stipulation underscores the boundary the field has imposed on itself. It is not about organizing or managing as general processes; it is about knowledge to support the industrially produced organizational subgroup known as 'management.'

45 Pfeffer and Baron (1988) is a vivid application of this assumption.

Whether one sees one's role as supporter of the *status quo*, scientist or social critic – or elements of all three – effective action to influence this emerging order will be greatly assisted by understanding of the historical and cultural processes through which the Federalist/industrial 'manager' has been constructed.

Total Quality Management and Business Process Re-engineering

In a decade, TQM/BPR has gone from being touted as the invincible key to Japanese management to being called a tired fad. If this becomes the fate of BPR, it will not be surprising. How this has been able to occur without discussion of the critical potential of TQM/BPR says more about the limits of management discourse than it does about the merits of this school of thought.[46]

The first thing many organizations did when committing to TQM/BPR efforts was to send workers to classes where they were taught statistical quality control tools. Treating TQM/BPR as a tool to be used immediately rather than as a challenge to one's ways of thinking about organizing is, as they say, 'as American as apple pie.' The 'real' (that is, Federalist) American *already* knows what to think about problems. All s/he needs is good tools and the freedom to use them. It is also very American to seek a return to the freedom from limits that characterized pioneering reality. As those who have been involved in any organizational change effort know, change comes slowly and with great effort. Yet the contemporary US evangelist of Quality claims it to be 'free' and achievable 'without tears.'[47] Three centuries after the Plymouth colony, the good American still has credibility discovering Utopia. A common justification for the allegedly limited potential of TQM/BPR in the US is that it requires group cooperation and Americans are an individualistic bunch. There is no denying that the *ideology* of individualism plays a major role in shaping US work behaviors, but it has been a century since cooperation and interdependence became the structuring principles of work in industrial/post-industrial settings. To recognize individualistic bias as a problem to be addressed would be appropriate. To claim it as a basis for dismissing TQM/BPR is to deny the existence of large-organization work relationships, privileging instead an extinct Federalist order. But, of course, since it is not permissible within the current discourse to recognize that it disappeared in the 1880s, it is not necessary to face the impossibility of bringing it back.

46 I consider Scientific Management, Total Quality Management and Business Process Re-engineering to represent a single, coherent line of thought through the history of management. Each has contained insights and blinders specific to its time and context, but all share a paradigmatic philosophy that 'organization' represents a network of product-related workflows. This view exists in marked contrast to the industrial managerial view of organization as authority hierarchies based on functional areas.

47 Philip Crosby, *Quality Without Tears* (1985), *Quality is Free* (1979).

What has been lost to Procrustes is, arguably, the most radical insight of TQM/BPR, the realization that functional division of work and authority is inappropriate to effective large-organizational performance (and perhaps has been since the 'second industrial revolution'). This is a 'paradigmatic' problem of the first order. It requires moving from a reality based on work function and task to one based on work process flow. It requires a leap similar to the 'phenomenological shift' discussed in Chapter 6. TQM/BPR suggest a remapping of authority in organizations. Instead of chopping work problems up into 'accounting problems,' 'personnel problems,' 'production problems,' et cetera, a process-oriented focus follows work processes across functional areas. One need not inhale the superheated rhetoric of recent popular books documenting TQM/BPR successes to see that there is much at stake: the organization which successfully adopts a process orientation can gain significant production and marketing advantages relative to time, cost and flexibility,[48] but in this organization what constitutes authority and who will hold it will have changed. This is perhaps the most significant shift in the dynamics of large organizations in this century. But how does one escape an industrially bounded American discourse to ask the hard questions raised by this shift?

Hierarchical divisions within functionally bounded 'fiefdoms'[49] are the current structure within which organizational authority and reward flow. This system took at least a half-century to coalesce. To suggest that a serious remapping of these relationships will be accomplished by sending a few workers to statistical quality control classes is laughable, but so is the view that a shift toward process-centered authority relationships can be avoided by dismissing TQM/(BPR?) as a fad. But how can one effect change when those who have the power to support change have gained that power through rising within functional hierarchies, giving them the greatest vested interest in the *status quo*? What effect would this product-centered view of work have on an organizational order in which the operational unit has been losing prominence for more than a century to a corporate-level general office whose reality is centered on financial, not product-related, phenomena?[50]

One instance of new thinking that could be stimulated by the portion of TQM/BPR thinking lost to Procrustes is in the area of work/family. The status of work/family issues is dramatically changed if one applies the TQM/BPR principle of thinking about the domestic unit as supplier partnership. To envision the home as a *supplier* – of worker health, education and welfare, of relational skills and relational workers – suggests that work/family should not be thought of in terms of work *versus* family. Rather, 'Home Incorporated' must be thought of as an equal partner, one

---

48 Peters (1992); Hammer and Champy (1993).

49 This explicit, if casual, feudal reference is frequently made in corporate settings.

50 For Chandler (1962) this dominance is practically the defining feature of the modern industrial organization.

with whom one negotiates for mutual advantage. This suggests that both ignoring the home and dictating terms of work transfer to the home are inappropriate practices for the successful TQM/BPR organization.

A final question, largely overlooked by the critical community, is what potential for resistance lies in the challenge to established authority relationships posed by TQM/BPR. If a process-centered organization will require new process 'owners,' new criteria for reward, new boundaries relating to job definition, discretionary authority and organizational commitment to worker learning, what voices will participate in defining the new relationships? The critical purist may find an anti-TQM/BPR position intellectually expedient, but to remove oneself from the discourse of organizing may not be the most effective form of engagement. This is admittedly a complex dilemma, not entirely unlike one faced in the last century when labor was divided between those seeking to retain control of the labor process and those willing to accede to collective bargaining within a managerially controlled order.

Pay-for-performance/outcome-centered work

As organizational environments come to require more discretionary efforts on the part of the worker, one increasingly hears advocates of compensation schemes in which pay is linked to performance. That this is appropriate is defensible; that it represents something new indicates a serious lack of perspective. In 1850, all but a few free, male workers (that is, those upon whose interests social structures were based) were paid for performance. Scientific Management's advocacy of piece-rate schemes and 'high-priced labor' reflected the inadequacy of flat-rate wages at the turn of the century. Scanlon plans and profit sharing have indicated a desire to connect compensation to performance throughout this century. If the flat-rate wage or salary has remained the dominant form of payment for labor, one has to ask what interests it has served.

Chapter 2 began with two voices of outrage. Abraham Zaleznik decries a management culture that confuses busy-work with achievement. Judith Bardwick, under the imprimatur of the American Management Association, finds workers 'entitled,' expecting rewards for their efforts rather than their accomplishments. That these conditions do not produce high-performance organizations is quite plausible, but the authors' outrage suggests a lack of perspective leading to misplaced blame. This book has traced the broad outlines of the bitter social transformations through which it became normative to be a 'wage worker for life.' Workers (managers or operatives) who did not develop this attitude were first purged as syndicalists, anarchists and radicals; later they were trained through disciplinary practices to develop the right 'sentiments' toward work. Today, they expect a paycheck regardless of their level of contribution to 'value added'? *Quelle surprise*!

Why can presumed experts on organizing blame the worker for processes laboriously constructed against the worker's express intentions? It helps greatly that the process of construction has been largely forgotten. This is facilitated by the narrow scientism fashionable in organization studies. Historical study is 'merely' anecdotal; the field has 'progressed' to rigorous data collection. Here science and culture support each other. The Federalist is a self-knowing, self-motivated figure responsible for his/her actions. The Federalist citizen creates society, but the reverse is not true. It stands to reason, then, that if workers are 'entitled' it is because they choose to be and they should be criticized for this choice.

Contributing to this reasoning is a dichotomization of US thought. If individuals are influenced by their social setting, they are not accountable for their actions. One is *either* self-determining *or* an automaton free of moral responsibility. This has become the axis of Liberal/Conservative assumptions to such a degree that it seems to occur to nobody that one could be socially produced as a subject *and* still held accountable for one's actions. Within this simplistic, jingoistic and moralizing perspective, it is impossible to develop a complex picture of the worker as simultaneously a product of flat-payment compensation and a participant in its sedimentation. The worker cannot be conceptualized as having a 'nature' profoundly influenced by this system and also having self-awareness. For instance, forty years of research have gone into determining whether work is a 'central life interest' (CLI) of the employee.[51] Even if one believes this question can be answered in such general terms, work remains a central life *practice*. Would it not be more useful to ask how varying social influences and organizational structures influence the *construction* of worker attachment to, or alienation from, the job? Townley (1993, 1994) has suggested a re-framing of human resource management that would permit such an understanding. This can be facilitated by excavating the historical and cultural baggage that has become attached to views of employee nature.

International management or post-colonial studies?[52]

Viewed historically, the recent prominence of 'international management' is a curious phenomenon. By the time the US *emerged* as an industrial power in the *1890s*, 'the conquest of the international markets' was occurring (Simons, 1912: 309). Throughout the present century, US firms have routinely produced, purchased and sold abroad. It caused no crisis of American management consciousness when Servan-Schreiber predicted that by the 1980s the world's third largest industrial power, 'after the United States and Russia, will not be Europe, but *American industry in Europe*' (1967: 3; emphasis in the original). Could it be that the long-established American mindset of 'US first and the rest nowhere,' noted by Lawson

---

51 Cf., Dubin (1956) and the research this has spawned.
52 I would like to thank CSPP student Utama Sandjaja for his valuable assistance in bringing many of these sources to my attention.

(1903: 5) was upset by the oil shocks of the 1970s, by the loss of several industry sectors to East Asian countries and the loss of global hegemony enjoyed by the US automobile industry? The present business school emphasis on international management cannot reflect recent international- ization of organizations, because such internationalization is not a new phenomenon. What it may reflect, which would be a new trend, is the passing of centralized control and profit accrual from the US to other countries. International management is perhaps a euphemism for 'manag- ing' to resist this diffusion of economic power.

This phenomenon is reinforced within management education, in part for very different reasons. As shown in earlier chapters, the university has been structured by the changing needs of various times. Today, one demographic reality of the American university is declining US enrollment in the face of a growing 'export market' as the economies of other nations, especially in the so-called 'third' world, grow, permitting their students to study in the schools of the world's dominant economic power. At one, superficial, level, this has resulted in competition to market schools to non-US students as institutions cognizant of the multitude of problems and perspectives faced by businesses worldwide. Beneath the addition of a little international case material, however, what is exported worldwide is a curriculum with a knowledge base developed on a primarily US work force, embedded values reflecting the American Dream of freedom, competition and individuality, and a discipline still geared to the core problems of an industrializing US.[53]

As a source of perspective on the limits of a discourse bounded by 'international management,' one might consider the debates on 'post- colonial theory' which have appeared throughout the humanities and social sciences, although their influence to date on management theorizing has been minimal.[54] A central object of post-colonial debates has been the continued dominance of the West in other cultures despite the post-Second World War collapse of empires in a political sense. This heterogeneous body of thought has gone beyond accepting the sufficiency of incorporating diverse cultures into an already existing body of knowledge and has challenged the dominance institutionalized in the Western/US 'capitali- zation' of knowledge. For instance, Weeks (1990) argues that colonization is occurring as long as knowledge is primarily funded from a central core of countries and journal publication is centralized in this core, restricting the development of localized centers of learning. She adds, '[m]any third world academics cite the need for social scientists to take a definite political stance.

---

53 Recent situations in which I have heard the claim that the US produces culturally bound knowledge and exports it as if it were universal (accompanied by the claim that it is the dominant source of management knowledge in its export market) include Clegg et al. (1994), Janssens and Steyaert (1994), and personal conversations with academics affirming their view that this situation exists in their experience in Sweden, France and Indonesia.

54 Calás et al. (1993) are among the few to have utilized post-colonial theory within organizational studies. Useful texts for background include Chatterjee (1986), Said (1979), Spivak (1988), Williams and Chrisman (1994).

They consider a "neutral" social science to be really the same as a Western one' (Weeks, 1990: 237). Alatas (1993) also argues for decentralizing knowledge production, calling for an 'indigenization' of discourse. In psychology, Misra and Gergen (1993) argue the need for *psychologies*, that is, multiple forms of regionally-appropriate knowledge not universalized into a single overarching framework of Western science.[55]

One might ask how objectivity can be ideological. At the level of method, consider the function of scientific modeling. One seeks a parsimonious model for capturing broadly generalizable phenomena. In the 1950s and 1960s, organizational science underwent a strong neopositivist shift[56] with the express goal of becoming an applied arm of the social sciences 'as engineering stands with respect to the physical sciences, or as medicine to the biological' (Thompson, 1956: 103). The goal was to establish that there is 'a generic administrative process' that is 'not only constant and universal in some respects, but is also a variable in an equation of action' (Litchfield, 1956: 9). This was not a change of direction, but it did constitute a narrowing of topics and methods. If one adds race as a 'mediating variable,' the model loses parsimony; requisite sample size rises, increasing the time and funding needed to conduct a study. Add gender and the problem is exacerbated. Add culture, sexual orientation, disability, et cetera, and before long the model is conceptually muddy and logistically unworkable. If, as do most current organizational researchers, one understands objectivity to mean statistical reliability, validity, significance and lack of bias, the 'progress' of knowledge simply does not permit more than marginal attention to 'confounding' factors like other belief systems and cultural practices.[57] As we have seen with the issue of gender, family and the work transfer of relational practices, accounting for worker sex fails to address many effects of socially constructed identities (see the section on work/family in this chapter, pp. 176–80). To 'do diversity' seriously would mean rethinking the

---

55 This may be read as an argument against science by those of a neopositivist bent, but it need not be. The authors suggest uses for a scientific inquiry that does not demand, as its first criterion, universal prediction and control.

56 Consider, for instance, the first fifteen years of *Administrative Science Quarterly*, which showed a narrowing from many forms of research and theorizing to a 'rigorous' reporting of hypothesis-testing data. Or compare the blend of quantitative data gathering and informed anthropological methods evident in Roethlisberger and Dickson's classic study (1939) with the parochialism of the 'qualitative-quantitative' debates of the 1970s and since (cf., Jick, 1979, in the context of Morgan and Smircich, 1980).

57 Some may find the examples of gender, sexual orientation and disability odd in this context. I, however, see the boundary between diversity and international issues as thoroughly artificial except in regard to legal/financial aspects of national policy. One of the major barriers to understanding the dynamics of asymmetrical power relations between identity groups is the disciplinary mechanism through which each comes to be regarded as a separate domain. While there is value to coming together around a single identity issue (consider the success of women's studies), there is also the danger that marginal groups will be disempowered by an institutional partitioning process that provides no forum for discussing the general issue of dominance and marginality.

dominant philosophy and methodology of organizational science to accommodate, not simply other *data*, but other *ways of understanding data*.

At another level, consider the myth of progress as a core value of the American Dream. Throughout vast areas of Africa, Asia and elsewhere are peoples who exhibited little desire to 'progress' until forcibly disenfranchised from traditional cultural practices while simultaneously being offered the products of industrial society as symbols of 'getting ahead' (this continues today with Coke, Big Macs, Levis, Camels – and management texts). Takaki (1993), by bringing together issues of cultural and national diversity, shows how the idea of societal evolution has cloaked the subordination of Others within the rhetoric of neutral science.[58] In a world of finite limits, a belief system with a core value of growth is pernicious. A century after the closing of the frontier, the US is still a culture seeking a 'new frontier,' a 'last frontier' – anything but limits. This metaphorically addictive thinking is strongly reflected in US business and society. Consider automobiles, a highly symbolic US product. The oil shortages of the 1970s produced a consciousness that oil is a limited resource. Legislation required higher fuel economy in new cars. The Detroit automakers responded with downsized vehicles and more technologically sophisticated engines. Once gasoline became plentiful, this period was reinterpreted. It had not been a permanent sign that fuel was limited, it had simply been a bad time precipitated by bad people – Japanese automakers and the OPEC cartel. The Reagan election precipitated a period of purging any constructive lessons that might have been learned from oil shock and stagflation. The amnesia and denial of the 1980s left a four trillion dollar national debt as a legacy, but in the mid-1990s, cars and engines are becoming larger and larger, with the 'all American' V-8 engine resurgent. A 1995 Camaro ad boasting a 5.7 liter engine (at least three times the displacement required for adequate transportation) explicitly ties fuel squandering to the American Dream, asking 'is this a great country or what?' As this book goes to press, my drive to work takes me past a billboard offering a 250 horsepower Oldsmobile as an 'American Dream.' And, speaking of power . . .

Power in organizations: the discourse of objectivity

Why is it that so little is said about power in organizations when (as Talcott Parsons wrote in volume one of *Administrative Science Quarterly*) 'the central phenomenon of organization is the mobilization of *power* for the attainment of the goals of the organization' (Parsons, 1956: 225; emphasis in

---

58 To dismiss this as bad science is thoroughly inadequate. The racism, nationalism and elitism perpetuated as objective knowledge could not be eradicated through better internal and external controls on data collection. Neither are they the result of deliberate distortion on the part of researchers. What makes it possible to marginalize cultural groups in the name of objectivity is a refusal and/or inability to examine the cultural value system(s) within which the objective mechanisms of scientific inquiry are embedded and through which 'data' takes on meaning as interpretation.

the original). To theorize organizing without mentioning power is a bit like electrical engineers theorizing circuitry without mentioning amperes or volts. Once again, historical perspective is useful for explaining this oddity.

Recall the bitter struggle precipitated between employers and occupational groups by the organization of scale. This was the birthplace of Scientific Management, which claimed to have knowledge transcending vested interest. In a period where coercive power was being exercised to the detriment of everyone's interests,[59] scientific approaches to work sublimated power to the higher authority of objective truth. 'Power,' when spoken of directly, came to mean simply the (generally inappropriate) coercion of person B by the self-aware actions of person A. In the perfect organization, then, there would be no power because, science having shown the most appropriate path toward the goal, all would follow it. Reaching the goal would benefit all parties, employers, employees and consumers. Thus the power of organizing itself was conceptualized as natural or quasi-natural, residing in societal *progress*, the laws of the *environment* and the universal laws of human *behavior*.

The price paid for this formulation was that it seriously constrained the study of options and recognition of the socially constituted basis of organizational life. To suggest that power relations be changed in society is to be tainted with the 'power perspective'[60] and dismissed as one who sees society as a hegemonic plot of the strong against the weak. If one accepts an evolutionary perspective, this view cannot have validity because what exists has been validated as superior simply by its having been selected over possible alternatives. The social constitution of social structures can be admitted to this discourse because it is possible to simultaneously hold constructivist and evolutionary perspectives.[61] What cannot be admitted to any degree is the social construction of *subjectivity*, that is, the construction of 'human nature.' Enveloping these questions is the paradox that, although organizational science has itself become a significant force in the construction and maintenance of present organizational relations, it is not possible to speak of the operation of this power without being labeled anti-scientific because the conceit of organizational science is that it simply observes empirical relationships – it does not have a normative agenda.

Any reasonable observer would have to concede that there are differences of voice, reward and influence in large organizations. The question is not if power differentials exist, but whether they are justified. In the twentieth-century organization in the US these differentials have been justified with reference to natural law and Federalist cultural values. The problem this poses for theorizing the post-industrial is that if one cannot analyze power

---

59 I personally believe that capital's interests were ultimately served fairly explicitly while labor's interests, where served, were largely a byproduct of rising productivity, but that is not central to the point being made here.

60 E.g., Von Glinow (1988); Gerpott and Domsch (1985).

61 An explicit, and influential example is Weick (1969).

relationships at all, one certainly cannot analyze how they might be changing. There are very good reasons why the discourse of objectivity might have emerged from the conflicts of industrialization, but these conflicts are not the central problems of the present day. To blindly insist on the scientific superiority of the discourse of objectivity, in the absence of compelling evidence of its success, is to enact the dynamics of dysfunctional family abuse at a societal level. It prevents asking with an open mind what benefits might accrue from promoting a discourse of advocacy.[62]

Productivity and efficiency

What does IBM sell? Most people would say computers and/or office products. But for the better part of a century, the Watsons and their successors appear to have understood that they were selling a *relationship*. One of the world's largest corporations was never driven primarily by productivity or efficiency as much as it was by a relational ethos that made being the most productive producer unnecessary. Consider this example from personal experience. The healthcare software firm in which I was a manager had developed a data base package comparable to an IBM product, but offering twice the performance at half the price. For a DP manager, purchase of this product was equivalent to having $180,000 added to his/her budget. The product should have sold itself. Why then did sales people see potential clients' eyes glazing over as they pitched this product? What we had missed as an organization – and what has often been missed in analyses of IBM – is that the world's largest computer company *never* sold computers; computers were simply a medium for delivering the irreplaceable product – security. You would have the report you needed for your 8.00 am board meeting if IBM had to charter a private jet to fly your data in from Tierra del Fuego. In return, the client organization had only to relax, focus on its business, and write very large checks to IBM. To disturb such a relationship for the sake of a mere productivity improvement would have been short-sighted indeed.

Other things being equal, productivity and efficiency are, of course, contributors to financial success, but other things are *never* equal! To want to maximize the overall effect of the organization within the constraints imposed by finite material and human resources is a relatively uncontroversial goal – but watch out for that semantic eclipse! Productivity is a product of ratio-nal, numeric disciplinary thinking. Industrial productivity is expressed as a ratio of *measurable* inputs and outputs. If one comes to see reality in terms of productivity ratios, complex interrelationships and intangible factors such as communicating and facilitating enter the realm of the 'not quite real.' As the problems of 'knowledge intensive firms'[63] become more critical to understand than those of production-line environments,

---

62 This was one of the points I argued in Jacques (1992b).
63 E.g., Starbuck (1992).

most of what is important to understand is pre-defined as peripheral or non-existent by a discourse centered on productivity and efficiency.

Only one segment of industrialized economies have ever been driven by overriding concerns of productivity and efficiency. That is the segment built upon lowest-cost, standardized, stable, tangible products produced in a low-skill, technology-driven environment. There was a time when this segment dominated work life, but its influence has been declining now for something like half a century. Today, for every situation meeting this description, there are many more where concerns of productivity and efficiency take a back seat to concerns of quality, innovation, flexibility, worker knowledge and maintenance of client relationships. Rather than asking how businesses of the twenty-first century can be productive and efficient to meet the challenges of global competition, it might be more *'productive'* to ask: How does the discourse of industrial productivity and efficiency constitute an obstacle to thriving as a twenty-first-century organization? This will be further illustrated in the following sections which connect work/family issues and knowledge work in a way counterintuitive to industrial common sense.

Work/family: beyond 'women's issues;' beyond women and men

Two demographic trends have contributed to the surfacing of work/family tensions as central problems of organizing. First, working men are less likely to have stay-at-home wives who can act as unpaid support staff for the worker. Secondly, workers are increasingly likely to be women (single or in committed relationships) whose overall work life includes a 'second shift'[64] of primary responsibility for a household in addition to their 'real' job or career. Because employers have historically been able to assume both the unlimited commitment to wage work of the employee as well as silent support in the domestic arena from a homemaker, it is almost impossible for discussions starting from industrial common sense to avoid framing work/family tensions primarily as a conflict – the merits of being 'family friendly' depend on the degree to which family support policies increase worker productivity. Such logic may seem unassailable, but it is flawed.

The work of society is done in both domestic and formal organizational sites. The skills for doing society's work are developed in both areas. To arbitrarily focus on the formal organization only in the study of organizing prevents following the flow of work and skill development back and forth across the mobile boundary separating the public and the private.[65] It

---

64 Hochschild (1989).

65 Another study waiting to be undertaken is the mapping of the curious and privileged space business has come to occupy *between* the public and the private. Such organizations are largely freed of the social responsibilities of governmental and 'public sector' agencies. This is related to the nineteenth-century shift to legitimating (noted previously) the corporation as an aggregation of the individual rather than as a subdivision of the state. Thus the corporation claims individual freedoms rather than civil state responsibilities. At the same time that the

removes from organizational discourse the potential for understanding the social origins of potentially critical workplace skills and attitudes and behaviors. For instance, consider the relationship between facilitating knowledge-intensive work and the primarily domestic sphere of *relational practice*.[66]

The traditionally masculine sphere of business is shaped by an ethos of competition, especially in US management circles. The traditionally feminine sphere has been consigned primary responsibility for relationship maintenance.[67] While this does not predetermine the individual qualities a man or woman will bring to the organization, it does indicate a powerful set of forces telling the organization member how s/he is *expected* to behave, both at work and in the broader world.

In the industrializing US, as society became specialized into a domestic sphere of consumption and an organizational sphere of production, relational practice was de-emphasized in the organizational sphere. Women, the traditional bearers of relational responsibility, became less integral to production.[68] Male businesses centered on character underwent a 'masculinization' into practices centered on scientific objectivity and Darwinian competition. This has been little affected by the increasing presence of, and research on, women in management.[69] This is not to say

corporation is 'private' relative to the public good, it is 'public' relative to personal responsibility. The welfare of the individual worker and his/her family is relegated to the private sphere of domestic responsibility through a unilaterally determined labor contract which presumes that the worker's choice to work for an employer constitutes a free agreement to sell labor for the market rate. This is the extent of the 'contract;' the employer assumes no responsibility for the worker beyond the workplace (except by choice, in which case the employer claims recognition as benevolent). Thus, the corporation has the combined rights of the domestic sphere and the state with the responsibilities of neither.

66 It is reflective of the early stages of theorizing this work that theorists do not even have a commonly recognized term for it. In my earlier work, I have used the awkward neologism 'caring/connecting' work to emphasize that while such work involves the sentiment of caring, it is not simply affect; the *act* of connecting is equally central. The better term 'relational practice' I owe to Joyce Fletcher (see Fletcher, 1994a).

67 This has been a tenet of conservative anti-feminist thought as well as a central theme of women's studies. One stream of theorizing influential to the authors cited in this section includes the work of Chodorow (1978), Miller (1976), Gilligan (1982) and the literature their work has engendered (cf., Jordan et al., 1991; Grimshaw, 1986). This work has been based on the observation that – presumably through socialization – men tend to develop a relatively autonomous self, identified through individuation, while women tend to develop a more permeable *self-in-connection*. This does not, in my opinion, necessarily homogenize or essentialize the sexes by implying that men or women are inherently the possessors of any particular characteristic. It does, however, point to a double conditioning of social experience by which women are encouraged to construct their identities through connection rather than separation and by which social practices related to such connection – *relational practices* – come to be seen as appropriate for women to carry out in organizations and in society as a whole.

68 In the workplace, that is. Women remained integral, but in supporting roles.

69 Cf., Powell (1994). What is present in Powell constitutes an excellent summary of this area of research; what is absent offers a representative example of its boundaries (note that I am distinguishing 'women in management' research from gender research in general; this is because it has constituted the main stream of organizational gender research in the US).

that relational practices have been eliminated from organizations. They have, however, become relatively invisible because they do not constitute objects of knowledge, the basis for reward or a source of authority.

Recently, some theorists have claimed that the widely lamented need for relational managers who can support and facilitate, rather than direct and control, knowledge-intensive work can be remedied by bringing women's alleged relational skills back into the workplace.[70] As Tom Peters (1990) himself pithily expressed it, 'the best new managers will listen, motivate, support: isn't that just like a woman?' This thinking captures one important point: relational skills are increasingly critical for effectively organizing and these skills cannot currently be found in the norms of the industrial workplace.

However, the simplistic solution of adding women indicates a lack of perspective in that it fails to recognize that women in the workplace have achieved organizational prominence to the degree that they have been able to work within the norms of that organization. Taking a broader historical perspective, it might be more useful to ask how the industrial transformation of society has interacted with gendered sex role socialization to marginalize, not women, but the entire domain of relational practice.[71] Both Kolb (1992) and Huff (1990) comment on the complex and poorly understood relationship between relational work, gender coding and devaluation. In previous work, commenting on the hidden 'managing' performed through the relational practices of hospital nurses, I observed that caring in organizations has been most often represented as a personal/interpersonal affective activity. 'What has not yet been voiced is the role of *caring as a structural practice* . . . making the work of the entire organization possible and effecting its quality of performance' (Jacques, 1993: 1; emphasis in the original). However,

> [s]eeking to represent [these] work activities . . . leads to the realization that *there is an entire economy of work practices that begins out of sight and ends at what theorists of work consider to be the beginning of analysis. An innate characteristic of this work is that, when it is performed competently, the worker and the work disappear, leaving no evidence that something had to be done in the first place.* (Jacques, 1992a: 247; emphasis in the original)

Fletcher (1994a) in a study of relational practices among engineers makes it clear that such practices do not simply disappear. They are subject to systematic organizational processes through which they 'get disappeared.' The three elements identified by Fletcher are that: (1) Such work practices get labeled as appropriate to the home rather than the workplace; (2) There is no language to describe such practices as competent work behaviors; (3) Such activities are gender-coded as pertaining to 'women's work,' a labeling

---

70 Helgeson (1990), Jelinek and Adler (1988), Loden (1985), Rosener (1990). Some potential problems with this line of thinking have been discussed in Calás et al. (1991), Calás and Smircich (1993) and Fletcher (1994b).

71 Women have also been marginalized, which is an important issue as well. The two issues are also interrelated, but they should not be confused; they are not one and the same.

detrimental to the workplace credibility of men *or* women. If one follows this line of reasoning, it suggests that a key resource for understanding and managing in the knowledge-intensive environments that will supposedly characterize post-industrial work, has become socially coded as *inappropriate to the workplace*. This cannot be solved by increasing the numbers of women in the workplace if both men's and women's workplace credibility is contingent upon the suppression of 'domestic' and 'feminine' relational practices.

From this perspective, only a small portion of the relationship between the formal organization and the domestic sphere is covered by the present 'work/family' dialogue, bounded as it is by consideration of which benefit packages and work policies will produce a 'family-friendly' workplace. Within the structure of the current discussion, family[72] can hardly be posited in any role except as a competitor with the workplace for the time and attention of the worker. What has been overlooked is the positive contribution of the family as a *supplier*. The family performs uncompensated relational work for the organization in maintaining the physical and mental well-being of the worker[73]. It also provides 'free' training by developing the relational skills workers bring to the workplace. In the case of nurses and secretaries (and to a lesser degree, many personal service occupations), the very structure of the occupation relies on an ethos brought into the workplace from the domestic sphere, yet these skills are not formally supported work in the organization. This is a very one-sided form of partnering inconsistent with current thinking about post-industrial organizations as cooperating networks of internal and external suppliers and customers. The industrial organization could attempt to get a free ride at the expense of the domestic sphere because relational skills in the workplace were not central to the problems of mechanized mass production. The free ride is now ending. In knowledge intensive environments, competitive advantage will go to the organization that can successfully 'partner' with 'Home Incorporated;' doing so will be facilitated by knowing the dynamic processes through which the current relationship between the corporation and the home came about. This suggests several questions that go well beyond issues of family-friendly benefit policies, or even issues of women and men in management:

- How can 'work transfer' between the home and corporate workplace be better understood so that the supply of critical domestic resources can be

72 By 'family' I mean any combination of adults and children who think of themselves as a relatively stable domestic group. The issues discussed here are not specific to heterosexual couples with children.

73 This has been less overlooked by Marxist theorists since the landmark paper by Hartmann (1981), which suggests a conceptual starting point for theorizing domestic labor which can be useful for the reader of any ideological stripe. Unfortunately, because of the intellectual distance between Marxist thought and the mainstream of organization studies, this critique of the labor theory of value has not led to a similar rethinking in organizational studies.

developed and supported (for example, domestic 'training' in relational consciousness)?
- How can theorists better understand the potential work transfer between organizations by which public sector and voluntary organizations may assume the feminized role of supplying to the corporate sector services socially coded as domestic (for example, unemployment, counseling, retraining, health and literacy programs)?
- What would be necessary for domestic labor to be included within the authorized body of knowledge about work (for example, understanding the management of a household as legitimate management experience; valuing research of domestic practices as legitimate management research)
- What are the power dynamics of corporate/domestic work transfer (for example, what forces control the movement of work from one sphere to the other; who benefits from this movement; who does not?)?
- What knowledge must be gained in order to theorize the domain of relational practices in organizations (for example, Jacques, 1992a; Fletcher, 1994a, above)?
- How do some (primarily relational) practices come to be coded as 'women's work' and, through that coding, come to be seen as appropriate to the domestic sphere and inappropriate to the workplace? How does this differentially affect the opportunities of men and women? How does this make it difficult or impossible to represent and theorize certain valuable practices?

To address these questions will require more than adding a few new variables or topics to present-day organizational knowledge. Management knowledge itself has developed within the industrial division of home and workplace. *L'employé*, the subject upon whom management knowledge is based, reflects, in the words of Friedan, 'a standard of perfection in the workplace set in the past by and for men who had wives to take care of all the details of living' (1981: 80). 'He' (whether male or female) is physically produced and maintained through domestic labor, 'his' beliefs and values are significantly influenced by domestic socialization, and 'his' performance is supported by a hidden network of relational practices in the workplace. To understand the post-industrial worker, new boundaries will have to be drawn around what is work; new assumptions will have to be adopted regarding the nature of the working subject. As the following sections suggest, 'knowledge work' may be more than simply expertise; the knowledge worker may be other than the traditional employed professional.

Knowledge work as expertise

Two 'hot' topics today are knowledge work and organizational learning. There are compelling reasons to study these topics. Knowledge in organizations is fast becoming the critical determinant of success. Conceptualization of these problems, however, continues to reflect an industrial, or even pre-industrial, worldview. This book has argued that the emergence of *l'employé* was the point at which it became insufficient to merely assure the worker's labor. It was when his/her discretionary commitment, which could not be coerced, became critical that the mechanisms in place today for 'developing' and 'handling' workers coalesced. If the central problem of 'managing' the 'employee' has been one of knowledge, it is unlikely that the *emerging* worker can be distinguished from the traditional employee by this quality. One could argue that what is emerging is the *learning worker*, one whose value does not lie in what s/he knows but in the combination of discretion and skill that permit one to change what one knows.

The problem of the learning worker is that s/he is not controlled or developed through existing organizational practices. Disciplinary society learned to capitalize knowledge, in the Weberian 'files,' in procedure and in 'human capital.' One can assess a worker's level of knowledge. Examination permits both guided development of that knowledge and reward based upon its elaboration. Clearly marked certification of knowledge summarized in the personnel record can be linked to authority in terms of promotion and job assignment. Knowledge, in Hofstadter's apt term, is frozen; it can be 'handled.' None of these practices effectively controls the learning worker; learning is fluid. Where individuals learn – for instance, the intellectual capital of software developers – it is too easily retained as a personal, rather than an organizational asset. There are not even well-established guidelines for beginning to debate the question of who has a right to claim the value of worker learning.

The legacy of industrial thinking is present in current discussions of knowledge work that casually refer to these workers as either 'expert' or 'professional.' Professionalization, as I have argued (in Chapter 6), is an industrial mode of capitalizing knowledge through horizontally and vertically hierarchized experts. To think of the knowledge worker as an expert or professional is to apply a filter to the worker which permits only those aspects of the work which reflect an industrial reality to show through. Only to the extent that it can become possible to understand work that is knowledge-intensive, but other-than-professional, will it become possible to let this new subject into managerial discourse.

A similar argument can be made that understanding the 'learning organization' will first require removing industrial blinders. The book which popularized this term, Peter Senge's *The Fifth Discipline* (1990), is less a book about organizational learning than it is about individual learning in organizations. It can be a very useful book if one wishes to apply systems theory to problems of today's organizations, but as a theory of emerging work practices *The Fifth Discipline* builds on little that was not well articulated in Weick's *Social Psychology of Organizing* (1969). This is not criticism of Senge, but merely a distinction between individual learning in organizations and the learning of organizations as an entity. Starbuck (1992), almost in passing, suggests a much more promising conceptual foundation for thinking about learning from a distinctly organizational perspective.

Besides knowledge held in individual people, one can find knowledge in: (a) capital such as plant, equipment, or financial instruments; (b) firms' routines and cultures; and (c) professional cultures. People convert their knowledge to physical forms when they write books or computer programs, design buildings or machines. . . . People also translate their knowledge into firms' routines, job descriptions, plans, strategies and cultures. (Senge, 1990: 718–19)

A defining problem of the industrial was the capitalization of knowledge, through formalization, professionalization and machines themselves. A defining problem of post-industrial organizing will be the capitalization of learning. How will learning be accumulated, and applied? Who will own it? Who will shape the directions in which it develops? Here, US organizational science again encounters the ghost of Freeman Hunt. To a US reader, *The Fifth Discipline* appears to be about organizational learning because what could an organization be except the sum of what individuals do within it? This is not a specifically industrial bias. It can be traced back through the Quakers, Puritans, Hume and others to the earliest records of Anglo-US society.[74] It has survived a century of industrial society in which influence moves through the system and the group, not the individual. Before it can imagine the post-industrial, it will have to imagine the industrial. Thinking of the post-industrial in terms of non-subjective theories of management, leadership and learning may require a new epistemology, a 'knowledge theory of value.'[75]

Some Problems in Developing a 'Knowledge Theory of Value'

To study organizations is to study the processes through which the production and exchange of value takes place. But what has value? Studying the circulation of money can function, within very wide limits, as a study of value, but ultimately this only begs the question. Money has no inherent value; it simply *signifies* value. What does it signify? As Gintis and Bowles show, 'any basic resource can be considered an acceptable basis for value theory' (1981: 19). In industrial economies, this has been narrowed from a general question of moral philosophy (the field of Adam Smith) to a contest between labor theory and utility theory.[76] Both have been loaded with a heavy layer of ideology because, since Ricardo, labor theory has largely disappeared among pro-capitalist economists. Thus, elaboration of value as labor, which is not inherently radical, has been done largely by Marxist and post-Marxist thinkers. Since Marshall, neoclassical thinking about value has been solidly in the domain of utility. These are the two industrial possibilities for thinking about value: things have value because people prefer them to other things; or things have value because they embody the effort over time of those who have produced them and/or brought them to the market.

74 Cf., Macfarlane (1978).
75 Naisbitt (1982).
76 Cf., Wolff and Resnick (1987) for a primer.

Perhaps it is time to revisit the basic question of value. It is an axiom of industrial thinking that goods are composed of some combination of capital and labor. To date, knowledge has been hidden within these categories. If knowledge is becoming 'the central "factor of production" in an advanced, developed economy' (Drucker, 1968: 264),[77] would it offer new possibilities to invert the traditional relationship and think of capital and labor in terms of knowledge value? One could look at capital markets and the financial functions of the firm as processes for accumulating and distributing knowledge. Similarly, one could imagine machines and organizational practices as the sedimented knowledge (rather than labor) of those who have produced them. And, of course, one can imagine the 'human capital' of the worker as their ability to learn, rather than their ability to work. In most post-industrial situations, nearly everyone possesses the physical capacity to do nearly every job. What distinguishes one worker from another is knowledge – or perhaps learning.

Within a knowledge theory of value, the ability to learn represents the ability to change the capitalized store of value. It adds to the wealth of the individual, occupation, organization and/or society. Thus, within a knowledge theory of value it is not knowledge itself that is important – that was the central problem of an industrial reality – it is the ability to *change* knowledge, that is, to learn. The inadequacy of present theory to make this a central problem of analysis is possibly the key barrier to visualizing a post-industrial order. This is equally a problem for managerialist and Marxist/socialist thinkers. Both utility theory and labor theory reflect a historical period in which the central issue is to understand and legitimate relationships pertaining to industrial capital. Just as an earlier age would have developed other legitimating narratives centered on land ownership and rents, it is possible that the most industrialized societies of the world are entering a form in which social equity, privilege and exclusion, will be argued around the control of knowledge. But the legitimating narratives for these contests have yet to be developed.

Meanwhile, a concise example of the problem is present in today's educational practices. Examining them is useful: first, as a means of moving toward a 'post-industrial' university; second, for understanding the blinders imposed by our own educations; and, third, as an example to help clarify the industrial mode of controlling and using knowledge in organizations.

Knowledge and the university

Do professors exist to teach students content or to teach them to learn? This is a complex question. Certainly content would be seen as totally irrelevant by very few. There may also be a tension between the values of individual

---

77 Unlike *Post-capitalist Society* (1993), an angry polemic which gives the impression that Drucker actually knew *more* in 1968 than he remembers today, *The Age of Discontinuity* is an insightful early analysis of the problems of 'the knowledge economy.'

professors and the effects created by the institutional systems of which we are part.[78] If one looks at the norms and practices institutionalized in the current educational system in general, and management education in particular, one finds the entire process geared to the capitalization and certification within the student of *knowledge*. Ability to *learn* may be fostered as a byproduct of the system, but it escapes the system of institutional controls. What are the control points in academe? Curricula, examinations, grades, tenure and promotion are prominent.

High value is placed[79] on standardized curricula centered on the *textbook* – learning of others that has been frozen and packaged. Instructors know that summarizing the 'key points' of the text will generate less resistance from the relatively alienated student body than will attempts to disturb their ways of thinking and learning. If this were true of some students, it might be attributable to them, but when it is produced in class after class, one must look at the system. No one has ever seen a two year-old who was not curious, so where did all these inert twenty year-olds come from? The experiential movement has challenged this norm, but has remained fairly marginal. In addition, most 'experiential' classroom exercises are directed toward 'debriefings' in which the students will find out what they are *supposed* to have learned based on experiential textbook material. Open-ended learning, as espoused by those such as Dewey or Montessori, remains uncommon.

How do students wish to be evaluated? Some may prefer essay exams, others papers, still others objective tests; but most will expect the examination, regardless of format, to be evaluated as a regurgitation of the knowledge of others presumed to be experts, that is, the class readings or the professor's notes. This is not the fault of students, who are trying to determine how to use their education to find a place in society. As relatively passive carriers of societal values, however, students are a valuable source of insight into what is expected of the university by the world within which it is embedded. One goes to the university to learn the key facts of a body of expertise in order to be certified as having knowledge of social value. This extends beyond the classroom examination to the grading scheme in a neat pyramid. Examinations add up to completed course credits and course credits add up to a degree, certified with a grade-point average measured to the third decimal place.

The university promotion and tenure system (in the US, an artifact of industrialization) reinforces these relationships in two broad ways. First, in the classroom the professor is strongly influenced by student evaluations. These, in turn, are strongly influenced by the professor's ability to convey

78 There is the ongoing question of the degree to which expressing critical opinions within the institutional structure of academe upholds that structure regardless of the content of the opinions; cf., Jacoby (1987).

79 In varying degrees and with exceptions, of course. This is a description of a complex culture, but, like any culture, it is governed by certain norms.

what are presumed to be the key facts of the subject area and to be clear about which of them will be on the examination. Second, in doing research, the professor is often evaluated by largely quantitative criteria based on the number of articles, the number of citations and the status ranking of the journals in which s/he has published. All of these criteria are best met by research which builds upon rather than challenging currently popular topics, methods and points of view. Since the prize of tenure and/or promotion is highly valued and the criteria for achieving it are fuzzy, the professor is strongly rewarded for adding slightly to the established text, teaching it as fact and reifying the process of industrial education.

In the management disciplines, to use McLuhan's famous phrase, the medium is indeed the message. The graduating college senior who has forgotten the key variables of expectancy theory has still learned to appear at a scheduled time, to sit in rows and columns of desks, to be hierarchically ranked by grade level and 'quality' point average, to seek answers, not to raise questions. S/he has learned to do the task at hand without questioning its relevance. Industrialized education thus contributes to producing the task-centered worker 'discovered' by organizational psychology. As they leave school and become 'the employee,' they are re-discovered by replicating and confirmatory research. In the production of this organizational member, one can see an institutional response to the labor question and the works management question from which the management disciplines emerged.

The cliché of academia is that it is a medieval institution unresponsive to changing times. In a short-term sense, the university is unresponsive in that there is no control point from which a concerted change effort can be launched. In a larger sense, however, one should not overlook the 'industrial revolution' which transformed university practices in a manner congruent with the transformation of manufacture and exchange. In the US especially, many of the 'medieval' trappings of the university were *established* during this industrial transformation (see Table 6.1 on p. 130). In asking what should be the structure of a post-industrial university, a certain measure of respect is in order, but reverence for the past would be based on mythologizing a golden age that never existed.

Relations with the academy were not a necessary condition for the creation of large organizations. The university entered at a relatively late point. Today, it seems quite natural that success in business is dependent upon business education, but this was not always the case. Need the relationship continue? Braudel (1981, 1982, 1984) offers examples from over five centuries of institutions and industries moving out of, as well as into, the emerging capitalist order. Farming became capitalist where profit margins were sufficient, but remained a peasant industry where margins were narrow or uncertain. Industry aggregated when profits could be made on a large scale and reverted to small shop or cottage production when profits were higher in other areas. The dominant voice within capitalist production and exchange has shifted freely between the extracting, producing, trading and financial sectors. 'The chief privilege of capitalism, today as in the past, remains the ability to *choose*' (Braudel, 1982: 621; emphasis in the original). Is there any reason to imagine that the relationship between the university and business should be immune from this contingency?

In the emergence of organizational discourse, two distinctive roles have been played by the university. One has been that of custodian (through the language and values of the sciences) of the founding values of the discourse of objectivity. The second, related, role has been to certify, through degree programs, the objective expertise of the industrial manager and professional. It is impossible to overestimate the facilitating value of these roles when they emerged a century ago, at a point where the institutions of US society were widely believed to be in imminent danger of self-immolation at the hands of the vested interests of capital and labor. The authority of the discourse of *maneggiare* rested in its ability to 'objectively' represent knowledge of what constituted 'a fair day's work for a fair day's pay.' Its arm's length relationship to knowledge provided a basis for constituting a new, socially safe, discourse of work. The current privileged position of the management disciplines in the university perhaps owes more to this discursive role than to the discipline's ability to produce a science of organizing. In 1990, Oliver Williamson asserted that an 'incipient science of organization' is *beginning* to emerge[80], but Williamson's view was shared by Freeman Hunt – writing in 1857.

The intervening 134 years span the history of *l'employé*. S/he has been produced, lived and is now declining. If production of a science of the employee has not been a requirement for the academy's entry into the disciplinary relations of organizing, it seems unlikely that rigor and validity will slow the unravelling of these relationships should practitioner and academic discourses of work diverge. It is dangerously complacent not to ask what value industrial education can offer to post-industrial society. If educational relations with business and society were transformed in the nineteenth century by changes in the social organization of work, is it not likely that the transformation of industrial society, accelerating since the 1950s, may eventually result in yet another configuration of the relationships between education, business and society? *How would the university have to be transformed to produce the* ***ability to learn***, *rather than* ***static knowledge***, *as the product by which it is legitimated in society?* How could the academic be rewarded for learning, rather than knowing?

Memory Against Forgetting: Completing the Questions

Prerequisite to consideration of any of the above problems is reclaiming the history of organizational knowledge. This is not necessarily the end of

---

80 (Stone, 1991: 816).

organizational science, but it requires a new understanding of the *meaning* of science. Between universal truth and relativism there is a vast domain of the quasi-true based on knowledge of the quasi-real. The quasi-real has a durability and a regularity that can be represented in hypotheses (although it also has meanings which elude hypotheses.[81] The quasi-real is not the deliberate construction of cabals, nor is it the product of natural forces. Its origin is ultimately social; thus intentional action of persons and groups is meaningful. It is also beyond rational social control; thus it may at times approximate the operation of natural processes. For instance, hydraulic models are useful for modeling traffic flow on a highway, but unlike fluid molecules, drivers (sometimes) have self-awareness. Thus traffic laws, which have no hydraulic analog, are also relevant to understanding traffic.

Within a quasi-real organizational science, the methods, models and topics currently in use could still be applied and the accumulated findings of the field could still have meaning. Their meanings, however, would have to be understood as provisional, regularities based upon an order of relationships subject to change. Science would be one (not *the*, but *one*) legitimate way of telling a story to make sense of social experience. The benefit for the *status quo* of organizational knowledge is that this offers a way out of the truth trap referred to in Chapter 2. It permits communities of researchers to pack what they think they will need in the future and move on. The down side is that the absence of environmental necessity (that is, absolute reference points for truth and reality) would require science and scientists to be more accountable for the implications of their knowledge than is currently the norm in organizational studies.[82] This would require completing the questions structuring organizational research to include reflection upon: (1) Who benefits and loses from knowledge; (2) How knowledge is conditioned by the perspective of the knower; (3) How existing knowledge came to be accepted as legitimate; and (4) How the apparently real has been constructed over time and is a dynamic rather than a static reality.

For instance, the question 'what motivates the worker?' has been treated as an adequate formulation for research. A more appropriate question if social reality is treated as quasi-real might be 'what motivates the worker to do task work structured by others?' The question of organizational commitment has been structured largely as an obligation of the worker; 'what factors influence worker commitment?' A more complete question

---

81 Lyotard (1984) summed this up well when he noted that science is a subset of learning, which is a subset of knowledge in general. What can be represented scientifically is that which is (a) available for repeated observation, and (b) which can objectively be judged according to rules of inclusion/exclusion by experts. The latter criterion is most difficult to establish unless the phenomena are measured. These criteria structure a broad, but less than universal, domain within which science can be legitimated as useful.

82 This is another point regarding which organizational science is curiously archaic. The detached objectivity of the scientist invokes a dream perhaps best embodied by the international particle physics community between the 1890s and the 1930s – a dream thoroughly shattered by the complicity of this community in Hiroshima and the nuclear age.

might be 'what is the quid pro quo the organization must provide in order to establish a relationship of mutual commitment between the worker and the organization?' Completing implicit portions of questions would help to contextualize past research. For instance, the field has not asked 'what is leadership?,' but has asked 'what is leadership as the property of an individual whose specialized function is to be *a leader?*' The same restriction has bounded research on management as a function. Recognition of this boundary would permit conceptualization of leadership and management as *non-subjective processes* whose flow through the organization may or may not be embodied by the specialized subgroup claiming that process as an identity (that is, 'leaders,' 'managers').

Researching the quasi-real would also require retaining questions often forgotten about the meaning of basic concepts such as 'the organization.' Both managerial practice and organizational research accept the existence of an entity called 'the organization' and frequently appeal for legitimacy to the idea of acting 'for the good of the organization.' But what is 'the organization?' Examples can easily be produced of 'the organization' acting against every possible stakeholder: employees, managers, investors, suppliers, consumers, and the community. Is there a reality to 'the organization' beyond the naked contract of incorporation? Which shifting interests are being served when, at any given point, someone claims to be operating for the organization? Similarly, 'the employee,' 'management' 'the consumer,' and other homogenized labels would have to be thought of as provisional and contestable.

A final question might be put in terms of Kuhn's (1962/1970) distinction between normal science and paradigm shift. The structuring dream of organization studies has been the vision of creating an applied behavioral science. This is a normal science dream; it presumes the steady accumulation and application of knowledge. There is nothing wrong with a normal science dream if the social context of inquiry is stable. It is not. Whether one thinks in terms of the post-industrial, the postmodern or some other label, there is an increasingly prevalent belief that the foundations of knowledge and the social relations they both produce and reflect are shifting. For an applied science, this creates insurmountable problems in determining what knowledge to apply. This has been abundantly reflected in the turmoil of organization studies in the last two decades or so. In such turbulent times, the fundamental questions again arise: What is the purpose of organizational knowledge? On what can it be based? For whom is it being developed?

It is not at all unthinkable that 'management' will turn out to have been an historically bounded chapter in the story of organizing.[83] The development of industry is intertwined with the development of capitalism, but the two

---

83 Hollway (1991) attempts to show how the general question of how to organize industrial work (managing) was reduced to the more specific question of how to control the worker within industrial organizations (management).

are not synonymous. There are examples of non-capitalist industry and non-industrial capitalism. Post-industrialism is related to, but more limited than, postmodernism and postmodernism is intertwined with critique of capitalism. Rather than asking what will be the future of 'management,' it might be more appropriate to return to two broader questions that have been dormant[84] since the coalescence of managerial society: 'what is the role of organizing in society?' and 'what is the role of research knowledge in organizing?'

. . . And the Wisdom to Know the Difference

There is a ubiquitous aphorism attributed variously to Alcoholics Anonymous, native Americans, Reinhold Niebuhr, and perhaps others. With minor variations, it reads:

> Grant me the courage to change the things I can
> The patience to accept the things I cannot change
> And the wisdom to know the difference.

Why does this require wisdom? In any society, at any point in time, most social relations are more or less unchangeable. Societies change slowly, even through 'revolutions.' Consider the persistence of the Russian Tsarist bureaucracy through the Communist revolution or the durability of the frontier as a force shaping American thought decades after it ceased to exist as a relevant physical space. Even the great figures of history are often (perhaps always?) more the products than the producers of a time. Had evolution not come to be centered on *The Origin of Species*, others would soon have articulated similar thoughts. Edison would soon have been beaten to the discovery of a functioning light bulb.

But, this should not lead to overly deterministic views of social change. The Federalist belief in the self-determining individual may be an anachronistic nuisance, but unless human intentionality has the potential to make *some* difference, there is little point in writing or reading books such as this. This is why the 'wisdom to know the difference' is as elusive as it is critical. We live in curious times; flows of rivers are routinely re-engineered, but 'flows' of capital, market forces, are treated as environmental phenomena. This trend has accelerated in the US in recent years with the ascendancy of pseudo-economic models such as those of population ecology.[85] Whether or not these models 'accurately' describe the dynamics of organizational change they have the effect of focusing knowledge on the deterministic element of organizing – the effect of 'the environment.' Regardless of how much or how little the human situation can be influenced, it would seem that the goal of knowledge should be to maximize the utility of intentional

---

84 I see these questions actively debated from the 1870s into the twentieth century, but since Barnard (1938) the answers have become automatic, habitual and taken for granted.

85 The ur-document of this school of thought is Hannan and Freeman (1977).

action.[86] Toward this goal, knowledge of deterministic relationships can be valuable, but it cannot be sufficient. It is limited to telling us what to avoid or accept, not what to aspire to change.

Neither will the further accumulation of data lead to courage, patience or wisdom. Data-driven research provides only data. The construction of data into interpretations and goals is an extra-scientific project deeply embedded in social values. High 'body counts' and rigorous designs will produce, at best, reliability and validity. They can never be expected to provide a critically reflective vision of the good society, or inform debate between alternative visions of that society. The data will serve any master. To create what Graff has termed 'reflective second-order discourse about practices' (1990: 584) in organizational studies requires accepting that the value and limits of empirical testing cannot be determined by empirical tests; these are questions of value, philosophy and morality. Creation of such a dialogue does not require the rejection of scientific inquiry, only the acknowledgement that data does not produce social truth, that inquiry must be embedded within a broader dialogue about the uses of inquiry.[87] In this project, historical perspective can be invaluable. Indeed, it would be difficult to avoid.

The social world is in constant motion. All that appears solid is in the process of change. Practices may endure for centuries, but, like rivers, they flow in recognizable channels. Their origins and their deltas may be diffuse; their paths may be long, meandering, and changeable, but they can be navigated by one attuned to their dynamic patterns. The metaphor of river navigation is especially appropriate to the social researcher because the phenomena of study are fluid. All markers placed by the researcher must be considered provisional. The navigator cannot measure and record the position of each wave. S/he must constantly seek to understand the currents of change and the new patterns of reality they are producing. Technical data plays an important role in modern navigation, but it functions as a tool for enhancing informed judgment – not as a substitute for judgment. Accumulated knowledge – the level of the river, the position of the sand bar, the weather forecast – is not held to be either timeless truth or error. Its truth at one point in time sensitizes the pilot to look for certain conditions at a later point, but the *content* of the pilot's knowledge is worth nothing unless applied by one whose distinctive skill is the ability to *learn* and to make informed *judgments*.

But one cannot learn the currents by looking at the river at one point in time. Even so-called 'longitudinal' studies, valuable as they are in their own right, span a virtually instantaneous historical moment. They will

---

86 This is indeed an assumption and not a fact, but it is an assumption that would be widely shared by the consumers of research knowledge (if one assumes research is done to increase knowledge of the domain studied rather than solely for promotion and tenure. This second assumption is the more controversial assumption).

87 Cf., Jacques (1992b).

not reflect the specter of seventeenth-century perfectionism informing Hackett, Buycio and Guion's (1989) finding about the relationship of 'work ethic' to absenteeism. They will not connect the core values of participation and empowerment in Organizational Development to the ideal of the yeoman farmer, carried from fifth-century Jutland to England, from seventeenth-century England to 'New' England and from twentieth-century America to the businesses of the world, packaged as objective, organizational science. Neither will analysis uninformed by historical perspective show that the values and institutions embedded in contemporary American management knowledge of 'the employee' reflect an omnicompetence and independence that vanished from society no later than 1920.

Hopefully, the form of historical perspective reflected in this book shows that much effort today is being spent hammering on intractable and/or irrelevant issues. It may be too early to know what the core issues of post-industrial societies will be, but it is probably safe to say they will not be those central to US society a century ago. Perhaps, if these artifacts of the industrial US can be understood as temporary formations in the river of social life, researchers and practitioners can loosen our obsessive grasp on these temporary constructions to focus instead on the changing currents. Perhaps by querying the historical basis of our own common sense we can increase our 'wisdom to know the difference.' As Margaret Schaffner (1907: 132) reminded us at the beginning of our industrial age, '*No industrial relation can long survive the reasons for its being.*'

Bibliography

Addams, J. (1910/1981) *Twenty Years at Hull House*, New York: Signet.

Alatas, S.F. (1993) 'On the indigenization of academic discourse,' *Alternatives*, 18(2): 307–38.

Alvesson, M. & Wilmott, H. (eds) (1992a) *Critical Management Studies*, London: Sage.

Alvesson, M. & Wilmott, H. (1992b) 'On the idea of emancipation in management and organization studies,' *Academy of Management Review*, 17(3): 432–64.

Andreano, R. (ed.) (1962) *The Economic Impact of the American Civil War*, Cambridge, MA: Schenkman Publishing Co.

Ariès, P. & Duby, G. (eds) (1987) *From Pagan Rome to Byzantium*, Vol. 1 in *A History of Private Life* series, Cambridge, MA: Belknap.

Ashmos, D.P. & Huber, G.P. (1987) 'The systems paradigm in organization theory: correcting the record and suggesting the future,' *Academy of Management Review*, 12(4): 607–18.

Ashton, R.H. (1906) 'Organization of the operating department of railroads,' in E.R. Dewsnup (ed.), *Railway Organization and Working*, Chicago, IL: University of Chicago Press, pp.141–6.

Autry, J.A. (1991) *Lost Profit [sic]: The Art of Caring Leadership*, New York: Avon.

Baer, A.K. (1917) 'How we lifted hiring out of the rut,' in A.W. Shaw Co. (ed.), *Handling Men*, Chicago: A.W. Shaw Co., pp. 9–12.

Baer, C. (1991) 'The feminist disdain for nursing,' *New York Times*, 23 February, p. 24.

Bardwick, J.M. (1991) *Danger in the Comfort Zone: Boardroom to Mailroom – How to Break the Entitlement Habit That's Killing American Business*, New York: AMACOM.

Barley, S.R. & Kunda, G. (1993) 'Design and devotion: surges of rational and normative ideologies of control in managerial discourse,' *Administrative Science Quarterly*, 37(2): 363–99.

Barnard, C. (1938) *The Functions of the Executive*, Cambridge, MA: Harvard University Press.

Barthes, R. (1972) *Mythologies*, New York: Farrar, Strauss & Giroux.

Baudrillard, J. (1989) *America*, London: Verso.

Belchem, J. (1990) *Industrialization and the Working Class: The English Experience, 1750–1900*, Portland, OR: Areopagitica Press.

Bell, D. (1973) *The Coming of Post-Industrial Society*, New York: Basic Books.

Bellah, R.N., Madsen, R., Sullivan, W.M., Swidler, A. & Tipton, S.M. (1985) *Habits of the Heart: Individualism and Commitment in American Life*, New York: Harper & Row.

Benner, P. & Wrubel, J. (1989) *The Primacy of Caring: Stress and Coping in Health and Illness*, Menlo Park, CA: Addison-Wesley.

Berger, P.L. & Luckmann, T. (1967) *The Social Construction of Reality*, New York: Doubleday.

Berle, A.A. & Means, G.C. (1932) *The Modern Corporation and Private Property*, New York: Harcourt, Brace & World, Inc.

Bettis, R.A. & Donaldson, L. (eds) (1990) 'Theory development forum: market discipline and the discipline of management,' *Academy of Management Review*, 15(2): 367–535.

Beyer (1991) 'Presidential address: being professional, given at the annual Academy of Management Presidential Luncheon,' *Academy of Management News*, 21(4): 1, 2, 10–12.

Bingham, W.V. (1925) 'What industrial psychology asks of management,' *Bulletin of the Taylor Society*, 9(6), in B.V. Moore & G.W. Hartmann (eds) (1931), *Readings in Industrial Psychology*, New York: D. Appleton-Century Company, pp. 29–33.

Bion, W. (1959) *Experiences in Groups*, New York: Basic Books.

Blackford, K.M.H. & Newcomb, A. (1914) *The Job, The Man, The Boss*, Garden City, NY: Doubleday, Page & Co.

Blackler, F., Reed, M. & Whitaker, A. (1993a) 'Editorial introduction: knowledge workers and contemporary organizations,' *Journal of Management Studies*, 30(6): 851–62.

Blackler, F., Reed, M. & Whitaker, A. (1993b) 'Epilogue: an agenda for research,' *Journal of Management Studies*, 30(6): 1017–20.

Bledstein, B. (1976) *The Culture of Professionalism*, New York: W.W. Norton.

Bloomfield, M. (1916) 'The new profession of handling men,' *Industrial Management*, (52)1: 441–6.

Boje, D.M. & Dennehy, R.F. (1993) *Managing in the Postmodern World: America's Revolution Against Exploitation*, Dubuque, IA: Kendall/Hunt.

Boorstein, D. (1960) *The Lost World of Thomas Jefferson*, Boston, Beacon Press.

Bordo, S. (1986) 'The Cartesian masculinization of thought,' *Signs* 11(3): 439–56.

Borsodi, R. (1929) *This Ugly Civilization*, New York: Simon & Schuster.

Bowditch, J.L. & Buono, A.F. (1994) *A Primer on Organizational Behavior*, 3rd Edn, New York: Wiley.

Bradford, W. (1856/1981) *Of Plymouth Plantation 1620–1647*, New York: The Modern Library.

Brandeis, L.D. (1914) *Business – A Profession*, Boston, MA: Small, Maynard & Co.

Braudel, Fernand (1981) *Civilization & Capitalism 15th–18th Century: Vol. 1 The Structures of Everyday Life*, New York: Harper & Row.

Braudel, Fernand (1982) *Civilization & Capitalism 15th–18th Century: Vol. 2 The Wheels of Commerce*, New York: Harper & Row.

Braudel, Fernand (1984) *Civilization & Capitalism 15th–18th Century: Vol. 3 The Perspective of the World*, New York: Harper & Row.

Braudel, F. (1986) *The Identity of France, Volume 2: People and Production*, New York: Harper Perennial.

Braverman, H. (1974) *Labor and Monopoly Capital*, New York: Monthly Review Press.

Brown, M.W. (1927) *The Superfluous Man*, Cincinnati, OH: The Standard Publishing Co.

Bruce, R.V. (1987) *The Launching of Modern American Science*, New York: Knopf.

Bureau of the Census (1975) Washington DC: United States Government Printing Office.

Burke, J. (1985) *The Day the Universe Changed*, Boston, MA: Little, Brown & Co.

Burns, S. (1975) *Home, Inc.*, New York: Doubleday.

Burns, T. & Stalker, G.M. (1961) *The Management of Innovation*, London: Tavistock.

Burrell, G. & Morgan, G. (1979) *Sociological Paradigms*, Portsmouth, NH: Heinemann.

Business Week (1990) 'The *Business Week* 1000: America's Most Valuable Companies,' Special Issue, 5 April.

Byers, M.L. (1908) *Economics of Railway Operation*, New York: The Engineering News Publishing Co.

Byrne, J.A., Depke, D.A. & Verity, J.W. (1991) 'IBM, what's wrong, what's next?,' *Business Week*, 17 June, pp. 24–31.

Calás, M.B. (1987) 'The postmodern in the management disciplines,' unpublished doctoral dissertation, University of Massachusetts, Amherst, MA.

Calás, M.B. (1992) 'An/other silent voice? Representing "Hispanic Woman" in organizational Texts,' in A.J. Mills & P. Tancred (eds), *Gendering Organizational Analysis*, Newbury Park, CA: Sage, pp. 201–21.

Calás, M.B. & Smircich, L. (1987) 'Organizational culture: a critical assessment,' in F. Jablin, L. Putnam, K. Roberts and L. Porter (eds), *Handbook of Organizational Communication*, Newbury Park, CA: Sage, pp. 228–63.

Calás, M.B. & Smircich, L. (1993) 'Dangerous liaisons: the "feminine-in-management" meets "Globalization,"' *Business Horizons*, March/April.

Calás, M.B., Jacobson, S.W., Jacques, R. & Smircich, L. (1991) 'Is a woman-centered theory of management dangerous?,' Paper presented at the Academy of Management annual meeting, Miami, FL.

Calás, M.B., Smircich, L., Chio, V.C.M. and Holvino, E. (1993) 'Unbounding organizational analysis: questioning "Globalization" through third world women's voices,' Symposium presented at the annual meeting of the Academy of Management, Atlanta, GA.

Campbell, R.F., Fleming, T., Newell, L.J. & Bennion, J.W. (1987) *A History of Thought and Practice in Educational Administration*, New York: Teachers College Press.

Cantor, N.F. (1993) *The Civilization of the Middle Ages*, New York: HarperCollins.

Carnegie, A. (1913) *The Empire of Business*, New York: Doubleday.

Carnegie, A. (1920) *Autobiography of Andrew Carnegie*, Boston, MA: Houghton Mifflin.

Carpenter, E. (1921) *Civilization: Its Cause and Cure*, New York: Charles Scribner's Sons.

Carr-Saunders, A.P. & Wilson, P.A. (1933) *The Professions*, Oxford: Oxford University Press.

Census of the United States of America (1850), United States Bureau of the Census, Washington, DC: United States Government Printing Office.

Champlin, J.M. with Champlin, C.D. (1993) *The Visionary Leader*, New York: Crossroad.

Champy, J. (1995) *Reengineering Management: The Mandate for New Leadership*, New York: Harper Business.

Chandler, A. (1962) *Strategy and Structure*, Cambridge, MA: MIT Press.

Chandler, A. (1990) *Scale and Scope: The Dynamics of Industrial Capitalism*, Cambridge, MA: Belknap.

Chandler, G. (1992) 'The source and process of empowerment,' *Nursing Administration Quarterly*, 16(3): 65–71.

Chappell, T. (1993) *The Soul of Business: Managing for Profit and the Common Good*, New York: Bantam.

Chatterjee, P. (1986) *Nationalist Thought and the Colonial World: A Derivative Discourse*, Minneapolis, MN: University of Minnesota Press.

Chernow, R. (1990) *The House of Morgan: An American Banking Dynasty and the Rise of Modern Finance*, New York: Atlantic Monthly Press.

Chodorow, N. (1978) *The Reproduction of Mothering*, Berkeley, CA: University of California Press.

Clegg, S. (1994) 'Social theory for the study of organization: Weber and Foucault,' *Organization*, 1(1): 149–78.

Clegg, S., Dwyer, L., Gray, J., Kemp, S., Marceau, J., & O'Mara, E. (1994) 'Leadership and management needs of embryonic industries,' A research report for Midgley & Company on behalf of the Industry Task Force on Leadership and Management Skills.

Collins, E.G.C. & Devanna, M.A. (1990) *The Portable MBA*, New York: Wiley.

Covey, S. (1990a) *Principle-Centered Leadership*, New York: Simon & Schuster.

Covey, S. (1990b) *The 7 Habits of Highly Effective People*, New York: Simon & Schuster.

Croly, H. (1909) *The Promise of American Life*, New York: The Macmillan Company.

Crosby, P. (1979) *Quality is Free*, New York: McGraw-Hill.

Crosby, P. (1985) *Quality Without Tears*, New York: Nal-Dutton.

Crowther, S. (1917) 'There's a solution for labor troubles: an interview with John D. Rockefeller, Jr.,' in A.W. Shaw Co. (ed.), *Handling Men*, Chicago, IL: A.W. Shaw Co., pp. 82–90.

Culler, J. (1986) *Ferdinand de Saussure*, Rev. Edn, Ithaca, NY: Cornell University Press.

Cushman, P. (1990) 'Why the self is empty: toward a historically situated psychology,' *American Psychologist*, 45(5): 599–611.

Daft, R.L. & Lewin, A.Y. (1990) 'Can organization studies begin to break out of the normal science straightjacket?,' An editorial essay, *Organization Science*, 1(1): 1–9.

Davis, J.P. (1905/1961) *Corporations*, New York: Capricorn.

Davis, M.M. (1921) *Immigrant Health and the Community*, New York: Harper and Brothers.

De Certeau, M. (1984) *The Practice of Everyday Life*, Berkeley, CA: University of California Press.

De Tocqueville, A. (1835/1956) *Democracy in America* [abridged], New York: Mentor.

Deal, T.E. & Kennedy, A.A. (1982) *Corporate Cultures: The Rites and Rituals of Corporate Life*, Reading, MA: Addison-Wesley.

DeBrizzi, J.A. (1983) *Ideology and the Rise of Labor Theory in America*, London: Greenwood Press.

DePree, M. (1989) *Leadership is an Art*, New York: Doubleday.

Dewing, A.S. (1920) 'The early trust movement outlined,' in R.E. Curtis (ed.) (1931), *The Trusts and Economic Control*, New York: McGraw-Hill, pp.13–19.

Dewsnup, E.R. (ed.) (1906) *Railway Organization and Working*, Chicago, IL: University of Chicago Press.

Disston, F. (1917) 'How we hold our men,' A.W. Shaw Co. (ed.), *Handling Men*, Chicago, IL: A.W. Shaw Co, pp.67–81.

Dominiak, G.F. & Louderback, J.G. (1985) *Managerial Accounting*, 4th Edn, Boston:, MA: Kent.

Donham, W.B. (1922) 'Essential groundwork for a broad executive theory,' *Harvard Business Review*, 1(1): 1–10.

Dopp, K.E. (1902) *The Place of Industries in Elementary Education*, Chicago, IL: University of Chicago Press.

Dorfman, J. (1969) *The Economic Mind in American Civilization 1865–1918*, Vol. 3, New York: Augustus M. Kelley.

Drever, J. (1929) 'The Human Factor in Industrial Relations,' originally published in C.S. Myers (ed.), *Industrial Psychology*, London: Thornton Butterworth Ltd, pp. 16–17. Republished in B.V. Moore & G.W. Hartmann (1931), *Readings in Industrial Psychology*, New York: D. Appleton-Century Company, p. 26.

Dreyfus, H.L. & Rabinow, P. (1983) *Michel Foucault: Beyond Structuralism and Hermeneutics*, 2nd Edn, Chicago, IL: University of Chicago Press.

Drucker, P.F. (1968) *The Age of Discontinuity*, New York: Harper & Row.

Drucker, P.F. (1988) 'The coming of the new organization,' *Harvard Business Review*, (66)1: 45–53.

Drucker, P.F. (1991) 'The new productivity challenge,' *Harvard Business Review*, 69(6): 69–79.

Drucker, P.F. (1993) *Post-capitalist Society*, New York: Harper Business.

Dubin, R. (1956) 'Industrial workers' world: a study of the "central life interests" of industrial workers,' *Social Problems*, January, pp.131–42.

Duby, G. (ed.) (1988) *A History of Private Life: Revelations of the Medieval World*, Vol. 2, 5 vols) (general editors: P. Ariès & G. Duby), Cambridge, MA: Belknap.

Edison, T.A. (1917) Aphorism cited in A.W. Shaw Co. (ed.), *Handling Men*, Chicago, IL: A.W. Shaw Co., p. 81.

Elliott, E.A. (1989) 'The discourse of nursing: a case of silencing,' *Nursing & Health Care*, 10(10): 539–43.

Elliott, M. (1994) 'Take me to your leader,' *Newsweek*, 25 April, p. 67.

Etzioni, A. (ed.) (1969) *The Semi-Professions and Their Organization*, New York: The Free Press.

Ewen, S. (1976) *Captains of Consciousness: Advertising and the Social Roots of the Consumer Culture*, New York: McGraw-Hill.

Fagan, James O. (1909) *Labor and the Railroads*, New York: Houghton Mifflin.

Fayol, H. (1916) *Administration Industrielle et Générale*, Paris: Durod.

Fierman, J. (1994) 'The contingency workforce,' *Fortune*, 24 January, pp. 30–6.

Fisher, B. (1917) 'Profit sharing – its successes and failures,' in A.W. Shaw Co. (ed.), *Handling Men*, Chicago, IL: A.W. Shaw Co., pp. 153–8.

Fletcher, J. (1994a) 'Toward a theory of relational practice in organizations: a reconstruction of "real" work,' Unpublished doctoral dissertation, Boston University, MA.

Fletcher, J. (1994b) 'Castrating the female advantage: feminist standpoint research and management science', *Journal of Management Inquiry*, 3(1): 74–82.

Flexner, A. (1915) 'Is social work a profession?,' *School and Society*, 1(4): 901–11.

Follett, M.P. (1925/1942) *Dynamic Administration*, compiled and edited by H.C. Metcalf & L. Urwick, New York: Harper.

Foner, P.S. (1962) *History of the Labor Movement in the United States*, Vol. 1, New York: International Publishers.

Ford, H. (1922) *My Life and Work*, Garden City, NY: Doubleday Page & Co.

Foucault, M. (1972a) *The Archaeology of Knowledge*, New York: Pantheon.

Foucault, M. (1972b) *The Discourse on Language*, New York: Pantheon.

Foucault, M. (1973a) *Madness & Civilization: A History of Insanity in the Age of Reason*, New York: Random House.

Foucault, M. (1973b) *The Order of Things: An Archaeology of the Human Sciences*, New York: Random House.

Foucault, M. (1975) *The Birth of the Clinic: An Archaeology of Medical Perception*, New York: Random House.

Foucault, M. (1979) *Discipline & Punish: The Birth of the Prison*, New York: Random House.

Foucault, M. (1980) *The History of Sexuality, Vol. I: An Introduction*, New York: Random House.

Foucault, M. (1984a) 'The ethic of care for the self . . .,' *Philosophy and Social Criticism*, July.

Foucault, M. (1984b) 'What is Enlightenment?,' in P. Rabinow (ed.) *The Foucault Reader*, New York: Pantheon, pp. 32–50.

Friedan, B. (1981) *The Second Stage*, New York: Summit Books.

Friedson, E. (1983) 'The theory of professions: state of the art,' in R. Dingwall & P. Lewis (eds), *The Sociology of the Professions*, New York: St Martin's Press.

Friedson, E. (1984) 'Are professions necessary?,' in T.L. Haskell (ed.), *The Authority of Experts*, Bloomington, IN: University of Indiana Press.

Frost, P.F. (1988) 'Rekindling the flame: researching the meaning still embedded in the culture construct,' Symposium presented at the annual meeting of the Academy of Management, Anaheim, CA.

Frost, W.J. (1973) *The Quaker Family in Colonial America*, New York: St Martin's Press.

Fry, L.W. & Smith, D.A. (1987) 'Congruence, contingency, and theory building,' *Academy of Management Review*, 12(1): 117–32.

Galbraith, J.K. (1958) *The Affluent Society*, New York: Houghton Mifflin.

Galbraith, J.K. (1967) *The New Industrial State*, Boston, MA: Houghton Mifflin.

Galbraith, J.K. (1983) *The Anatomy of Power*, Boston, MA: Houghton Mifflin.

Garson, B. (1977) *All the Livelong Day: The Meaning and Demeaning of Routine Work*, New York: Penguin.

Geneen, H. (1984) *Managing*, New York: Avon.

Georgano, G.N. (1982) *The New Encyclopedia of Motorcars: 1885 to the Present*, 3rd Edn, New York: E.P. Dutton.

George, H., Jr. (1905) *The Menace of Privilege*, New York: Grosset & Dunlap.

Gerpott, T.J. & Domsch, M. (1985) 'The concept of professionalism and the management of salaried technical professionals: a cross-national perspective,' *Human Resource Management*, (24)2: 207–26.

Gerth, H.H. & Mills, C.W. (1946) *From Max Weber: Essays in Sociology*, New York: Oxford University Press.

Gilbreth, L.M. & Cook, A.R. (1947) *The Foreman in Manpower Management*, New York: McGraw-Hill.

Gillespie, R. (1991) *Manufacturing Knowledge: A History of the Hawthorne Experiments*, Cambridge: Cambridge University Press.

Gilligan, C. (1982) *In a Different Voice*, Cambridge, MA: Harvard University Press.

Gintis, H. & Bowles, S. (1981) 'Structure and practice in the labor theory of value,' *Review of Radical Political Economics*, 12(4): 1–26.

Gioia, D.A. & Pitre, E. (1990) 'Multiparadigm perspectives on theory building,' *Academy of Management Review*, 15(4): 584–602.

Glazer, N. (1993) *Women's Paid and Unpaid Labor: The Work Transfer in Health Care and Retailing*, Philadelphia, PA: Temple University Press.

Goodman, N.G. (1945) (ed.)*A Benjamin Franklin Reader*, New York: Thomas Y. Crowell.

Gordon, J.S. (1988) *The Scarlet Woman of Wall Street: Jay Gould, Jim Fisk, Cornelius Vanderbilt, the Erie Railway Wars, & the Birth of Wall Street*, New York: Weidenfeld & Nicolson.

Gordon, S. (1991a) *Prisoners of Men's Dreams*, Boston, MA: Little, Brown & Co.

Gordon, S. (1991b) 'The Crisis in Caring,' *Boston Globe Magazine*, 10 July, pp. 22–6.

Graff, G. (1990) 'Other voices, other rooms: organizing and teaching the humanities conflict,' *New Literary History*, 21: 817–39.

Greenleaf, R.K. (1977) *Servant Leadership: A Journey into the Nature of Legitimate Power and Greatness*, New York: Paulist Press.

Grimshaw, J. (1986) *Philosophy and Feminist Thinking*, Minneapolis, MN: University of Minnesota Press.

Haas, H.G. with Tamarkin, B. (1992) *The Leader Within: An Empowering Path of Self-Discovery*, New York: Harper Business.

Habermas, J. (1987) *The Philosophical Discourse of Modernity*, Cambridge, MA: MIT Press.

Hackett, R.D., Buycio, P. & Guion, R.M. (1989) 'Absenteeism among hospital nurses: an ideographic-longitudinal analysis,' *Academy of Management Journal*, 32(2): 424–53.

Hackman, Oldham, Janson & Purdy (1975) 'A new strategy for job enrichment,' *California Management Review*, 17(4): 57–71.

Haines, H.S. (1919) *Efficient Railway Operation*, New York: Macmillan.

Haller, J.S. (1981) *American Medicine in Transition 1840–1910*, Urbana, IL: University of Illinois Press.

Hammer, M. (1995) *Reengineering Management: The Mandate for New Leadership*, New York: Harper Business.

Hammer, M. & Champy, J. (1993) *Reengineering the Corporation: A Manifesto for Business Revolution*, New York: Harper Business.

Hampden-Turner, C. (1990) *Creating Corporate Culture: From Discord to Harmony*, Reading, MA: Addison-Wesley.

Hannan, M.T. & Freeman, J. (1977) 'The population ecology of organizations,' *American Journal of Sociology*, 82(5): 929–64

Haraway, D. (1988) 'Situated knowledges: the science question in feminism and the privilege of partial perspective,' *Feminist Studies*, 14(3): 575–99.

Harré, R. & Gillett, G. (1994) *The Discursive Mind*, London: Sage.

Hartmann, H. (1981) 'The unhappy marriage of Marxism and feminism: towards a more progressive union,' in L. Sargent (ed.), *Women and Revolution*, Boston, MA: South End Press.

Hays, J.W. (1917) 'Your right in your employees' inventions, in A.W. Shaw Co. (ed.), *Handling Men*, Chicago, IL: A.W. Shaw Co., pp. 193–200.

Hays, S.P. (1957) *The Response to Industrialism 1885–1914*, Chicago, IL: University of Chicago Press.

Healy, K.T. (1940) *The Economics of Transportation in America*, New York: The Ronald Press.

Hegel, G.W.F. (1807/1977) *Phenomenology of Spirit* (translated by A.V. Miller), Oxford: Oxford University Press.

Helgeson, S. (1990) *The Female Advantage: Women's Ways of Leadership*, New York: Doubleday.

Herm, G. (1976) *The Celts*, New York: St Martin's Press.

Hobbes, T. (1651/1969) *Leviathan*, Cited in W.T. Jones (1969) *A History of Western Philosophy: Hobbes to Hume*, 2nd Edn, Vol. III, New York: Harcourt, Brace, Jovanovich.

Hochschild, A. (1989) *The Second Shift*, New York: Avon.

Hofstadter, R. (1963) *Anti-Intellectualism in American Life*, New York: Vintage.

Hogg, A. (1906) *The Railroad in Education*, 15th Edn, Louisville, KY: John P. Morton and Company.

Holbrook, S.H. (1953/1985) *The Age of the Moguls: The Story of the Robber Barons and the Great Tycoons*, New York: Harmony Books.

Holder, C.F. (1913) *The Quakers in Great Britain and America*, New York: The Neuner Company.

Hollway, W. (1991) *Work Psychology and Organizational Behavior*, London: Sage.

Holmes, G. (ed.) (1988) *The Oxford History of Medieval Europe*, Oxford: Oxford University Press.

Hoskin, K.W. & Macve, R.H. (1988) 'The genesis of accountability: the West Point connection,' *Accounting, Organizations and Society*, 13(1): 1–24.

Howe, L.K. (1977) *Pink Collar Workers: Inside the World of Women's Work*, New York: Avon.

Hoyt, E.P., Jr. (1966) *The House of Morgan*, New York: Dodd Mead & Co.

Huey, J. (1994a) 'The new post-heroic leadership,' *Fortune*, 21 February, pp. 42–50.

Huey, J. (1994b) 'The leadership industry,' *Fortune*, 21 February, pp. 54–6.

Huff, A.S. (1990) 'Wives – of the organization,' Paper presented at the Women and Work Conference, Arlington, TX, 11 May.

Hunt, F. (1857) *Worth and Wealth: Maxims for Merchants and Men of Business*, New York: Stringer & Townshend.

Industrial Management (1916) 'Human-Being Management,' 52(10): 398–400.

International Correspondence Schools (1901) *The Businessman's Handbook: A Convenient Book of Reference for Business Men*, Scranton, PA: International Textbook Co.

Jacobson, S.W. & Jacques, R. (1990) 'Of knowers, knowing and the known: a gender framework for re-visioning organizational and management scholarship,' Paper presented at the annual meeting of the Academy of Management, San Francisco, CA.

Jacoby, R. (1987) *The Last Intellectuals: American Culture in the Age of Academe*, New York: Basic Books.

Jacques, R. (1992a) 'Re-presenting the knowledge worker: a poststructuralist analysis of the new employed professional,' Unpublished doctoral dissertation, University of Massachusetts, Amherst, MA.

Jacques, R. (1992b) 'Critique and theory building: producing knowledge "from the kitchen,"' *Academy of Management Review*, 17(3): 582–606.

Jacques, R. (1993) 'Untheorized dimensions of caring work: caring as a structural practice and caring as a way of seeing,' *Nursing Administration Quarterly*, 17(2): 1–10.

Jacques, R. & Fletcher, J. (1994) '"Getting disappeared": relational work and invisibility in organizations,' Presentation in the symposium 'Bringing work relationships into the foreground of organizational research,' annual meeting of the Academy of Management, Dallas, TX.

Janssens, M. & Steyaert, C. (1994) 'Language and translation: a problem or asset in management,' Presentation for the symposium 'Language: a barrier to organizational understanding,' annual meeting of the Academy of Management, Dallas, TX.

Jelinek, M. & Adler, N.J. (1988) 'Women: world class managers for global competition,' *Academy of Management Executive*, February, pp. 7–19.

Jenks, L.H. (1960) 'Early phases of the management movement,' *Administrative Science Quarterly*, (3)1: 421–47.

Jick, T.D. (1979) 'Mixing qualitative and quantitative methods: triangulation in action,' *Administrative Science Quarterly* 24(3): 602–11, reprinted in J. Van Maanen (ed.) (1983), *Qualitative Methodology*, Beverly Hills, CA: Sage, pp. 135–49.

Johnson, D. (1987) 'Doctors' dilemma: unionizing,' *New York Times*, 13 July, Section D4, p. 1.

Johnson, P. (1976) *A History of Christianity*, New York: Atheneum.

Jones, E.D. (1916) *The Administration of Industrial Enterprises: With Special Reference to Factory Practice*, New York: Longmans, Green and Co.

Jones, W.T. (1969) *A History of Western Philosophy: Hobbes to Hume*, 2nd Edn, Vol. III, New York: Harcourt, Brace, Jovanovich.

Jones, W.T. (1975) *A History of Western Philosophy: Kant and the Nineteenth Century*, Revised Edn, Vol. IV, New York: Harcourt, Brace, Jovanovich.

Jordan, J.V., Kaplan, A.G., Miller, J.B., Stiver, I.P. & Surrey, J.L. (1991) *Women's Growth in Connection: Writings From the Stone Center*, New York: The Guilford Press.

Josephson, M. (1934/1962) *The Robber Barons*, New York: Harcourt, Brace & World.

Kanter, R.M. (1977) *Men and Women of the Corporation*, New York: Basic Books.

Kanter, R.M. (1989a) 'The new managerial work,' *Harvard Business Review*, 67(6): 85–92.

Kanter, R.M. (1989b) 'Why cowboy management is bad for American business,' *Working Woman*, April, pp. 134–6, 166.

Kaufman, S.B. (ed.) (1986) *The Samuel Gompers Papers, Vol. 1: The Making of a Union Leader, 1850–86*, Urbana, IL: University of Illinois Press.

Keller, A.G. (1915/1973) *Societal Evolution*, Port Washington, NY: Kennikat Press.

Keller, E.F. (1983) *A Feeling for the Organism: The Life and Work of Barbara McClintock*, New York: W.H. Freeman.

Kerr, S. & Jermier, J.M. (1978) 'Substitutes for leadership: their meaning and measurement,' *Organizational Behavior and Human Performance*, 22(3): 375–403.

Kietchel, W. (1993) 'How we will work in the year 2000', *Fortune*, 17 May, pp. 38–45.

Kolb, D.M. (1992) 'Women's work: peace making in organizations,' in D.M. Kolb and J.M. Bartunek (eds) *Hidden Conflict in Organizations: Uncovering Behind-the-Scenes Disputes*, 63–91. Newbury Park, CA: Sage.

Kuhn, T.S. (1962/1970) *The Structure of Scientific Revolutions*, 2nd Edn, Chicago, IL: University of Chicago Press.

Kundera, M. (1981) *The Book of Laughter and Forgetting*, New York: Penguin.

Lancaster, H. (1994) 'A new social contract to benefit employer and employee,' *Wall Street Journal*, 29 November, p. B1.

Langton, J. (1984) 'The ecological theory of bureaucracy: the case of Josiah Wedgwood and the British pottery industry, *Administrative Science Quarterly*, 29(2): 330–54.

Laslett, P. (1960) *John Locke: Two Treatises on Government, A Critical Edition with an Introduction and Apparatus Criticus, Rev. Edn*, New York: Mentor.

Laurie, B. (1989) *Artisans into Workers: Labor in Nineteenth-Century America*, New York: Farrar, Strauss & Giroux.

Lawler, J. (1991) 'Author: workers seek approval for effort, not output,' *USA Today*, 26 November, p. 6B.

Lawrence, P. & Lorsch, J. (1967) *Organization and Environment*, Cambridge, MA: Harvard University Press.

Lawson, W.R. (1903) *American Industrial Problems*, Edinburgh: William Blackwood & Sons.

Lescohier, D.D. (1930/1967) 'What is the effect and extent of technical changes on employment security?,' in *American Management Association Personnel Series, Numbers 1–21, 1930–1935*, New York: Kraus Reprint Corporation, (1): 3–18.

Lichtenstein, B.M., Smith, B.A. & Torbert, W.R. (1995) 'Leadership and ethical development: balancing light and shadow,' *Business Ethics Quarterly*, 5(1): 97–116.

Link, H.C. (1924) *Employment Psychology*, New York: Macmillan.

Litchfield, E.H. (1956) 'Notes on a general theory of administration,' *Administrative Science Quarterly*, 1(1): 3–29.

Litterer, J. (1959/1986) *The Emergence of Systematic Management as Shown by the Literature of Management from 1870 to 1900*, New York: Garland.

Littré, Émile (1966) *Dictionnaire de la Langue Française, Vol. 2*, Paris: Gallimard/Hachette.

Locke, J. (1703/1960) *Two Treatises on Government*, New York: Mentor.

Loden, M. (1985) *Feminine Leadership*, New York: Times Books.

Lowell, A.L. (1923) 'The profession of business,' *Harvard Business Review*, 1(2): 129–31.

Lyotard, J.F. (1984) *The Postmodern Condition: A Report on Knowledge*, Minneapolis, MN: University of Minnesota Press.

Macfarlane, A. (1978) *The Origins of English Individualism*, Oxford: Basil Blackwell.

Machiavelli, N. (1537/1952) *The Prince*, New York: Mentor.

Madden, D. (ed.) (1970) *American Dreams, American Nightmares*, Carbondale, IL: Southern Illinois University Press.

Marglin, S. (1974) 'What do bosses do: the origins and functions of hierarchy in capitalist production,' *Radical Review of Political Economics*, Summer.

Martin, Edward Winslow (1877/1971) *The History of the Great Riots and of the Molly Maguires*, New York: Augustus M. Kelley.

Marx, K. (1867/1967) *Capital, Vol. 1*, New York: International Publishers.

Marx, K. (1947) *The German Ideology: Part One with Selections from Parts Two and Three and Supplementary Texts*, New York: International Publishers.

Mather, C. (1692/1991) 'A discourse on the wonders of the invisible world,' in *Cotton Mather on Witchcraft*, New York: Dorset Press, pp. 34–66.

Mayo, E. (1922) 'The irrational factor in society,' *The Journal of Personnel Research*, 1(10): 419–26.

McCaffrey, J.K.M. (ed.) (1964) *The American Dream: A Half-Century View from American Magazine*, Garden City, NY: Doubleday.

McCallum, Daniel C. (1856) 'Superintendent's report,' in A.D. Chandler (ed.) (1965), *The Railroads: The Nation's First Big Business*, New York: Harcourt, Brace & World, pp. 101–8.

McCraw, T.K. (1984) 'Business and government: the origins of the adversary relationship,' *California Management Review*, 26(2): 33–52.

McGregor, D. (1960) *The Human Side of Enterprise*, New York: McGraw-Hill.

McKinley, W. (1994) Message posted to the Academy of Management Organization and Management Theory Internet bulletin board <OMT@listproc.stfx.ca>, Vol. 3, Issue #182, 19 August.

McQuarrie, F. (1992) 'Elitism or diversity: "women in management" reconsidered,' Paper presented at the annual meeting of the Academy of Management, Las Vegas, NV.

Midgeley, M. (1985) *Evolution as a Religion*, New York: Methuen.

Miller, J.B. (1976) *Toward a New Psychology of Women*, Boston, MA: Beacon Press.

Miller, D.S. & Norton, V.M. (1986) 'Absenteeism: nursing service's albatross,' *Journal of Nursing Administration*, 16(3): 38–42.

Millikan, R.A. (1924) *Science and Life*, Boston: The Pilgrim Press.

Mills, A.J. & Tancred, P. (eds) (1992) *Gendering Organizational Analysis*, Newbury Park, CA: Sage.

Mills, C.W. (1956) *White Collar*, New York: Oxford University Press.

Mims, R. & Lewis, E. (1989) 'A portrait of the boss,' *Business Week*, 20 October, pp. 23–8.

Mintzberg, H. (1968) 'The manager at work – determining his activities, roles, and programs by structured observation,' Doctoral dissertation, MIT, Cambridge, MA.

Mintzberg (1971) 'Managerial work: analysis from observation,' *Management Science*, 18(1): B97–B110.

Mintzberg, H. (1979) *The Structuring of Organizations*, Englewood Cliffs, NJ: Prentice-Hall.

Misra, G. & Gergen, K.J. (1993) 'Beyond scientific colonialism: a reply to Poortinga and Triandis,' *International Journal of Psychology*, 28(2): 251–4.

Mitchell, T.R. & James, L.R. (1989) 'Situational vs. dispositional factors: competing explanations on behavior,' *Academy of Management Review*, 14(3): 330–2, 401–7.

Moore, B.V. & Hartmann, G.W. (eds) (1931) *Readings in Industrial Psychology*, New York: D. Appleton-Century Company.

Morgan, G. & Smircich, L. (1980) 'The case for qualitative research,' *Academy of Management Review*, 5(4): 491–500.

Morgan, K.O. (ed.) (1988) *The Oxford History of Britain*, Oxford: Oxford University Press.

Morris, R. (1920) *Railroad Administration*, 2nd Edn, [1st Edn, 1910], New York: D. Appleton & Co.

Murphy, C.D. (1917a) 'Living up to your employment system,' in A.W. Shaw Co. (ed.), *Handling Men*, Chicago, IL: A.W. Shaw Co., pp. 13–23.

Murphy, C.D. (1917b) 'The building of men,' in A.W. Shaw Co. (ed.), *Handling Men*, Chicago, IL: A.W. Shaw Co., pp. 138–42.

Naisbitt, J. (1982) *Megatrends*, New York: Warner.

Naisbitt, J. & Aburdene, P. (1985) *Re-Inventing the Corporation*, New York: Warner.

Navin, T.R. (1950) *The Whitin Machine Works Since 1831*, New York: Russell & Russell.

Newell, A. & Simon, H.A. (1976) 'Computer science as empirical inquiry: symbols and search,' *Communications of the ACM*, 19(3): 113–26.

Newman, K.S. (1988) *Falling From Grace: The Experience of Downward Mobility in the American Middle Class*, New York: The Free Press.

Niven, M.M. (1967) *Personnel Management 1913–63*, London: Institute of Personnel Management.

Nordhoff, Charles (1875/1962) *The Communistic Societies of the United States*, New York: Hillary House Publishers.

Norman, R. (1976) *Hegel's Phenomenology: A Philosophical Introduction*, New York: St Martin's Press.

Nussbaum, B. (1991) 'I'm worried about my job!,' *Business Week*, 7 October, pp. 94–104.

O'Connor, S.J. & Lanning, J.A. (1990) 'The end of autonomy? Reflections on the post-professional physician,' Paper presented at the Academy of Management annual meetings, San Francisco, CA, August.

Ommer, W.I. (1917) 'Why we are replacing men with women,' in A.W. Shaw Co. (ed.), *Handling Men*, Chicago, IL: A.W. Shaw Co., IL, pp. 47–56.

O'Reilly, M. (1994) 'Reengineering the MBA,' *Fortune*, 24 January, pp. 38–47.

Ouchi, W.G. (1981) *Theory Z*, New York: Avon.

Ozanne, R. (1979) 'United States labor-management relations, 1860–1930,' in K. Nakagawa (ed.), *Labor and Management*, Proceedings of the Fourth Fuji Conference (The International Conference on Business History), Tokyo: University of Tokyo Press, pp. 77–95.

Packard, V. (1958) *The Hidden Persuaders*, New York: Pocket Books.

Pais, A. (1982) *'Subtle is the Lord': The Science and the Life of Albert Einstein*, Oxford: Oxford University Press.

Parkinson, C.N. (1957) 'Parkinson's Law, or the rising pyramid,' in *Parkinson's Law and Other Studies in Administration*, Boston: Houghton Mifflin, pp. 2–13.

Parsons, T. (1956) 'Suggestions for a sociological approach to the theory of organizations, Parts I and II,' *Administrative Science Quarterly*, 1(1): 63–85 and 1(2): 225–39.

Partridge, W.E. (1887) 'Capital's need for high-priced labor,' *Transactions of the ASME*, 8: 269–94.

Pelavin, E. (1995) 'Bringing women's voices to the organization: the experiences of working mothers of adolescents.' Doctoral dissertation, California School of Professional Psychology, Alaeda, CA.

Perkins, Charles E. (1885) 'Administering a great railroad system' in A.D. Chandler (ed.) (1965) *The Railroads: The Nation's First Big Business*, New York: Harcourt, Brace & World, pp. 118–25.

Perrow, C. (1973) 'The short and glorious history of organizational theory,' *Organizational Dynamics*, (1)1: 8–20.

Perrow, C. (1981) 'Disintegrating social sciences,' *NYU Education Quarterly*, Winter, pp. 2–9.

Perrow, C. (1986) *Complex Organizations: A Critical Essay*, 3rd Edn, New York: Random House.

Person, H.S. (1926) 'The management movement,' in H.C. Metcalf (ed.), *Scientific Foundations of Business Administration*, Baltimore, MD: Williams & Wilkins.

Peters, T. (1987) *Thriving on Chaos: Handbook for a Management Revolution*, New York: Knopf.

Peters, T. (1990) 'The best new managers will listen, motivate, support: isn't that just like a woman?' *Working Woman*, September, pp. 216–17.

Peters, T. (1992) *Liberation Management*, New York: Knopf.

Pfeffer, J. (1993) 'Barriers to the advance of organizational science: paradigm development as a dependent variable,' *Academy of Management Review*, 18(4): 599–620.

Pfeffer, J. & Baron, J.N. (1988) 'Taking the workers back out: recent trends in the structuring of employment,' in B.M. Staw & L.L. Cummings (eds), *Research in Organizational Behavior, Vol. 10*, London: JAI Press, pp. 257–303.

Porter, G. (1973) *The Rise of Big Business, 1860–1910*, Arlington Heights, IL: Harlan Davidson.

Porter, H.F. (1917a) 'Growing' your own executives,' A.W. Shaw Co. (ed.), *Handling Men*, Chicago, IL: A.W. Shaw Co., pp. 127–37.

Porter, H.F. (1917b) 'Giving the men a chance – what it's doing for Ford,' in A.W. Shaw Co. (ed.), *Handling Men*, Chicago, IL: A.W. Shaw Co., pp. 167–82.

Porter, M.E. (1980) *Competitive Strategy: Techniques for Analyzing Industries and Their Competitors*, New York: The Free Press.

Porter, M.E. (1985) *Competitive Advantage: Creating and Sustaining Superior Performance*, New York: The Free Press.

Porter, M.E. (1990) *The Competitive Advantage of Nations and Their Firms*, New York: The Free Press.

Powell, G.N. (1994) *Women & Men in Management*, 2nd Edn, Newbury Park, CA: Sage.

Printers' Ink: A Journal for Advertisers (1938) '50 years 1888–1938, section two,' 28 July.

Prude, J. (1983) *The Coming of Industrial Order: Town and Factory Life in Rural Massachusetts 1810–1860*, Cambridge: Cambridge University Press.

Quick, H. (1913) *On Board the Good Ship Earth*, Indianapolis, IN: Bobbs-Merrill Co.

Quine, W.V.O. (1953) *From a Logical Point of View*, Cambridge, MA: Harvard University Press.

Ramanathan, K.V. (1982) *Management Control in Nonprofit Organizations: Text & Cases*, New York: Wiley, pp. 210–11.

Reay, B. (1985) *The Quakers and the English Revolution*, New York: St Martin's Press.

Reece, B. (1895) 'First principles in railroad management,' *The Engineering Magazine*, IX(4): 617–22.

Reich, R.B. (1983) *The Next American Frontier*, New York: Penguin.

Rindova, V. (1994) 'Theories X, Y and Z BC: concepts of management in ancient China,' Presentation in the symposium 'How modern is modern management,' annual meeting of the Academy of Management, Dallas, TX.

Riordan, W.L. (1963) *Plunkett of Tammany Hall*, New York: E.P. Dutton & Co.

Roberts, W. (1986) *Leadership Secrets of Attila the Hun: A Metaphorical Primer*, New York: Peregrine.

Robbins, S.P. (1990) *Organization Theory: Structure, Design & Applications*, 3rd Edn, Englewood Cliffs, NJ: Prentice-Hall.

Roethlisberger, F.J. & Dickson, W.J. (1939) *Management and the Worker*, Cambridge, MA: Harvard University Press.

Roomkin, M.J. (1989) *Managers as Employees*, New York: Oxford University Press.

Rose, R.C. & Garrett, E.M. (1992) *How to Make a Buck and Still be a Decent Human Being*, New York: Harper Business.

Rosener, J.B. (1990) 'Ways women lead,' *Harvard Business Review*, 69(6): 119–25.

Rouche, M. (1987) 'The Early Middle Ages in the West,' in P. Veyne (ed.) *A History of Private Life: From Pagan Rome to Byzantium*, Vol. 1, 5 vols (general editors P. Ariès & G. Duby), Cambridge, MA: Belknap, pp. 411–550.

Rowse, A.L. (1959) *The Elizabethans and America*, New York: Harper & Brothers.

Rudolph, F. (1962) *The American College and University: A History*, New York: Vintage.

Said, E.W. (1979) *Orientalism*, New York: Vintage.

Salter, M.S. (1973) 'Taylor incentive compensation to strategy,' *Harvard Business Review*, 51(2): 94–102.

Sanger, D.E. (1988) 'The moment of truth for Big Blue,' *New York Times*, 3 January, Section 3, pp. 1, 6.

Sarfatti Larson, M. (1984) 'The production of expertise and the constitution of expert power,' in T.L. Haskell (ed.), *The Authority of Experts*, Bloomington, IN: Indiana University Press, pp. 28–80.

Schabas, M. (1990) *A World Ruled by Number: William Stanley Jevons and the Rise of Mathematical Economics*, Princeton, NJ: Princeton University Press.

Schaef, A.W. (1987) *When Society Becomes an Addict*, San Francisco, CA: Harper & Row.

Schaef, A.W. & Fassel, D. (1988) *The Addictive Organization*, San Francisco, CA: Harper & Row.

Schaffner, Margaret Anna (1907) 'The labor contract from individual to collective bargaining,' *Bulletin of the University of Wisconsin*, 2(1): 1–182.

Schein, E.H. (1985) *Organizational Culture*, San Francisco, CA: Jossey-Bass.

Schneider, H. (1914) 'Selecting young men for particular jobs,' *Bulletin of the National Association of Corporation Schools* [subsequently *Management Review*], 1(7): 9–19.

Schwartz, R.M. (1989) *Servant Leaders of the People of God: An Ecclesial Spirituality for American Priests*, New York: Paulist Press.

Scott, J.W. (1990) 'Deconstructing equality-versus-difference: or, the uses of poststructuralist theory for feminism,' *Feminist Studies*, 14(1): 33–50.

Scott, W.D. (1903) *A Theory of Advertising*, Boston, MA: A.W. Shaw Co.

Scott, W.D. & Clothier, R.C. (1923) *Personnel Management: Principles, Practices, and Point of View*, Chicago, IL: A.W. Shaw Co.

Senge, P.M. (1990) *The Fifth Discipline: The Art and Practice of the Learning Organization*, New York: Currency Doubleday.

Servan-Schreiber, J.J. (1967) *The American Challenge*, New York: Atheneum.

Shaiken, H. (1977) 'Craftsman into baby sitter,' in I. Illich, I.K. Zola, J. McKnight, J. Kaplan & H. Shaiken (eds), *Disabling Professions*, New York: Marion Boyars, pp. 111–27.

Shaw, A.W. (1916) *An Approach to Business Problems*, Cambridge, MA: Harvard University Press.

Shaw, A.W. Co. (1917) *Handling Men*, Chicago, IL: A.W. Shaw Co.

Sheehan, J.J. (1989) *German History 1770–1866*, Oxford: Clarendon Press.

Shipman, P. (1994) *The Evolution of Racism*, New York: Simon & Schuster.

Showalter, E. (1987) 'Critical cross-dressing: male feminists and the woman of the year,' in A. Jardine & P. Smith (eds), *Men in Feminism*, New York: Methuen, pp. 116–32.

Siler, J.F. (1990) 'Pressure on Professionals,' *Business Week*, 23 July, pp. 24–5.

Simons, A.M. (1912) *Social Forces in American History*, New York: Macmillan.

Skinner, B.F. (1971) *Beyond Freedom & Dignity*, New York: Bantam.

Sloan, A.P. (1964) *My Years With General Motors*, New York: MacFadden.

Slocum, C.H. (1917) 'Shaping men to the work,' in A.W. Shaw Co. (ed.), *Handling Men*, Chicago, IL: A.W. Shaw Co., pp. 143–50.

Slotkin, R. (1992) *Gunfighter Nation: The Myth of the Frontier in Twentieth-Century America*, New York: Harper Perennial.

Smircich, L. (1983) 'Concepts of culture and organizational analysis,' *Administrative Science Quarterly*, 28(2): 339–58.

Smircich, L. & Calás, M.B. (1987) 'Organizational culture, a critical assessment,' in F. Jablin, L. Putnam, K. Roberts & L. Porter (eds), *The Handbook of Organizational Communication*, Beverly Hills, CA: Sage.

Smircich, L. & Calás, M.B. (1990) 'What feminist theory offers organization and management theory or why go from culture to gender?,' Paper presented at the annual meeting of the Academy of Management, San Francisco, CA.

Smith, A. (1776/1937) *The Wealth of Nations*, New York: Random House.

Smith, P. (1984) *The Rise of Industrial America: A People's History of the Post-Reconstruction Era*, Vol. 6, New York: Penguin.

Smith, T.K. (1994) 'What's so effective about Stephen Covey,' *Fortune*, 12 December, pp. 116–26.

Socialist Review (1991) 'Post-Fordism: flexible politics in the age of just-in-time production,' 21(1). Special issue.

Solvay, E. (1898) *Le Productivisme Social*, Annals of the Institute of Social Sciences, tome IV, pp. 411–37, Brussels. Cited in Urwick, L. (1956) *The Golden Book of Management*, London: Newman Neame Ltd.

Sombart W. (1906/1976) 'Why is there no Socialism in the United States?' White Plains, NY: M.E. Sharpe.

Spence, G. (1989) *With Justice For None: Destroying an American Myth*, New York: Times Books.

Spivak, G.C. (1988) *In Other Worlds: Essays in Cultural Politics*, New York: Routledge.

Stanley, D.A. (1917) 'Helping employees to save,' in A.W. Shaw Co. (ed.), *Handling Men*, Chicago, IL: A.W. Shaw Co., pp. 183–92.

Starbuck, W.H. (1992a) 'Learning by knowledge-intensive firms,' *Journal of Management Studies*, 29(6): 713–40.

Starbuck, W.H. (1992b) 'Surmounting our human limitations,' in R. Quinn & K. Cameron (eds), *Paradox and Transformation: Toward a Theory of Change in Organization and Management*, Cambridge, MA: Ballinger.

Starbuck, W.H., Rindova, V., Garvey, M.L., Kuperman, J.C., Jain, S. and Eisner, A.B. (1994) 'How modern is modern management,' Symposium presented at the annual meeting of the Academy of Management, Dallas, TX.

Starr, P. (1982) *The Social Transformation of American Medicine*, New York: Basic Books.

Staw, B.M. (1985) 'Repairs on the road to relevance and rigor: some unexplored issues in publishing organizational research,' in L.L. Cummings & P.J. Frost (eds), *Publishing in the Organizational Sciences*, Homewood, IL: Irwin.

Steinbeck, J. (1938) 'The Leader of the People,' in *Of Mice and Men and Short Stories*, New York: P.F. Collier, pp. 283–303.

Steinmetz, C.P. (1918) 'Presidential Address [of the Association],' *Bulletin of the National Association of Corporation Schools* [subsequently *Management Review*], 5(1): 3–7.

Stevens, R.P. & Schoberg, G. (1990) *Servant Leadership*, New York: Shaw.

Stone, K. (1974) 'The origins of job structures in the steel industry,' *Review of Radical Political Economics*, Summer: 350–81.

Stone, M.M. (1991) 'Organization theory from Chester Barnard to the present and beyond,' Oliver E. Williamson (ed.) [book review], *Academy of Management Review*, 16(4): 815–17.

Struck, F.T. (1930) *Foundations of Industrial Education*, New York: John Wiley & Sons.

Sweeney, J.J. & Nussbaum, K. (1989) *Solutions for the New Work Force: Policies for a New Social Contract*, Cabin John, MD: Seven Locks Press.

Takaki, R. (1979) *Iron Cages: Race and Culture in 19th-Century America*, Seattle, WA: University of Washington Press.

Takaki, R. (1993) *A Different Mirror: A History of Multicultural America*, Boston, MA: Little, Brown & Co.

Tarbell, I.M. (1902) 'Ida M. Tarbell on the methods of the Standard Oil Company,' in R. Hofstadter (ed.), *The Progressive Movement 1900–1915*, New York: Simon & Schuster.

Tarbell, I.M. (1925) *The Life of Elbert H. Gary: The Story of Steel*, New York: D. Appleton & Co.

Tate, W.E. (1967) *The Enclosure Movement*, New York: Walker and Co.

Taylor, A. (1994) 'Iacocca's Minivan,' *Fortune*, 30 May, pp. 57–70.

Taylor, F.W. (1895) 'A piece rate system being a step toward a partial solution of the labor problem, *Transactions of the ASME*, 16: 856–903.

Taylor, F.W. (1911) *The Principles of Scientific Management*, New York: Norton.

Terry, S.H. (1869) *The Retailer's Manual*, Newark, NJ: Jennings Brothers.

Thomas, L.I. (1917) 'The high cost of labor that comes and goes,' A.W. Shaw Co. (ed.), *Handling Men*, Chicago, IL: A.W. Shaw Co., pp. 91–102

Thompson, A.A. & Strickland, A.J. (1987) *Strategic Management: Concepts and Cases*, Plano, TX: Business Publications.

Thompson, J.D. (1956) 'On building an administrative science,' *Administrative Science Quarterly*, 1(1): 102–11.

Thompson, J.D. (1967) *Organizations in Action*, New York: McGraw-Hill.

Thoreau, H.D. (1854) 'Walden,' in J.W. Krutch (ed.) (1962), *Walden and Other Writings*, New York: Bantam, pp. 105–352.

Thoreau, H.D. (1863) 'Life without principle,' in J.W. Krutch (ed.) (1962), *Walden and Other Writings*, New York: Bantam, pp. 353–74.

Toffler, A. (1980) *The Third Wave*, New York: Bantam.

Towne, H.R. (1884) 'A drawing office system,' *Transactions of the ASME*, 5: 193–205.

Towne, H.R. (1886) 'The engineer as an economist,' *Transactions of the ASME*, 7: 428–32.

Townley, B. (1993) 'Foucault, power/knowledge, and its relevance for human resource management,' *Academy of Management Review*, 18(3): 518–45.

Townley, B. (1994) *Reframing Human Resource Management: Power Ethics and the Subject at Work*, London: Sage.

Travers, R.M.W. (1983) *How Research Has Changed American Schools: A History From 1840 to the Present*, Kalamazoo, MI: Mythos Press.

Tuchman, B.W. (1978) *A Distant Mirror: The Calamitous 14th Century*, New York: Knopf.

Turner, F.J. (1893/1956) 'The significance of the frontier in American history, and contributions of the West to American democracy,' in G.R. Taylor (ed.), *The Turner Thesis Concerning the Role of the Frontier in American History*, Lexington, MA: D.C. Heath, pp. 1–33.

Urwick, L. (1956) *The Golden Book of Management: A Historical Record of the Life and Work of Seventy Pioneers*, London: Newman Neame Ltd.

Vail, C.H. (1907) *Modern Socialism*, Chicago, IL: Charles H. Kerr & Co.

Van de Ven, A.H. (1989) 'Special forum on theory building: nothing is quite so practical as a good theory,' *Academy of Management Review*, 14(4): 486–9.

Vance, C., Talbott, S., McBride, A. & Mason, D. (1985) 'An uneasy alliance: nursing and the women's movement,' *Nursing Outlook*, 33(6): 281–7.

Veblen, T. (1899/1983) *The Theory of the Leisure Class*, New York: Penguin.

Veblen, T. (1923) *Absentee Ownership and Business Enterprise in Recent Times: The Case of America*, New York: Scribner's.

Veyne, P. (ed.) (1987) *A History of Private Life: From Pagan Rome to Byzantium*, Vol. 1, 5 vols (general editors: P. Ariès & G. Duby), Cambridge, MA: Belknap.

Veyne, P. (1987) 'The Roman Empire,' in P. Veyne (ed.) *A History of Private Life: From Pagan Rome to Byzantium*, Vol. 1, 5 vols (general editors: P. Ariès & G. Duby), Cambridge, MA: Belknap, pp. 1–234.

Vogel, L. (1990) 'Debating difference: feminism, pregnancy and the workplace,' *Feminist Studies*, 16(1): 9–32.

Vollmer, H.M. & Mills, D.L. (1966) *Professionalization*, Englewood Cliffs, NJ: Prentice-Hall.

Von Glinow, M.A. (1988) *The New Professionals: Managing Today's High-Tech Employees*, Cambridge, MA: Ballinger.

Vroom, V. (1964) *Work and Motivation*, New York: John Wiley & Sons.

Wachhorst, W. (1981) *Thomas Alva Edison: An American Myth*, Cambridge, MA: MIT Press.

Watkins, M.W. (1927) 'Certain causes emphasized [from "Industrial Combinations and Public Policy"],' in R.E. Curtis, (ed.) (1931), *The Trusts and Economic Control*, New York: McGraw-Hill, pp. 19–22.

Weber, M. (1904/1958) *The Protestant Ethic and the Spirit of Capitalism*, New York: Scribner's.

Webster, J. & Starbuck, W.H. (1988) 'Theory building in industrial and organizational psychology,' in C.L. Cooper & I. Robertson (eds), *International Review of Industrial and Organizational Psychology*, New York: Wiley, 93–138.

Weeks, P. (1990) 'Post-colonial challenges to grand theory,' *Human Organization*, 49(3): 236–44.

Weick, K.E. (1969) *The Social Psychology of Organizing*, Reading, MA: Addison-Wesley.

Weick, K.E. (1989) 'Theory Construction as disciplined imagination,' *Academy of Management Review*, 14(4): 516–31.

Welles, E.O. (1994) 'It's not the same America,' *Inc.*, May, pp. 82–98.

White, R. & Jacques, R. (1995) 'Operationalizing the postmodernity construct for efficient organizational change management,' [title is tongue-in-cheek] *Journal of Organizational Change Management*, 8(2): 45–71.

Wiebe, R.H. (1967) *The Search for Order 1877–1920*, New York: Hill & Wang.

Wiggam, A.E. (1922) *The New Decalogue of Science*, Indianapolis, IN: The Bobbs Merrill Co.

Wiggam, A.E. (1924) *The Fruit of the Family Tree*, Garden City, NY: Garden City Publishing Co. Inc.

Williams, P. & Chrisman, L. (eds) (1994) *Colonial Discourse and Post-Colonial Theory: A Reader*, New York: Columbia University Press.

Wolff, R.D. & Resnick, S.A. (1987) *Economics: Marxian versus Neoclassical*, Baltimore, MD: Johns Hopkins University Press.

Woodward (1965) *Industrial Organization: Theory and Practice*, London: Oxford University Press.

Yates, J. (1989) *Control Through Communication: The Rise of System in American Management*, Baltimore, MD: Johns Hopkins University Press.

Yukl, G.A. (1989) *Leadership in Organizations*, 2nd Edn, Englewood Cliffs, NJ: Prentice-Hall.

Zaleznik, A. (1989) *The Managerial Mystique*, New York: Harper & Row.

Zuboff, S. (1988) *In the Age of the Smart Machine*, New York: Basic Books.

Author Index

Subject Index

Printed in the United Kingdom
by Lightning Source UK Ltd.
9714100001B/26-45

4599

9 780803 979161